How Things Shape the Mind

How Things Shape the Mind

A Theory of Material Engagement

Lambros Malafouris

The MIT Press
Cambridge, Massachusetts
London, England

MIT Press books may be purchased at special quantity discounts for business or sales promotional use. For information, please email special_sales@mitpress.mit.edu.

Set in Stone Sans and Stone Serif by Toppan Best-set Premedia Limited. Printed and bound in the United States of America.

Library of Congress Cataloging-in-Publication Data

Malafouris, Lambros.
How things shape the mind : a theory of material engagement / Lambros Malafouris ; foreword by Colin Renfrew.
    p.   cm
Includes bibliographical references and index.
ISBN 978-0-262-01919-4 (hardcover : alk. paper) 1. Neuroanthropology. 2. Material culture. 3. Archaeology. 4. Cognition and culture. 5. Neuropsychology. I. Title.
QP360.6.M35   2013
612.8—dc23
2012045908

10 9 8 7 6 5 4 3 2

Contents

Foreword by Colin Renfrew   ix
Acknowledgments   xiii

1 Introduction   1
Chronesthesia, the prehistory of mind   1
Recasting the boundaries of the mind   2
At the tip of the blind man's stick   4
What is the difference that makes a difference?   8
Setting the scene   10
The realm of material engagement   15
A synopsis of the book   17

I Cognition and Material Culture

2 Rethinking the Archaeology of Mind   23
In search of the ancient mind   23
Where is the mind?   24
Cognitivism   25
Re-presentation: Looking at the other side of the engram   26
Dismantling Hawkes' ladder   31

3 The Material-Engagement Approach: A Summary of the Argument   35
How to carve mind at its joints   36
Boundaries, paths, and analytical units   36
Understanding evolvability: The developmental challenge   38
"Vital materiality": How to take material culture seriously   43

Metaplasticity   45
Material engagement: The analytical nexus   50
An ontological recommendation   51

II   Outline of a Theory of Material Engagement

4   The Extended Mind   57
Beyond cognitivism: Thinking outside the brain   57
The embodied mind   59
The distributed-cognition approach   66
Remembering through, or how a Linear B tablet helps you forget   68
The intelligent use of clay   69
Were it to happen in the head: From "parity" to "complementarity" and
beyond   73
The hypothesis of the constitutive intertwining of cognition with material
culture   77
Things matter: The coupling-constitution fallacy   81
Being where? The locational fallacy   82
The affect of engagement   85

5   The Enactive Sign   89
Moving beyond representation   89
The fallacy of the linguistic sign   90
Searching for the properties of the material sign   94
The enactive logic of the material sign   96
Projections through matter   99
Material anchors and integrative projections   103
Making numbers out of clay   106
Learning to count in the Neolithic   111
The material sign and the meaning of engagement   116

6   Material Agency   119
Material culture and agency   119
Toward a non-anthropocentric conception   122
Actor-Network Theory   123
The argument for material agency   130
Methodological fetishism   133

Intentionality and secondary agents   135
Agency and intentionality   136
Rethinking "things" as agents   144
Ask not "What is an agent?" but "When is an agent?"   147
A conceptual talisman   148

III   Marking the Mental: Where Brain, Body, and Culture Conflate

7   Knapping Intentions and the Handmade Mind   153
Homo faber: Prosthetic gestures   153
The tools of the Stone Age   155
Where does the knapper end and the stone tool begin?   161
Tools for a plastic mind   164
The "handaxe enigma" revisited   169
Reassembling the mind of the toolmaker   172
Enactive intentionalities: The merging of flesh with stone   173
Tools are us: A "cyborg" species   177

8   Thoughtful Marks, Lines, and Signs   179
Mark-making humans   179
The prehistory of mark making   181
What is so special about these marks? The tyranny of modernity   183
From "deliberateness" to "symbolic or representational intent"   185
Were they symbols?   187
What kind of line? Getting outside the engraver's mind   190
Learning to see: On being conscious of marks and pictures   194
The liberation of sight   200
Becoming symbol-minded   205

9   Becoming One with the Clay   227
Thrown on the wheel   227
At the potter's wheel: Agency in action   209
Agency and "sense" of agency   213
"I did it": The problem of agency   215
Agency in pottery making   221
Time, agency, and material engagement   222
Situated bodies and the feeling of clay   225

10 Epilogue: How Do Things Shape the Mind?   227

Methodological ramifications   228
What is it to be human?   230
Homo faber   232
Homo symbolicus: When is a symbol?   234
Unlearning modernity   239
At the tip of the blind man's stick: "We have never been modern"   243
The spike of culture   248

Notes   251
References   257
Index   293

Foreword

This challenging work, *How Things Shape the Mind*, qualifies as one of the most important contributions of recent years to the study of human origins. Since any study of the origins of humankind has to deal with the archaeological record, the book clearly makes a major contribution to the emerging field of cognitive archaeology—the archaeology of mind. Yet its scope and its consistent application of Material Engagement Theory take it much further than the flints and potsherds of the archaeological record, permitting it to examine in a deep way how the human mental capacities that have their primary location in the brain (within the skull) are not separable in any serious consideration from their expression in action. This is effected through the body of the individual, and then through artifacts— the material things we utilize in any action. This expression in action also operates through the activities undertaken by other people who are in communication with that active individual, or are influenced by the things, the external symbols (objects, signs, writing), so created. The insep- arability of thought, action, and material things is a basic principle of Material Engagement Theory. Its development here by Lambros Malafouris has significant implications not only for scholars studying human origins but for all those seeking to understand the foundations of human action and the roots of sociality.

With *How Things Shape the Mind* Lambros Malafouris offers a deeper understanding of a central question: What is it to be human? Just what is it that distinguishes us humans from other animals? He does so not only in the restricted sense of describing the evolutionary path followed by our species, but with the much broader aim of analyzing just what it was that changed as humankind developed from ape-like ancestors. This involves formulating a clear view of the nature of mind. The crux, it turns out, is how we interact with the world, and with things in the world. This process of human engagement with the material world is the focus of Malafouris' analysis. The product of this analysis is Material Engagement Theory.

In this remarkable book, Malafouris undertakes a fundamental review of the way we seek to understand human prehistory. He demonstrates that separating mind and body is unhelpful when we are talking about human action. That dualism, which has been dominant in Western thought since the time of Descartes, has been a source of confusion that has proved difficult to overcome. Malafouris takes up the challenge by developing a theory of material engagement that foregrounds the role of things in the processes of human cognition. Only by rethinking the very nature of mind in this way is it possible to reexamine the process of the emergence of our species from our earlier ancestors and the important developments of human abilities and of culture as they are increasingly revealed by archaeological research.

Much of the evidence for these processes derives from the practice of archaeology. The focus is on the process of becoming human. But although the time span implied by that process extends back a million years and more, the outcome is very much in the present. We are all involved today, as members of the species *Homo sapiens* and as inheritors of the generations that have preceded us, in the human condition, which we all share. So the reassessment offered here of the nature of mind and of the processes of cognition, though rooted in the prehistoric past, is directly applicable to the present. It bears directly on what we are today, on the world we have together, over the generations, created, and on how each new generation accommodates to that world and then proceeds to change it.

It is a feature of the radical nature of Malafouris' reassessment of the development of human cognition that his discussion is as much philosophical as archaeological, certainly in the systematic discussions in parts I and II. Only in part III, where specific processes are discussed, do archaeological examples move into the foreground. There Malafouris shows how the processes of making things with the hands, exemplified by the production of tools in the Stone Age, shaped the processes of human cognition. He analyzes the production of marks and of symbols, using examples that pre-date the development of writing. And in his discussion of the potter's wheel he demonstrates that to separate body from mind in the discussion is fruitless, and that an approach is needed in terms of the potter's material engagement with the world he or she is in.

With the production of the first stone tools our ancestors took the first steps in the production of material culture. With the first engraved or painted signs they initiated the processes that led to the external storage of information and ultimately to writing. With modeling in clay and subsequently with the potter's wheel they went beyond the limitations of the body itself. With the constructions of the architect and the planner they began to develop the tectonic environment in which we all live and operate. These are the telling examples that Malafouris analyzes in part III, having introduced the Material Engagement approach in part I and outlined its theoretical foundations in part II. In part III he develops his critique of "cognitivism" (the misconception that the mind is simply a computer located within the brain) and argues that the mind is to be understood as embodied, indeed as extended beyond the body, and beyond the individual, and as interacting with the things of the material world.

All of this has a powerful impact on the field of cognitive archaeology. Cognitive archaeology is no longer seen as the attempt simply to reconstruct some early and elusive symbolic concepts, seen as situated at almost unattainable rungs up some notional ladder of inference. It is understood, rather, to be a program of exploration and investigation by which we can seek to understand the basic foundations of human society and culture. Yet although these issues certainly encompass the field of cognitive archaeology, they go well beyond its confines. They impinge on neuroscience, on ethology, and on sociology, and they raise a number of issues in philosophy.

This is a book with many implications for the theory and the practice of archaeology. It opens the way to a clearer understanding of the qualities and capacities that define us and constitute our essential nature, and of how they came about. It deals coherently and consistently with the question of how we have become what we are today, and indeed with the question of what it means to be human.

Colin Renfrew

Acknowledgments

This book has been a long time in preparation. The initial conception of the theory of material engagement I lay out in it began with my PhD thesis, but it has changed a lot, expanded, and evolved since then. Naturally, the ideas I set forth in the book did not come from nowhere. My debts are varied and great, extending across many people and institutions.

To begin with, I should single out a few people to whom I feel I owe a special debt of thanks. At the top of the list, without a doubt, is Colin Renfrew. He has been my mentor in the archaeology of mind, and it was he who first introduced me to the idea of material engagement. He has been a valuable teacher and a source of inspiration to me (he still is). He had faith in me at times when I had very little in myself. I owe him my greatest intellectual debt. I also want to acknowledge my longtime colleague and friend Carl Knappett. To Carl I am particularly grateful for invaluable help and for a series of stimulating discussions about cognition and material culture over the course of the last several years. Very special thanks are also due to Chris Gosden for believing in my work and supporting it. His encouragement and constructive criticism over the years have been invaluable and have played an active role in the shaping of my thinking.

I mentioned that the book took many years of growing before acquiring its final shape. It is also an interdisciplinary book. I have been influenced and excited by several authors working in different disciplines outside archaeology. Those deserving special mention include Andy Clark, Edwin Hutchins, and Tim Ingold, whose work and views are a major influence on all that I write.

Many institutions have contributed to the book. Much of the research and the early writing were carried out while I held a Balzan Postdoctoral

Research Fellowship at the McDonald Institute for Archaeological Research at the University of Cambridge (funded by the second part of the Balzan Prize awarded to Professor Colin Renfrew in 2004). I owe a debt of gratitude to the Balzan Prize Foundation for granting me this fellowship. I am also grateful to the McDonald Institute for offering a warm and stimulating environment for my research. A series of international symposia that provided the interdisciplinary testing ground for many of the ideas presented in this book were convened at the McDonald Institute. Some of the material originated or is based on parts or fragments of papers I presented and published there. The first of these symposia, titled The Cognitive Life of Things and co-organized with Colin Renfrew, took place in 2006. The second, titled The Sapient Mind: Archaeology Meets Neuroscience and co-organized with Colin Renfrew and Chris Frith, took place in 2007. Those two meetings helped me to frame and develop many of the questions I address in the book. There were another two conferences at the McDonald Institute that have helped me a great deal to conceive and develop some of the ideas on early imagery and the development of numerical thinking I present. The first of those conferences, held in 2005, was titled Material Beginnings; the second, held in 2006, was titled Measuring the World and Beyond. I want to thank the organizers, Iain Morley and Colin Renfrew. Thanks to all the speakers and participants at those meetings. Thanks in particular to Michael Wheeler, Merlin Donald, David Kirsh, Sander van der Leeuw, Nicholas Humphrey, Richard Harper, Scott H. Frey, Günther Knoblich, J. Scott Jordan, Andreas Roepstorff, Maurice Bloch, Niels Johannsen, and Fiona Coward for stimulating exchanges of ideas.

In the last few years I have also been fortunate enough to have been granted the opportunity to participate in some further stimulating conferences that have allowed me to develop my thinking on several issues: The Dialectics of Ancient Innovations (Freie Universität Berlin, 2011), The Body Shop (University of Texas, 2011), Origins of Pictures (Chemnitz, 2011), Vision and Activity (Hungarian Academy of Sciences, 2010), Experimentality in Nature (Institute for Advanced Studies, Lancaster University, 2010), and Multidisciplinary Approach to the Evolution of the Parietal Lobes (Centro Nacional de Investigación sobre la Evolución Humana Paseo Sierra de Atapuerca s/n, 2009). I want to thank Reinhard Bernbeck, Stefan Burmeister, Klaus Sachs-Hombach, Jürgen Streeck, Christian Meyer, Zsuzsanna Kondor, Stephanie Koerner, and Emiliano Bruner for organizing the above meetings, at which I benefited greatly from discussions with Iain Davidson, Charles Goodwin, Thomas Csordas, and other colleagues. I especially thank Fred Coolidge.

Equally important was the opportunity provided by the European Platform for Life Sciences, Mind Sciences, and the Humanities, funded by the Volkswagen Stiftung. For many useful discussions on a range of topics from different disciplinary perspectives, I should like to thank my collaborators in The Body-Project and the Neuroscience in Context project. I gained much from them. Thanks are due to Jan-Christoph Heilinger and Saskia K. Nagel for the wonderful conference, titled Human Nature and Its Alterability, that we organized together at the Berlin-Brandenburg Academy of Sciences and Humanities in 2009. I also owe a special debt of thanks to Manos Tsakiris for his invaluable help, especially with chapter 9.

I owe a deep debt to my current home, Keble College at the University of Oxford, where the book was completed. I would like to offer my thanks to the fellows of the college. I owe additional debts of gratitude to Tom Higham, Marc Brodie, and Jonathan Phillips, and to the Keble Advanced Studies Centre for its financial support of the ethnographic work on which chapter 9 is based. (I also should express my thanks to all the Greek potters I have been working with in the course of the last few years for their time and enthusiasm.) An especially big thank-you goes to my colleagues in archaeology and anthropology Lisa Bendall and Morgan Clarke—I highly appreciate your letting me work quietly and undisturbed during the final writing.

Denise Schmandt-Besserat deserves special thanks for her stimulation and generosity in supplying and allowing me to reproduce data and photographs. Thanks also to Dietrich Stout for many discussions on "neuroarchaeology" and for permission to use his photo of a handaxe. Also I am grateful to Giannis Galanakis and the Ashmolean Museum at Oxford for the Linear B photos.

I would also like to thank Philip Laughlin, Katie Persons, Paul Bethge, and all the other people at the MIT Press for their good work. I am particularly indebted to Philip for his early enthusiasm and continued support.

My greatest thanks, as always, to my wife Danae and my son Odyssea, the two individuals who, more than anyone else, have supported and inspired my work all these years. I am also grateful to Danae for providing feedback and editorial advice. To Odyssea I owe a special debt for all his good work with the drawings!

1 Introduction

Chronesthesia, the prehistory of mind

Prehistory, in addition to designating a vast span of time, also has a second, deeply philosophical sense: It is "the discipline by which we study ourselves and investigate the way we have come to be as we are" (Renfrew 2007, viii). The research field we call the archaeology of mind, or cognitive archaeology, can be understood along similar lines: It is a prehistory as much as it is a chronesthesis. By 'chronesthesia' I mean the form of consciousness that enables us humans to be aware, in the present, of our past and our possible future (Tulving 2002). Cognitive archaeology provides a memory path for reconstructing the autobiography, and thus the identity, of our species—who we are and how we got here. In a certain way, then, one could see the archaeology of mind as a form of consciousness as much as a philosophy, an anthropology, and a prehistory of human becoming. Of course, the kind of mental time travel this involves can be realized only through the material remains of the past—it is mental as much as it is physical. Individual memories now give way to long-term transformations of material signs and complex recursive interactions between people and things that lead from earliest human prehistory to the present. I suggest that the archaeology of mind, more than anything else, signifies this distinctively human search for understanding the intimate links between being and becoming. These are simple and, I hope, uncontestable statements. But precisely how could the ongoing and multifaceted archaeological quest for human identity be transformed into a coherent research program focusing on the long-term making and evolution of the human mind? A number of challenging questions immediately confront us: What might constitute an archaeological trace of human thought? What is the ontology of those material signs and traces? What questions should we ask of them? How can we identify, understand, and assess the different forms that they take? How are we to follow the cultural trajectories and make better use of the long-term biographies of the signs, lines, and traces that can be found in different phases of the archaeological record? These are important questions for cognitive archaeology. They remain largely unanswered.

In this book, I shall try to meet this challenge by laying the foundations of a theory of material engagement. Material Engagement Theory represents the effort of many years to build an interdisciplinary analytical framework able to recast the boundaries of the mind and redress the balance of the cognitive equation by bringing materiality—that is, the world of things, artifacts, objects, materials, and material signs—firmly into the cognitive fold. Highlighting the cognitive efficacy and the embodied dynamics of past and present material culture, I sketch a very different picture of the nature of interaction between persons and things. It is an open picture with permeable boundaries, and it is so for a very good reason: It maps a cognitive landscape in which brains, bodies, and things play equal roles in the drama of human cognitive becoming. The Material Engagement approach proposes a new way of thinking about minds and things that, I hope, will help us answer the question that is central to this book: How do things shape the mind?

Recasting the boundaries of the mind

I will briefly introduce the differentiating feature of the new theoretical framework of material engagement by raising an unexpected but extremely important question: Where does the mind stop and the rest of the world begin? This question, which hardly received any explicit attention in archaeology, recently became popular in the context of philosophical discussions of the embodied, extended, enacted, and distributed nature of the mind. (See, e.g., Clark and Chalmers 1998.)

Answering the question seems easy enough at first, which explains why the question may sound odd to some people: The mind is the sort of thing that thinks, and thinking is the sort of activity that takes place inside people's brains. We may still be far from reaching a consensus about what sort of stuff minds are made off, but mainstream philosophy and cognitive science appear to be in agreement about where we should be looking for the mind's stuff: inside the head.

I think this well-entrenched view is quite mistaken. As deeply intuitive as this assumption about the boundaries of the mind may be, it is largely misconceived. I will show that what at first seems obvious enough to be taken for granted is, on closer inspection, more of an acquired predisposition—one that continues to reiterate a "dualist," "internalist," and nowadays largely "neurocentric" view of mind. Such a view, I argue in this book, threatens to obscure much that is of value in the archaeology, the anthropology, and the philosophy of mind and in our understanding of the nature of the relationship between cognition and material culture.

Drawing on recent work on enactive, distributed, and extended cognition, I will suggest that, contrary to what classical cognitive science believes and cognitive archaeology often implicitly reiterates, what is outside the head may not necessarily be outside the mind. Natural as it may seem (especially from the perspectives of other disciplines) to point to the human brain as the seat of all that is truly mental, from an archaeological viewpoint I see no compelling reason why the study of the mind should stop at the skin or at the skull. It would, I suggest, be more productive to explore the hypothesis that human intelligence "spreads out" beyond the skin into culture and the material world. (See Knappett 2005; Gosden 2008; Malafouris and Renfrew 2010.)

I understand that a brain scan may seem more convincing as evidence for the active human mind than a mere assemblage of things from early human prehistory. However, I contend that it appears to be so only because of our learned convictions about what counts as a thinking process and about where one should be looking for constitutive ingredients of such a process. It is epistemological contingency, rather than metaphysical necessity, that makes us see, in the various objects, marks, gestures, and lines of human prehistory, merely external products of human thought rather than integral parts of it. I will argue that these common presumptions of "mentality over materiality" are historical conventions rather than *a priori* metaphysical truths. What in present-day neuroscience goes by the name *blood-oxygen-level-dependent* (BOLD)[1] represents only one among many possible ways to look for the material traces of human thought. Neuroimaging techniques go only halfway toward solving the traditional mind-body problem. No measurement of regional brain activity, however accurate it might be, can tell, in itself, the whole story. Although neuroscience indeed offers the best guide we have for discerning the intricate pathways and wirings of the neural structures and networks that support human cognitive operations, I see no reason why it should be trusted to reveal the location and the provenance of the stuff of which human minds and selves are made. Where do we look for the mind, then? How can we stop thinking about the mind-world relationship in a dualist way?

In this book, taking advantage of the strong archaeological preoccupation with long-term processes and the study of material culture, I intend to foreground the material basis of the human mind by looking beyond the skin and across the scales of time. Not only do I want to explore the different ways in which things become cognitive extensions or are incorporated by the human body; I also want to investigate how those ways might have changed since earliest prehistory, and what those changes mean for the ways we think. Thus, the reader should expect some serious questioning of conventional intuitions about the boundaries and whereabouts of the human mind—questioning that will lead us to rethink many classical archaeological assumptions about the shape of human cognitive evolution and the usefulness or validity of notions such as "cognitive modernity" and "behavioral modernity."

My starting point will be the classic example of the blind man's stick (Merleau-Ponty 1962; Polanyi 1962; Bateson 1973).

At the tip of the blind man's stick

[C]onsider a blind man with a stick. Where does the blind man's self begin? At the tip of the stick? At the handle of the stick? Or at some point halfway up the stick?
—Gregory Bateson (1973, 318)

Where do we draw, and on what basis can we draw, a delimiting line across the extended system that determines the blind man's perception and locomotion? Does the biological boundary of the skin apply in this case? More than four decades after Merleau-Ponty (1962), Polanyi (1962), and Bateson (1973) first raised the question of the blind man and his stick, it remains as timely as ever. (For a more detailed discussion, see Malafouris 2008b.) From an archaeological perspective, one need only replace the stick with any of the numerous artifacts and innovations that constitute the diverse archaeological inventory of prehistoric material culture to realize that there is much more at issue here than a mere philosophical puzzle. As will be explored throughout this book, our answers to some of the most fundamental questions about the emergence of human intelligence depend on precisely where one decides to draw the line between the mind and the material world.

I use the example of the blind man's stick as my point of departure for introducing the differentiating feature of my approach to the archaeology of mind mainly for two reasons. First, I believe it provides a refreshing analogy for the profound plasticity of the human mind. Using a stick, the blind man turns touch into sight. This "unnatural" rerouting of tactile processing to occipital visual cortex speaks of the reconfigurable "nature" of mind. In the context of archaeological thinking, this analogy serves to remind us that what we often see as a fixed human nature is more a flexible process of ongoing human becoming—a process still in progress and largely unfinished. Obviously there is more than cross-modal neural plasticity at issue here. The stick has its own interesting role. Tactile sensation is somehow projected onto the point of contact between the tip of the stick and the outside environment. This extension in the "body schema" also means that the brain treats the stick as part of the body. One could see in this emergent coalition between the blind man and the stick, which enables the making of vision out of touch, a powerful metaphor for what it means to be human. For it is indeed a similar coalition (or ontological unity) between cognition and material culture that, I suggest, drives human cognitive evolution. Unfortunately, the possibility of such an ontological coalition, or, in fact, of a co-extension of the mental with the physical, has been largely ignored. In this book I seek to encourage the reader to pay attention to the complex "cognitive ecologies" of material engagement inside which, as the anthropologist Edwin Hutchins suggests, "all of the elements and relations potentially interact with one another and . . . each is part of the environment for all of the others" (2010a, 99).

With the latter remark in mind, let me turn to the second reason why I have chosen the example of the blind man's stick to introduce the overarching hypothesis of this book: I believe this example provides one of the best diachronic exemplars of what I call the gray zone of material engagement, i.e., *the zone in which brains, bodies, and things conflate, mutually catalyzing and constituting one another* (Malafouris 2004). Mind, as the anthropologist Gregory Bateson pointed out, "is not limited by the skin" (1973, 318), and that is why Bateson was able to recognize the stick as a "pathway" instead of a boundary. Differentiating between "inside" and "outside" makes no real sense for the blind man. As Bateson notes, "the mental characteristics of the system are immanent, not in some part, but in the system as a whole" (ibid., 316). Yet for the external observer the question of the ontological status of the stick remains vague. How can a thing made of wood, plastic, or metal ever be seen as part of the machinery of human thought? On what grounds should we conceive of the stick as a component part of the blind man's living body? Are we not conflating conscious kinds and material kinds—agents and tools? The problem is complicated further if one considers that for the archaeology of mind the stick is not simply a "pathway along which differences are transmitted under transformation" (ibid., 318) but a *difference* in itself. Often the stick is, to use Marshall McLuhan's (1964) formulation, not the medium but the message.

Some of the difficulty of dealing with questions of the above type stems, as I will discuss in the next chapter, from the dominant internalist, representational, or computational thinking that characterizes cognitive sciences in general and cognitive archaeology in particular. Fortunately, a growing number of insightful and fertile perspectives that have recently emerged in cognitive science favor a view of the mind that is embodied, extended, and distributed rather than "brain-bound" and limited by the skin. The proposal I sketch in this book draws on some of these exciting theories. This does not mean, however, that I uncritically succumb to their premises as a whole. Few of the new theories take the study of material culture seriously. Despite the widely recognized need to expand the analytical units of human cognition in order to accommodate broader cognitive phenomena enacted through the body and the material world, we currently lack any kind of consensus on exactly what the nature of the inextricable ties between brains, bodies and things might be. The reason for that is not difficult to imagine: Most of the grounding assumptions that define what we know about the human mind, but also the ways by which we have come to know what we know about the human mind, have been premised and nurtured in the absence of materiality. (See Costall and Dreier 2006.) Perhaps a look at the history of Western thought can teach us that the study of *nous* always favored the order of Platonic essences and ideas over the messiness and fluidity of pre-Socratic becoming. Turning our back on the spirit of hylozoism, we became prisoners of our own purified categories of thought. Either things are altogether missing from the human noetic field or, at best, they are seen as epiphenomenal to the study of mind proper. In a way, then, things seem to exist in a state of ontological deprivation. This is strange in view of the way materiality conspicuously envelops our everyday thinking and sensory experience. The anthropologist of material culture Daniel Miller refers to this phenomenon as the "humility of things" (2010, 50). Beginning in early childhood, we constantly think through things, actively engaging our surrounding material environment, but we rarely become explicitly aware of the action potential of this engagement in the shaping of our minds and brains. Like the blind man, we do not sense the "stick"; we sense the presence or the absence of objects in the outside environment. Although the stick offers the means for this exploration, it becomes, through time and practice, incorporated and thus transparent. It is itself forgotten. Perhaps things are very good to think with, or through, but not so good to think about. The "immediate, sensual and assimilable" nature of the materiality that surrounds us (Miller 1987, 3) makes comprehending its importance extremely difficult. Things, like the blind man's stick, work best when in motion and unnoticed. However, the prosthetic "phenomenological osmosis" (Leder 1990) that characterizes our embodied skills and interactions with things is not a reason to abandon them. On the contrary, it is precisely the reason why things demand our attention.

As will be discussed in more detail in the following chapters, this kind of epistemic asymmetry in the way we continue to select the chief ingredients of the human cognitive recipe is not without serious implications. It is now important to note, however, that, for all the above reasons, understanding the relationship between cognition and material culture—what it is, how it changes, and what role the human body plays in forging those links—is of the utmost importance for the study of mind. This can be argued to be the case not only for archaeology and anthropology (disciplines dedicated largely, by their very nature, to the study of things) but also for the broad field of philosophy and the cognitive sciences (disciplines traditionally conceived as far removed from the material conditions of human life). Mind, as the philosopher Andy Clark notes in his book *Being There*, "is a leaky organ, forever escaping its 'natural' confines and mingling shamelessly with body and with world" (1997, 53). And it is precisely this powerful statement that I intend to follow in setting the foundations for a new archaeology of mind.

What is the difference that makes a difference?

What differentiates this book from other works in cognitive archaeology? Broadly speaking, this book, like many others, aims to provide a new account of the making of the human mind. What sets it apart from other similar studies is the way I intend to provide such an account. In particular, I seek to understand how human minds came to be what they are by taking material culture seriously. By "taking seriously" I mean being systematically concerned with figuring out the causal efficacy of things in the *enactment* and the *constitution* of human cognition. This book sets out to investigate the changing nature, and the different aspects, of the relationship between persons and things—that is, how they respond to and participate in each other's coming into being. In other words, it asks why we humans, more than any other species, make things, and how those things, in return, make us who or what we are.

One potential problem stemming from such a conception is that things, like minds, become very hard to define. "Thingness" and "mindness" are highly unsettled and ontologically fluid states. They remain formless and plastic, waiting to take the shape of our embodied projections, which inevitably vary in different times and places. But our inability to define what things and minds are does not mean that we cannot recognize them if we come across them. A common-sense understanding of these terms is sufficient to identify the target of our investigation and to serve our theoretical purposes. The problem is that common sense may not be the best guide to those issues. Should we then feel obliged to define an essence of what minds and things are? Take, for instance, the concept of 'mind'. Exactly what is it for a process to be cognitive? Without knowing what we mean by cognition, we are left clueless—or so it seems—about where we should look for it. Some philosophers argue that such a "cognitive agnosticism is untenable," and that, as a precondition for making "any progress on the Where-question," we "need a mark of the cognitive, i.e., an answer to the What-question" (Walter and Kastner 2012, 17). But do archaeologists and anthropologists actually require a definition of 'cognition'? I think not. Let me explain: I am not questioning whether what we call mind can be defined; I am questioning whether such a definition, foreclosing what we think cognition is and does, would be a useful starting point from an archaeological or an anthropological perspective. In fact, methodologically speaking, this lack of analytic precision about necessary and sufficient conditions, far from being problematic, can offer a tactical advantage well suited to the goal of this book, which is to redefine our conceptual vocabulary by shifting attention away from the sphere of closed categories of persons and things and toward the sphere of the fluid and relational transactions between them. There is an obvious link with previous dialectical approaches to the study of material culture, but there also are some important differences. For instance, a common thread that runs through the chapters of this book is that minds and things are continuous and interdefinable processes rather than isolated and independent entities. I argue that by knowing what things are, and how they were made what they are, you gain an understanding about what minds are and how they become what they are—and vice versa. Of course, simply to speak about relationality is not, nowadays, saying or assuming much. Phenomenology, ecological psychology, and anthropology offer a number of different ways of articulating the idea that the mind is relational.

We need a way to penetrate the specific cultural, social, and developmental dynamics through which these connections are effected and sustained, as well as an efficient way to describe the cognitive properties that arise from the co-constitution of people and things. Doing away with conventional ideas of mind will require a change of focus and a new conceptual vocabulary. Material Engagement Theory aims to offer such a conceptual apparatus. One of the principal objectives of this book is to change our understanding of what minds are, and what minds are made of, by changing what we know about what things are and about what things do for the mind. How is human thought built into and executed through things? Indeed, how do things shape the mind? Too much clarity and too great an emphasis on definitions could be misleading in a context where transgressing the common wisdom about minds and things is often a precondition for success. Material engagement, as a methodological stance, does not have to commit *a priori* to a certain ontological description about minds and things. In this sense, instead of asking what the concepts of minds and things mean, it might be more useful to ask about what kind

of concepts they are. (See Walter and Kastner 2012.) This surprisingly difficult question poses unprecedented challenges to archaeological and
anthropological research practice. I hope that this book will make some
important steps toward an answer.

Setting the scene

Let us take a closer look at the general research context and the problems
that motivated the writing of this book. In recent years, a number of
stimulating books have approached the question of the relationship
between cognition and material culture from various disciplinary angles,
including archaeology, anthropology, philosophy, and cognitive science.
Yet it can be argued that those studies lacked a unified theoretical framework able to accommodate the multiplicity of phenomena that characterize various levels and temporal scales of human experience.

Philosophical studies, for instance, reflective of a more general tendency
in the mainstream cognitive sciences that can be called "epistemic neglect
of the object," tend to leave material culture outside the cognitive equation
proper. As a result, most philosophical treatments remain epistemically
agnostic about material culture's properties and about its active role in
human life and evolution. Even embodied cognitive science (Anderson
2003; Wheeler 2005; Chemero 2009; Clark 1997, 2008a), which explicitly
recognizes the intrinsic relationship between brain/body and environment, often seems oblivious to the phenomenal properties of the material
medium that envelops and shapes our lives. Although the material world
is recognized as a "causal influence" rather than a "mere stimulus," it is
rarely seen as playing a "constitutive" role. On this construal, the cultural
object may be what triggers or mediates some cognitive process but is not
seen as having any important role or as being a part of the cognitive
network responsible for the implementation and realization of this process.
Despite stretching the mind as far as the body's surface, embodied cognition remains trapped inside the biological boundaries of the individual.
Moreover, although embodied and situated cognitive science has drastically expanded the territory of mind into the material world, it fails to
move beyond its computational heritage, leaving "a lingering ghost within
the machine" (Gosden 2010, 39). It seems that, at the present stage of
research, philosophy of mind remains skeptical and undecided about

entering the treacherous territory of the extended mind proper, which prevents the "missing masses" of materiality that in recent years (thanks primarily to the work of Bruno Latour) balanced the fabric of social theory from exerting a similar effect on cognitive science.

By the same token, the majority of studies in human cognitive evolution have yet to address the question of materiality proper. When one surveys the extended literature dedicated to debates over the origin of *Homo sapiens*, including both the literature that looks at the cognitive requirements of tool making and the literature that looks at the roles of various material innovations in the emergence of "modern" human intelligence, the absence of any real concern with the semiotic ontology of material culture is obvious. Things are treated, in the majority of studies, as epiphenomenal reflections of, or proxies for, pre-defined aspects of human thought. In other words, things have become passive markers in a pre-defined evolutionary journey. Most studies in human cognitive evolution see material culture as, at best, indirect archaeological evidence from which they infer or read, often without making clear how or by what method, the presence of a certain cognitive capacity or process (e.g., syntactic language or symbolic thinking). There is rarely any serious consideration of the roles that various forms of material culture might have played in bringing about these cognitive capacities and processes or in changing them over the long term. As Nicole Boivin rightly points out, if the influence of culture on human genetic and brain evolution has received little attention, "the specific capacities of human-created material and technological environments and activities to exert an evolutionary effect has received even less" (2008, 190). As a result, evolutionary studies in archaeology also largely fail to accommodate and account for recent transformations in human cognitive becoming. Moreover, the lack of interdisciplinary expertise and the lack of serious engagement with cognitive science mean that the cognitive processes under consideration often are very poorly understood.

Turning to the archaeology and anthropology of material culture, we are faced with a different problem. Although material culture now takes center stage, there is little concern with the study of human cognition. The majority of studies in those fields, although grounded on the assumption "that persons make and use things and that the things make persons" (Tilley et al. 2006, 4), have paid scant attention to the study of mind. The "materiality turn" in archaeology (see Hicks 2010) has rightly placed things at the core of the human social nexus, but has paid little attention to, or has taken a fairly conventional approach to, their cognitive dimensions and qualities. The problem that most researchers in the field of material culture fail to acknowledge is that in turning their backs on the cognitive life of things they blindly validate and implicitly succumb to preconceived notions of what the human mind supposedly is and how it works—notions that seriously undermine the study of material culture. With a few brilliant exceptions (e.g., Knappett 2005, 2011; Renfrew 2007; Boivin 2008), there has been little explicit concern with the archaeology of mind-world inter-action. Consequently, the "internalist" fallacy still dominates much of archaeological and anthropological thinking about what the mind is and does. No one can deny, of course, the important contributions of many archaeological and anthropological studies to recognizing the animate and meaningful character of things and helping us understand why and how things matter (Miller 1998, 2009). This book could have never been written in the absence of that well-established tradition. Nonetheless, it can be argued that the first attempts to reveal the material core of the social uni-verse have often undermined the active nature of material culture by placing the "social" over the "material" and by keeping the "social" and the "material" separate from the "cognitive." For example, Arjun Appadu-rai's focus on the intimate linkages between commodities and sociality, successful as it may have been in revealing the dynamic and transactional character of "things-in-motion" (1986, 5), nonetheless kept that motion a prisoner of some "closed" social universe. But surely this "motion" must have some effect on, or some leakage to, the human mind. Even Alfred Gell's treatment of object-agency and extended selfhood fails to consider the huge implications of the proposed "isomorphy of structure" between mind or consciousness and the material world for the study of mind. Extremely powerful metaphors, such as Gell's description of the Kula exchange system as "a form of cognition" in which "internal" and "outside" transactions have fused (1998, 231–232), are somehow left hanging in a parallel anthropological universe. Yet, as far as the study of mind as an extended and distributed phenomenon is concerned, the distance between Gell's (1998) example of New Zealand Maori meeting houses and Clark and Chalmers' (1998) example of Otto's notebook is smaller than one might think. As long as we fail to pay proper attention to this important domain of human phenomenology (that is, the relationship or interface between cognition and material culture), the much-advocated "return to things" will remain only partially realized. Material culture will remain one "of the most resistant forms of cultural expression in terms of our attempts to comprehend it" (Miller 1987, 3), and the human mind will continue to be perceived as a disembodied information-processing ghost captured in the laboratories of neuroscience.

Perhaps what cognitive scientists are doing in their laboratories, or how philosophers go on to resolve the mind-body problem, may not seem to be of much concern for most archaeologists. The same can be said, I am sure, in respect to Miller's claim about material culture; certainly this is also something that very few cognitive scientists and philosophers might be willing to bother with. It is this attitude that needs to change. In fact, it is already changing. What is needed is to fully embrace and accept the consequences of the fact that the science of mind and the science of material culture are two sides of the same coin.[2] This is precisely the blind spot that this book aims to overcome by showing that understanding material culture leads to an understanding the human mind and vice versa. I perceive in the above a unique opportunity for active interdisciplinary dialogue that will forever transform not only our understanding of the boundaries between minds and things but also our understanding of the boundaries between the disciplines involved in the study of mind. Two questions remain: How can this transformation be achieved? Which discipline would carry the main burden of this task?

So far as the second question is concerned, the position of this book is pretty clear. It is inevitable, and it may also be advisable, that archaeology, in view of its natural preoccupation with the material medium and the long term, should carry the principal burden of such a transformation. Cognitive archaeology, probably more than any other field of cognitive research, has the ability, and the epistemic obligation, to develop a systematic understanding of the relationship between cognition and material culture from its own unique perspective. The temporal depth and historical diversity of the archaeological object, coupled with a genuine systematic examination of the interaction between mind and matter in the course of human cognitive evolution, may well yield some insights into the current questions and debates over human embodiment and the boundaries of mind. Although questions of this sort have only quite recently received explicit attention in philosophical discourse, they remain well rooted in the history of archaeological thought and practice. As a characteristic example, consider the work of André Leroi-Gourhan, who pointed out decades ago "the uniquely human phenomenon of exteriorization of the organs involved in the carrying out of technics" (1993 [1964], 258). For Leroi-Gourhan, human evolution has been oriented toward placing *outside* what in the rest of the animal world is achieved *inside* (ibid., 235). His early insights into the "freeing" of tools and the operational synergy of tool and "gesture" can certainly be seen as having anticipated many subsequent philosophical arguments about the extended, enactive, and distributed character of human cognition. In some sense, for the archaeologist, human cognition was never entirely in the head. Unfortunately, this genuine though vague intuition about the whereabouts of the human mind was never transformed into a systematic theory about exactly what cognition is and what it does.

Now let us return to the first question: How can we achieve this transformative integration of the way we think about mind and matter? There are many different routes that one could follow in order to achieve that. As I will discuss in the following chapters, each of these different methodological paths has its own merits and presents its own unique problems, challenges, and opportunities. What may be simpler or more useful to point out in the context of this brief introduction is the way *not to* achieve this transformation. And the way not to achieve this transformation is by shifting the focus of attention away from the cognitive domain and focusing solely on the social domain of human material existence, as many proponents of social archaeology and of material-culture studies seem to suggest. This tendency should be avoided because it often turns things into a mere passive substratum for society to imprint itself upon. (See, e.g., Olsen 2003, 2010; Webmoor and Witmore 2008; Webmoor 2007; Shanks 2007.) It should be made clear, then, that the transformation we are after can be achieved only by recognizing that all these different domains (social, bodily, cultural, or material) are essentially inseparable parts of the ontological compound we call the human mind. Choosing to speak about the cognitive rather than the social life of things, or about the cognitive rather than the social aspects of human evolution, does not mean in any way that I wish to demarcate one domain of phenomena from the other, or to differentiate between two distinctive realms of experience, one psychological and one social. It is instead a methodological, or perhaps an analytical, strategy for approaching and viewing these two inseparable aspects of human life. This brings us to the realm of material engagement.

The realm of material engagement

Strangely enough, the realm of material engagement can be thought of as one of the most familiar existential territories that we humans come to know and, at the same time, as an unknown existential territory. For example, it is familiar when the hand grasps a stone and makes it a tool, yet it remains *terra incognita* in that, despite a long genealogy of analytic efforts, just what this grasping implies for humans remains elusive and refuses to be reduced and read in the form of a linear evolutionary narrative.

There are many reasons why this blind spot exists. I have already pointed out some of them, and I shall point to others in the chapters that follow. But there is one general point that nicely encapsulates them all. It concerns the way in which the artificial line between persons and things, or between mind and the material world, has kept our deeply rooted Cartesian visions and modes of thinking at a safe distance from our long-evolved "cyborg" character (Clark 2003). Much of current thinking about human cognition seems to have neglected that the way we think is the property of a hybrid assemblage of brains, bodies, and things. This has a number of negative implications. As I have already said, it has blinded philosophy and the cognitive sciences to the pervasive, diachronic influence, and the transformative potential, of things in human life and cognitive evolution, leaving the study of mind ontologically oblivious of and epistemically agnostic about the properties and the active nature of material culture. In addition, this ongoing "tyranny of the dichotomy between humans and nonhumans" (Latour 1994, 795), characteristic of what Latour (1999) calls the "modern predicament," has for decades provided assumptions and preconceptions that still color our perceptions of the human past and the prehistoric mind. As a consequence, even if a big part of present-day archaeological theory adopts a relational viewpoint, more often than not archaeology is unwilling to follow the consequences of such a conviction or remains in a state of confusion about what this might imply in practice. The general call for non-dichotomous thinking in archaeology

(e.g., Hodder 1999; Tilley 1994; Gosden 1994; Thomas 1996) seems analogous to the Müller-Lyer illusion (figure 1.1). Knowing that the lines between
the arrows are equal, we still perceive them as different. Similarly, knowing
that mind and matter are relational entities, we continue to approach them
through the distortive lenses of representation. It seems that the purifica-
tion project of modernity (Latour 1993) that habituated our minds to think
and talk in terms of clean divisions and fixed categories makes it very difficult to shift the focus away from the isolated internal mind and the
demarcated external material world and toward their mutual constitution
as an inseparable analytic unit.

Apparently, this common attitude and implicit approach to the world
of things ought to change. In fact it has been changing, especially in recent
decades, most recognizably in the domains of material-culture studies and
embodied cognitive science. But although philosophers, anthropologists,
and archaeologists have now come to recognize that "who we are is in
large part a function of the webs of surrounding structure" (Clark 2003,
174), escaping from our Cartesian prison requires more than a change
in our academic "language games." It often demands a willingness to
transgress the ontological tidiness of modernity, just as conceptual art
transgressed the aesthetic tidiness of the Renaissance. Such a thorough
recalibration of the archaeology's perceptual field is not an easy task; it will
involve a great deal of cognitive dissonance. In this sense, the principal
objective of this book is to provide the conceptual means for reducing the
dissonance by furnishing a novel way to understand the ontological con-

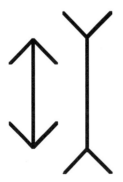

Figure 1.1
The Müller-Lyer illusion.

figurations and interconnections between cognition and material culture. Material engagement is the synergistic process by which, out of brains, bodies, and things, mind emerges.

A synopsis of the book

How have we gotten to where we are in our conceptions of what human mind is and does? Why does it matter, for archaeology, where the boundaries of mind are drawn? Precisely how does this relate to the study of material culture? In part I of the book (chapters 2 and 3) I provide a historical review and critique of cognitive archaeology and offer some preliminary remarks on the implications of the approach taken in this book for the study of cognition and material culture. In particular, chapter 2 briefly explores the ways in which archaeological and anthropological conceptions of the relationship between cognition and material culture have changed in the last 30 years or so. I explore the reasons why the majority of these conceptions continue to replicate the largely Cartesian predicament of modernity, and I try to identify the problems this causes for the archaeology of mind. In chapter 3, against this background, I summarize the Material Engagement approach and explain how that new theoretical framework could help us to overcome the problems. I discuss the epistemological foundation of and the metatheoretical assumptions behind this new way of looking at the intersection between cognition and material culture.

In part II (chapters 4–6), I set out Material Engagement Theory, focusing on the detailed exposition of the three main working hypotheses that make up the material-engagement approach: the extended mind, the enactive sign, and material agency.

In chapter 4, I explore the hypothesis of the extended mind. At issue here is a radical critique of the mind's location. I challenge the prevailing computational view of mind as an internal representational engine. Focusing on the example of the Mycenaean Linear B tablets, I attempt to clarify what the Extended Mind Hypothesis is and how precisely it relates to the perspectives of embodied, enactive, and distributed cognition. Against this philosophical background, I proceed to spell out my own hypothesis of the constitutive intertwining of cognition with material culture. The chapter ends with a series of archaeological and anthropological examples

This is the problem of cause again. How are things, actualized, actions caused? Surely some kind of representation is involved

exploring the implications of these ideas for the archaeology of mind and for the study of material culture.

In chapter 5, I explore the semiotic basis of material engagement, focusing on the semiotic dimension of material engagement and the nature of the material sign. I shift my focus from the traditional question of *what* a material sign means and place it upon the question of *how* it means. I start with what I call *the fallacy of the linguistic sign*, differentiating the material sign from the linguistic sign. The principal underlying assumption of my analysis is that, from a semiotic perspective, language and material culture differ substantially in the cognitive mechanisms that support their semiotic functions. More specifically, my suggestion is that the material sign does not primarily embody a communicative or representational logic but an *enactive* one. For *material semiosis* meaning is not a product of representation; it is a product of a process of conceptual integration between material and conceptual domains. I use a case study of the emergence of symbolic numerical thinking in the Neolithic of the Near East to explore that idea.

re represented?

In chapter 6, I pursue the question of agency and rethink the dualism between agents and things. Critically reviewing the use of agency in current sociological, anthropological, and archaeological theory, I challenge the deeply entrenched anthropocentric understanding of this notion as an attribute of the human individual. This challenge is followed by a suggestion for an alternative *symmetric* conceptualization that foregrounds the possibility of material agency in equal terms. From a non-anthropocentric perspective, I discuss *methodological fetishism* as a conceptual apparatus for studying the agency of things. I conclude the chapter by advancing the argument for material agency. My argument is that in the human engagement with the material world there are no fixed attributes of agent entities and patient entities and no clean ontological separations between them; rather, there is a constitutive intertwining between intentionality and affordance. Agency and intentionality may not be properties of things; they are not properties of humans either; they are the properties of material engagement.

What about bulls? believed

As I have said, part II of the book sets out and develops Material Engagement Theory. The central thesis that unites all the different levels is that the relationship between cognition and material culture is not one of abstract representation, or some other form of action at a distance, but one

re not what it is,
but what it does.

of ontological inseparability. This means that the understanding of human cognition is essentially interlocked with the study of the technical media-tions that constitute the central nodes of a materially extended and dis-tributed human mind.

But how, in practice, can we answer the question about whether "exter-nal" material resources can really function as literal extensions of some-one's mind? Can we do so by appealing to evidence found in archaeology and anthropology? In part III of the book (chapters 7–9), aiming to put the proposed theoretical scheme to the test, I shift my attention to a multi-scale analysis of the process of material engagement, using a number of characteristic archaeological and anthropological case studies ranging from earliest prehistory to the present.

In chapter 7, I focus on the tools of the Stone Age and the process of knapping (that is, striking flakes off a core). I examine, in particular, the prototypical stone tool: the Acheulean handaxe. How are we to understand the cognitive life of this object? What can it tell us about the traditional way we draw the line between cognition and material culture? Following the lines of Material Engagement Theory, I approach knapping as an *act of thought*—that is, a cognitive process that criss-crosses the boundaries of skin and skull, since its effective implementation involves elements that extend beyond the purely "mental" or "neural." With such an ontological foundation, my suggestion is that the stone held in the knapper's hand did much more than simply and passively offer the necessary "conditions of satisfaction" to the knapper's intention. Instead, I propose, the flaking intention is constituted, at least partially, by the stone and the marks left on its surface. In later periods, these marks, produced by different tech-niques, at different times, in different cultural settings, would become memory, symbol, number, and literacy—they would become us. I discuss these marks in chapter 8. How could an engraved ochre—or any other form of prehistoric marking, from incised bones to cave art—help us to under-stand the making of human mind? To answer this question, I attempt a comparative prehistory of mark making, aiming, on the one hand, to examine what connects or separates different assemblies of prehistoric marks (e.g., abstract geometric patterns, iconic depictions, or symbolic representations) and, on the other, to understand what, if anything, they tell us about the changing relationship between cognition and material culture. I show how those different kinds of material traces are more than mere indexes of human intelligence; they are, instead, the true marks of the mental, albeit of a mental that is truly indistinguishable from the physical.

In chapter 9, I attempt to situate the various aspects of my thesis in an ethnographic context that could better highlight the phenomenological requirements of the principal assertions of Material Engagement Theory. Striving to construct a cognitive ethnography by pursuing these issues, and placing special emphasis on the problem of agency and human creativity, I focus on the example of the potter's wheel. I show how the being of the potter is co-dependent and interweaved with the becoming of the clay.

In the epilogue (chapter 10), I attempt to pull the main findings of the preceding chapters together into a coherent argument about the relationship between cognition and material culture, the nature of extended cognition, and the cognitive life of things. How do things shape the mind? What implications follow from the seemingly unique human predisposition to reconfigure our bodies and extend our senses by using tools and material culture? A major methodological implication that Material Engagement Theory carries with it is that the observed changes in the material archaeological record should also be seen as indicative of possible plastic transformations and reorganizations in human cognitive architecture, rather than simply reflective of preexisting cognitive capacities or genetic changes. My aim in the epilogue is to stimulate critical discussion about how different forms of material culture (materials, artifacts, techniques, tools) may have provided, from prehistory to the present, a powerful mechanism of defining not only what we are but also what we want to become. This, I hope, will help us to achieve a better understanding of the meaning of stability and change in human beings. It will also transform the perceived role of cognitive archaeology and its future prospects in the study of mind.

I Cognition and Material Culture

2 Rethinking the Archaeology of Mind

In search of the ancient mind

Broadly defined as the "study of past *ways of thought* as inferred from material remains" (Renfrew 1994, 3, emphasis added) and analytically situated in the middle ground between functional processual and post-processual approaches, cognitive archaeology has launched a challenging research project in search of the mind behind the artifact. The overall goal, expressed in the words of James Bell, was "to incorporate mental, ideational, symbolic and other such elements into theories about prehistoric peoples" (1992, 48). This general objective has been pursued from various perspectives. With time, the initial skepticism about "paleopsychological" investigations (e.g., Binford 1965) gave way to a systematic research endeavor, overcoming many methodological problems and opening new fruitful avenues of archaeological research.

What we now call cognitive archaeology or the archaeology of mind fuses different schools of thought and research strands together in a highly interdisciplinary and rapidly growing research field with two broad foci of interest. The first focus is mainly concerned with human cognitive evolution—that is, with what might be called human speciation (e.g., Stout et al. 2008; Stout and Chaminade 2007, 2009; Bruner 2003, 2004, 2007; Mellars et al. 2007; Mellars and Gibson 1996; de Beaune et al. 2009; D'Errico 1995, 1998, 2001; D'Errico et al. 2003; Gibson 1993; Wynn and Coolidge 2003, 2004; Coolidge and Wynn 2004, 2005, 2009; Wynn 2002; Deacon 1997; Read and van der Leeuw 2008; Humphrey 1998; Henshilwood and Dubreuil 2009, 2011; Hodgson and Helvenston 2006; Holloway 1999; Mithen 1996; Davidson and Noble 1989, 1993; Noble and Davidson 1996; Malafouris 2007, 2008b, 2009, 2010a,b; Malafouris and Renfrew

2008). The second major focus of research is on more recent developments of our species, *Homo sapiens*, ranging from the transition to agricul-
ture and the development of literacy and complex societies to the study
of technology, art, religion, selfhood, and, in general, the interaction
between cognition and material culture (e.g., Renfrew and Zubrow 1994;
Renfrew and Scarre 1998; Renfrew et al. 2008, 2009; Renfrew 2001a,b,
2004, 2006, 2007, 2008; Knappett 2002, 2004, 2005, 2006; Gosden 2008;
Gamble 2007; Hodder 1993, 1999; Mithen and Parsons 2008; Malafouris
2004, 2008a,c, 2010a,c; Malafouris and Renfrew 2010b; Boivin 2008; Stout
2002).

The success of cognitive archaeology in its quest for disciplinary identity
is undeniable. The same, I am afraid, cannot be said of another epistemic
domain. At the basis of cognitive archaeology one can still detect a serious,
and rather paradoxical, methodological drawback. It relates to a simple yet
extremely important question: Where in the archaeological record do we
find cognition?

Where is the mind?

There are things that archaeologists can dig up and things that they
cannot. Most people would agree that minds are of the latter kind. Mental
states and processes are supposedly made up of a different sort of stuff and
take place in a different sort of realm. In view of this prevalent tendency
to equate mind with brain, and the concomitant assumptions about the
spatial boundaries of the human cognitive realm that this tendency carries
with it, it was natural that cognitive archaeology could only aspire to use
the "external" material residues that can be detected in the archaeological
record for producing indirect inferences about the "internal" mental
aspects of the prehistoric cognitive realm. On this construal, what we
archaeologists excavate is not the ancient mind itself but the material
consequences of non-material thinking—that is, the behavioral residues
left by the ways in which human thought was imposed on or reflected in
the material culture visible in the archaeological record. Then why ask an
archaeologist about the mind? The archaeologist Carl Knappett captures
this critical point succinctly in his book *Thinking Through Material Culture*
(2005, 168): "Aspiring to mentalism, but condemned to materialism, it is
hardly surprising that many archaeologists have given up to the former

altogether." Indeed, what is then left for archaeology to say about the mind that might be of any true interest?

It appears, then, that the archaeology of mind, largely preoccupied with developing the necessary means for ascending Christopher Hawkes' ladder of inference (1954), has failed to realize that the metaphor of the ladder itself was grounded upon a mistake of a very special kind: a category mistake. What this category mistake essentially implies is a dualistic conception of the relationship between mind and matter. Or, if I may elaborate on Gilbert Ryle's (1949) formulation of the fallacy involved, the archaeologist who is searching for the ancient mind *behind* the artifact is committing the same "category mistake" as the foreign visitor to Cambridge or Oxford who, having seen the colleges, the libraries, and the departments, asks to be shown the university.

As a consequence, the theoretical basis of cognitive archaeology, trapped in a Cartesian universe that separates the mental realm from the realm of materiality and practice, remained constrained by the premises of two problematic assumptions: the dictates of methodological individualism (Bell 1992) (that is, the foregrounding of the human individual as the appropriate analytic unit and ontological locus of human cognition) and the equation of the "cognitive" with the "symbolic" (see, e.g., Renfrew 1993, 1994) according to the principles of an essentially representational view of mind. (For a concise critique of these problems, see chapter 1 of Knappett 2005.)

Thus, the archaeology of mind has some serious methodological hurdles to overcome. Before proceeding, however, we need to understand how we have gotten to where we are in our conceptions of the mind, why these conceptions continue to replicate the largely Cartesian predicament of modern thought, and how Material Engagement Theory could help us change these conceptions.

Cognitivism

Once the famous Cartesian dichotomy between the "thinking thing" and the "extended thing" was drawn, a mechanism was needed to account for how those independent components or substances interact. To account for the so-called mind-body problem (see, e.g., Ryle 1949), the notion of symbolic representation was gradually introduced in philosophy of mind to bridge this huge ontological gap. The idea of representation furnished a simple mechanism by which we could feed our cognitive apparatus with facts and information from the "external world"; it also suggested how we materialize and externalize our mental contents by way of behavioral output to the world. The image of mind that gradually emerged could be seen metaphorically as a bucket filled with knowledge and information (Popper 1979). Cognitive processing happens in the head somewhere between perception and action. The philosopher Susan Hurley dubbed this the "sandwich model of cognition" (1998). That is to say, mind was viewed as a storehouse of passive internal representational structures and procedures—a "filing cabinet" capable of receiving and manipulating internally the sensory information received from the "outside" world. (For reviews, see Clark 1997 and Clark 2001a.)

Grounded on the premises of this broad representational thesis, cognitivism,[1] or the so-called computational view of mind, emerged during the 1960s as an attempt to redefine human conceptual architecture in the image of the digital computer, which was developing rapidly at that time (Gardner 1985; Dupuy 2000). A new powerful metaphor was spreading rapidly: that the mind is to the brain as a computer program is to the hardware of the computer on which it runs. This, to a large extent, remains the dominant paradigm in present-day cognitive science, as well as the implicit model behind most archaeological accounts of prehistoric cognition that conceptualize the human mind primarily through the idioms of representation and information processing. (For a concise discussion of this trend, see Mithen 1998, 8–10.)

What makes something a representation? Why is representation an important concept?

Re-presentation: Looking at the other side of the engram

Generally speaking, representation can be understood in a double sense: as an object that stands for, refers to, or denotes something, but also as the relationship between a thing and that which stands for or denotes it. More important for our current purposes, we can distinguish between two major types of representations: "External" representations are those material signs or sign systems that are publicly available in the world. Mental or "internal" representations can be understood as referring to the representational content of a certain intention or belief *about* the world.

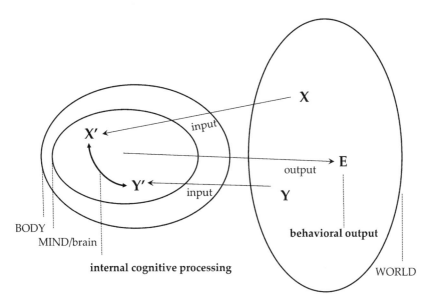

X & Y = things in the world
X′ & Y′ = representations of the real things (X & Y) inside the mind/brain
E = behavioral output

Figure 2.1
The internalist or representational view of mind.

Mental representations, in other words, provide an internal intracranial structure that makes it possible for the objects of thought and perception to be present *inside* the cognitive system, which is localized *inside* the head (figure 2.1). Their functional role is, in a way, closely associated with the physical neural vehicles that carry and code information about some states of affairs realized in the external world. More precisely, representation is conceived as the principal disembodied mechanism by which we feed our brains with information *from* the world, process that information, then externalize our mental contents *into* the world. On that construal, when we perceive, classify, remember, or simply think about an object X, we don't think about the "real" object; rather, we think about its internalized representational substitute or replicator, X′.

External representations have been studied for a long time and raise no real concerns from an archaeological or an anthropological perspective. However, no general consensus has been established about what "internal" representations are, what they do, and what neural structures realize them.

In my own view, "neurons" do not represent anything; neurons simply form plastic networks, which produce activation patterns that are structurally coupled with the rest of the human body and the material world. Still, representations are, according to the dominant computational theory of mind, the stuff of which our mental engines are made. This claim is "general enough to encompass the current range of thinking in cognitive science, including connectionist theories" (Thagard 1996, 10; see also Fodor 1981).

It was only natural that most archaeologists, given this strong "computationalist" or "internalist" tradition in philosophy and cognitive science, would see in this representational or "symbolic function" the defining feature of what it means to be a modern human cognizer. The thing to note, however, is that behind the undeniable advances in the study of the human mind that this paradigm has brought about one can easily find some very important shortcomings. For example, in implementing computational theory in the laboratories of artificial intelligence, it soon became manifest that, although simulations based on computational logic proved extremely effective in performing complex analytic tasks (such as running a program capable of winning a chess game), they were extremely ineffective in performing tasks as simple as instructing a robot to find its way out of a room without running into walls. In fact, when the first such autonomous devices were constructed by Grey Walter (1953), they had nothing to do with complex algorithms and representational inputs. Their kinship was with W. Ross Ashby's homeostat (1952) and Norbert Wiener's cybernetic feedback (1948) rather than with the complex representational structure of the by-that-time-famous Turing machine (Turing 1950). With simple electromechanical circuitry, Walter's "turtles" were capable of producing emergent properties and behavior patterns that could not be determined by any of their system components, effecting in practice a cybernetic transgression of the mind-body divide and materially exemplifying a model of human cognition the implications of which have yet to be realized and properly digested in cognitive science. (See Brooks 1991; Steels 2007.)

What the above implies for the computational model in question will not be pursued here in detail. (For details, see Dupuy 2000; Boden 1990; Clark 2001a,b.) However, to make a long story short and easier to comprehend, it is safe to argue that the major shortcoming of this paradigm was, and remains, that it provides a view of human cognition so purified and so detached from the world that in the end it resembles a "brain in a vat" (Putnam 1982)—that is, a disembodied input-output device characterized by abstract, higher-level logical operations. Using computational simulations as a method for gaining information about the human mind, you might learn a few things about the representational structures that support inferential logic and problem solving, but you will certainly also end up with a distorted picture of how those structures relate to the environment, and probably with no picture at all of how those structures are enacted in real-life situations and in different cultural settings. As the anthropologist Tim Ingold (1993, 431) remarks, "it makes no more sense to speak of cognition as the functioning of such a [computational] device than it does to speak of locomotion as the product of an internal motor mechanism analogous to the engine of a car. Like locomotion, cognition is the accomplishment of the *whole animal*, it is not accomplished by a mechanism interior to the animal and for which it serves as a vehicle." In other words, in most cases computationalism failed the test of ecological validity. As Andy Clark notes in his book *Being There*, evidence concerning the intimate role of the environment in thought processes implies that classical artificial intelligence "bundles into the *machine* a set of operational capacities which in real life emerge only from the interactions between machine (brain) and world" (1997, 64). Turing's algorithms and Chomskian grammars, however effective in mapping off-line analytical procedures of disembodied intellects, scored very low on cognitive tasks that involved embodied on-line engaging with the material world in real-life settings.

From the perspective of archaeology, I believe, it makes good sense to assume that the ancient mind whose operations we want to pursue and reconstruct in and through the material remains of the past is of the latter kind. It is a mind absorbed in, rather than detached from, the world, and principally preoccupied with doing "what computers can't do" (Dreyfus 1979). Consequently, to ground the challenging task of cognitive archaeology upon a model that conspicuously mistakes "the properties of the socio-cultural system for the properties of the person" (Hutchins 1995, 366), and for which material culture has a place in the mind only as a disembodied digit of information written somehow on the neural tissue, is not simply to undermine the whole project from the very start, but to deprive it of the possibility of making any significant contribution to the understanding of the human mind.

This is why I am extremely skeptical of the influence that notions like "symbolism," "symbolic storage," or "representational" capacities have in shaping, and in many cases defining, many archaeological and anthropological debates over the nature and the development of what is usually referred as "modern human cognition" or "behavioral modernity." Contrary to what a big part of present-day philosophy and cognitive science thinks a mind primarily does, I will argue in this book that we need to move beyond the limits of computation and free our minds from the legacy of representation. Approaching the engagement of mind with the material world on such a representational basis not only reiterates the myth of the "naked" brain, which reduces the cognitive life of things to an abstract internalized code of some sort; it also leads to an inherently dualistic conception of the complex co-evolutionary brain-culture spiral that characterizes hominin evolution. This "internalist" and "neurocentric" attitude threatens to obscure much that is of value in the archaeology of mind— especially our understanding of the nature of the relationship between cognition and material culture. I suggest, and I shall be discussing extensively in the following chapters, that representational phenomena and properties of the above sort are only the shadows of "the cognitive life of things." (Also see Malafouris and Renfrew 2010.)

Although I consider representationalism to be misleading in many important ways, I do not commit to a strictly non-representational stance. Though Material Engagement Theory can be certainly characterized, owing to its strong enactive basis, as an anti-representational framework (at least in relation to the two main premises of representationalism in classical cognitive science, namely an internalist view of human cognition and a computational understanding of what counts as a cognitive process proper), it does not deny representation altogether. Rather, it aims to ground representation on a more appropriate enactivist foundation. I understand that for some philosophers blending enactivism with representation, or what I call "enactive signification" (see chapter 5), may seem a contradiction in terms, but I hope that the concept will present no serious problems for archaeologists familiar with the semiotic qualities of material culture. No doubt material culture often represents, and thus the human mind can be seen as able to construct "external" representations. I want to argue, however, that this representational dimension of material culture doesn't exhaust its semiotic abilities (see also Boivin 2008, chapter 2; Knappett

2005, chapter 5), and that the fact that we are capable of constructing material representations doesn't necessarily imply that a similar representational function can be used to characterize the internal operations of our brains. In fact, insofar as "a signaling neuron uses as much energy as a leg muscle cell while running a marathon" (Allen 2009, 181), such an energetically expensive strategy makes little sense. What does this mean? To some extent, what I want to argue is similar to the proposal, recently put forth by the philosopher Pierre Steiner, that "the *only* representations that make up cognition are *external* (extracranial) representations" (2010, 237). Thus, for Material Engagement Theory, in contrast to what appears to be a common assumption in cognitive science, the only representations with any substantial or real implications for human cognition are to be found outside the head. Internal representations are simply a misleading attempt to explaining the unfamiliar intricate workings of the human mind and brain by way of a more familiar model: that of the external material symbol. In the context of Material Engagement Theory, the notion of "internal" representations can be retained only if it is used in the neural constructivist sense—that is, to refer some broadly defined "neural activation patterns in the brain that contribute to adaptive behaviour in the environment" (Westerman et al. 2007, 75). I shall be clarifying that in chapter 3. For present purposes, what should be emphasized about the relationship between the material-engagement approach and representation is that in mainstream cognitive science inner (within-the-skin) representations are often used as the criterion for what counts as cognitive in a way that would leave most external (beyond-the-skin) elements outside the cognitive equation. In contrast, for Material Engagement Theory the argument from representation works the other way around, for the only representations that count and that may have any true significance in the study of mind are those to be found, beyond skin and skull, in the outside world. For all these reasons, it would be fair to say that Material Engagement Theory requires us to rethink the idea of representation radically, but not necessarily to abandon it altogether.

Dismantling Hawkes' ladder

How, then, should we proceed? If the human mind is not the clearly demarcated information-processing representational device so neatly objectified in the familiar exemplar of the computer, what is it? And, indeed, where is it? Where do we draw a line between cognition and material culture? How can the cognitive properties that arise from the interaction of the person with the social and material world best be approached and described? In this book I seek to outline a fundamentally new outlook that I hope will help us to find answers to those questions. But whether or not we eventually come up with some good answers, one thing should be made clear: As long as cognition and material culture remain separated by the ontological gulf of representation, our efforts to understand the nature of either are doomed to failure.

All these problems with the use and abuse of representation in cognitive archaeology will become clearer as our discussion progresses. What is more useful to emphasize for now is that their gradual recognition resulted in several critiques within archaeology aiming at dismantling Hawkes' ladder of inference and recasting the narrow disembodied conception of human mind.

A major contribution in this direction has been made by the so-called interpretive or post-processual school of thought in archaeology—notably by Ian Hodder, who was one of the first to explicitly recognize the "active nature" of material culture and to foreground its meaningful social character. (See Hodder 1982, 1986, 1991.) We have also seen the development of conceptually new ways to approach some of the cognitive dimensions of material culture—for example, Daniel Miller's notion of objectification, defined as "the inevitable process by which all expression, conscious or unconscious, social or individual, takes specific form" (1987, 80). Moreover, Chris Tilley's work on material metaphors (1999) offered a new stance for examining the systematic linkages between material and conceptual domains. According to Tilley, material things, "unlike words," are "not just communicating meaning but actively doing something in the world as mediators of activity" (1999, 265). And we should not forget that it was the archaeologists Christopher Gosden (1994, 2008, 2010), Julian Thomas (1996), and Chris Tilley (1994) that first introduced phenomenology to archaeological thinking, or that the concept of material engagement obviously embodies such a phenomenological view of human existence. Thus, we may need a "temporal ethnography of the artefact" (ibid., 4) in order to understand the active, constructive character of things in human life.

More specifically from the perspective of cognitive archaeology, Colin Renfrew (2001a,b) was the first to attempt a significant methodological shift. Breaking the narrow equation between cognition and symbolism, he redefined the scope of cognitive archaeology, shifting the focus away from the abstract realm of the "symbolic" and toward the realm of "materiality" and "material engagement." There is an entire ontology implicit in the above suggestion, as well as accumulated experience and positive feedback from a variety of theoretical frameworks both within and outside the field of archaeology. The work of Carl Knappett further advanced the field of cognitive archaeology by offering a brilliant account on how "objects are bound up in humans in their guises as biological, psychological and social beings, as bio-psycho-social totalities" (2005, 169). Renfrew's discussion of the notion of weight may be useful in making this point explicit:

Weight has first to be perceived as a physical reality—in hands and arms, not just in the brain within the skull—before it can be conceptualized and measured. The mind works through the body. To localise it exclusively within the brain is not strictly correct. Moreover, we often think not only through the body, but beyond it. (Renfrew 2007, 119)

My aim is to build on the above ideas and make their philosophical and epistemological grounding more explicit. This book draws and extends on Renfrew's original proposal in order to construct a new cross-disciplinary foundation *toward a theory of material engagement* (Renfrew 2004; Malafouris 2004).

Material Engagement Theory can be seen as having much in common with many aspects of post-processual thinking and with the recent emphasis in archaeology on the "dialectical and recursive relationship between persons and things" (Tilley, Keane, Küchler, Rowlands, and Spyer 2006, 4). It also differs in many important respects, especially in its explicit emphasis on the cognitive life of things and the nature of the relationship between cognition and material culture. Hodder's recent theory of human-thing entanglement (2011a,b) is a good example. Entanglement Theory shares a great deal with Material Engagement Theory both in its "archaeological sensitivity to the complexities and practical interlacings of material things" (2011a, 175) and in its focus on the inter-connectedness and the practical temporalities of things. But whereas Entanglement Theory remains concerned with building "a particularly archaeological understanding of the social process" (2011a, 176), Material Engagement Theory focuses mainly on the process and the making of the human mind. Nonetheless, the two approaches are clearly complementary when it comes to answering the question of how humans and things have become entangled. What changes with Material Engagement Theory is our way of looking at things and the conceptual vocabulary we use to express the distinctively human ability to think through, with, and about the material world.

Where does all this leave us? I will quote Carl Knappett:

[W]ith our leitmotif of "thinking through material culture" the archaeologist need not be reduced to the unhappy state of being a frustrated mentalist condemned to materialism. If we accept that mind and matter achieve a codependency through the medium of bodily action, then it follows that ideas and attitudes, rather than occupying a separate domain from the material, actually find themselves inscribed "in" the object. (2005, 169)

In other words (and returning to Ryle's category mistake), there is no mind behind the artifact, just as there is no university apart from the labs, students, professors, libraries, and departments. The analogy may be crude, and the same can be said for the school of behaviorism from which it emanates, but it anticipates a basic point that is worth repeating again and again: that "the mental characteristics of the system are immanent, not in some part, but in the system as a whole" (Bateson 1973, 316).

3 The Material-Engagement Approach: A Summary of the Argument

The search for method becomes one of the most important problems of the entire enterprise of understanding the uniquely human forms of cognitive activity. In this case, the method is simultaneously prerequisite and product, the tool and the result of the study.
—Lev Vygotsky (1978, 65)

Exactly what does Material Engagement Theory (MET) aim to explain? How does it relate to standard ways of thinking in cognitive science and archaeology? (More important, how does it depart from them?) What, specifically, can MET bring to the study of mind? How can it help us to redefine material culture's place in and effect on the human cognitive system? The explanatory success of MET depends upon further clarification of these issues.

I should start by saying that MET seeks to provide an integrated archaeological perspective concerned with the interactions through time between cognition and material culture and with the consequences of these interactions for understanding the making of present and past ways of thinking. To that end, MET takes a comparative long-term view of human cognitive development and thus tends to be at variance with other established research frameworks in embodied cognitive science that remain largely individualistic and synchronic. More than that, it brings a fresh material culture perspective to the way human cognitive changes can be studied and understood.

The material-engagement approach is based on a number of mutually supporting concepts, postulates, and working hypotheses. Before I discuss them, it may be useful to acknowledge a basic theoretical commitment and aspiration: The aim of MET is to restate the problem of the interaction between cognition and material culture in a more productive manner by placing it upon a new relational ontological foundation.

How to carve mind at its joints

As I mentioned briefly in my introductory chapter, the anthropologist Edwin Hutchins uses the term *cognitive ecology* to describe a similar kind of relatedness. The study of mind in context, Hutchins argues, should be, first and above all, an attempt to uncover connectivity, that is, "the web of mutual dependence among the elements of a cognitive ecosystem" (2010b, 705). But how is that possible? If everything is (potentially) "connected to everything else," how do we choose where to draw the right boundaries for our analytical units? Fortunately, as Hutchins suggests, the density of connectivity varies within time and space, but also from one ecological assembly to another. Perhaps, then, we could follow Plato's advice and carefully "carve nature at its joints," placing the boundaries of our analytical units "where connectivity is relatively low" (*Phaedrus*, 265d–266a). An obvious problem arises: Connectivity is not *a priori*. Instead, it is based on assumptions that might emphasize some kinds of connections over others. This has the consequence of bringing certain phenomena to the center of attention while leaving some others unexplained or even rendering them invisible. Hutchins is, of course, fully aware of this problem: "Plato's advice is, alas, easier to state than to follow. . . . What looks like low connectivity under one theory may look like a region of high connectivity to another theory." (ibid., 706) At best, we can hope not to put delimiting lines where connectivity is high and dense but isn't of the sort that our current ontologies might be able to recognize.

It appears, then, that we have returned to where we started. Is there any way out of this circle? I suggest a possibility that might keep us from putting boundaries in the wrong place or assuming there is one center where in fact there are many. That is to abandon the logic of "boundaries" and "delimiting lines." (See Ingold 2006, 2008, 2010.) The purity of delimiting lines or of any concomitant neat analytical or metaphysical distinction cannot accommodate many of the phenomena I seek to investigate in this book.

Boundaries, paths, and analytical units

The foregoing remarks are meant to provide some hints about the logic behind the unit of analysis that the material-engagement approach takes as the focus of its study. To illustrate that better, it might be worthwhile to consider the question "What is human cognition, and where should we look for it?" If we accept the classical computational view that "cognition begins with an input to the brain and ends with an output from the brain," we should be looking to processes within the head (Shapiro 2011, 27). On this construal, what archaeologists can be said to excavate are the residues of past intelligent behavior and assemblages of material signs. Those cognitive traces, in other words, embody the possibility, and thus reiterate the archaeological aspiration, that if properly analyzed and interpreted they might give us a glimpse of what went on inside the head of the prehistoric individual. But notice the assumption here about where true cognitive states and processes are supposedly instantiated. Is such an assumption unavoidable?

MET rejects this classical computational ideal. As I mentioned in chapter 1, our deeply entrenched assumptions about the intracranial ontological boundaries of human cognition should be resisted. From an archaeological or an anthropological perspective, these common presumptions of mentality defined on the basis of brain-bound cognitive processes and genuine "non-derived representations" (see Adams and Aizawa 2008) should be treated as historical conventions rather than natural kinds. For one thing, most of our evidence about the evolution of human intelligence comes in the form of material culture rather than abstract ideas and brain tissue. For another, the more we come to learn and understand about things, the more they look like a genuine element of what it means to be a human cognizer. An important postulate of MET is that the sort of stuff that makes up the mind can be equally found located within and outside the skin. As far as the topology of human cognition is concerned, MET remains locationally uncommitted—as the computer scientist William Clancey put it (2009, 28), MET is committed to "antilocalization." Andy Clark, in his book *Supersizing the Mind*, also speaks of a similar indifference to the location of mental resources, which he calls "the Hypothesis of Cognitive Impartiality" (2008a, 121–123). Nonetheless, Clark's critique of the "brain-bound" mind seems to go only halfway. "In rejecting the vision of human cognitive processing as *organism bound*," he proposes, "we should not feel forced to deny that it is (in most, perhaps all, real-world cases) *organism centered*." (ibid., 123) For MET, the latter of Clark's statements cannot always be sustained. I will explore this decentralized view of mind and agency in part II of this book.

For present purposes, suffice it to say that, in the context of material engagement, boundaries are open and centers are shifting along the continuum of mediated action. The basic idea entertained here is very similar to the distributed-cognition approach and is nicely expressed by Hutchins:

> A good deal of contemporary thinking, and probably an even greater proportion of ancient thinking, happens in *interaction* of brain and body with the world. This seems innocent enough and many people take it to mean simply that thinking is something that happens in the brain as a consequence of interaction with the world. That is not the claim being made here. The claim here is that, first and foremost, thinking *is* interactions of brain and body with the world. Those interactions are not evidence of, or reflections of, underlying thought processes. They are instead the thinking processes themselves. (2008, 2112)

The theoretical power of MET lies precisely in providing a new means for studying the complex nature of the interactions between the internal and the external resources of human cognition as well as the role of cultural practices in the orchestration of human cognitive processes. The focus is on understanding the material world as a constitutive and efficacious part of the human cognitive system both from an ontogenetic and a phylogenetic perspective. Keeping this last point in mind, I will now try to situate MET in the context of other evolutionary and developmental frameworks of thinking.

Understanding evolvability: The developmental challenge

Material Engagement Theory, as an archaeological theory, seeks to describe and explain long-term change, particularly the processes by which human cognitive abilities grow, transform, and change. However, in contrast with more traditional approaches in cognitive archaeology, the material-engagement approach is not concerned with the task of associating specific human abilities with specific time periods and pre-fixed evolutionary stages. Specifically, whereas the majority of studies in cognitive and evolutionary archaeology seem to be primarily preoccupied with questions about when and where (e.g., where and when symbolic thinking and language first appeared in the archaeological record), MET asks primarily about the what, the why, and the how—for example: What is symbolic thinking? Why and how did symbolism emerge? What forms of signification count as symbolic *meta*-representational thinking? Knowing when and where things are happening in cognitive evolution is important and interesting but does not explain much in itself. What we need is an integrative comparative perspective able to identify the different ingredients of cognitive change (evolutionary or developmental) and the causal mechanisms that underlie them in different contexts of human cognitive becoming from the Early Stone Age to the present.

It follows from what I have said so far that the concern of MET with the cognitive development of our species might, to an important extent, be seen as a new form of evolutionary epistemology. Even though the general outlook of MET may seem to resemble that of evolutionary psychology (Cosmides and Tooby 1987; Barkow et al. 1992) or that of evolutionary archaeology (O'Brien and Lyman 2002; Shennan 2002), in fact it shares very few basic theoretical presuppositions with them. The material-engagement approach also differs from the prevalent cultural-evolution approach (Mesoudi 2011; Mesoudi et al. 2006; Durham 1990; Boyd and Richerson 1985). In particular, whereas MET sees cultural and biological evolution as an inseparable synergetic process, proponents of cultural evolution treat culture as a second, separate evolutionary system that acts in parallel to biological or genetic evolution. An advantage of the cultural-evolution approach is that properties of biological evolution can be directly applied to describe cultural phenomena. But I want to argue that the metaphoric logic behind the above premise is seriously problematic. Suffice it to say that for MET human intelligence is not situated simply in a basic interactive sense but in a deeper intra-active and temporally structured sense. This means that interaction elicited by our surroundings (human or nonhuman) not only influences our cognitive abilities and affective responses from the very beginning but also shapes the form and the constitutive mechanisms of interaction.

From the perspective of MET, understanding the co-evolution of brains, bodies, and things does not stop at the possible causal correlations that the changes observed in one of them might produce in the others. Another challenge is to discern the possible ways in which the actual nature of the relationship between them might have changed in the course of human evolution. Naturally, exploring the long-term effects of culture on the brain (and vice versa) is far more difficult. Despite years of research in many disciplines (for a good summary see Tomasello et al. 2005), the precise links between ontogeny and phylogeny remain far from obvious or straightforward. At present, learning and practice-related developmental plasticity appear to be the most promising avenues for building some analytical bridges between the short-term and the long-term aspects of human cognitive becoming. (See, e.g., Dupré 2008.)

For all the reasons cited above, if we want to situate the perspective of MET in the context of other current evolutionary and developmental frameworks of thinking, the intellectual kinship of our approach lies with more radical and interactive frameworks, such as developmental systems theory (Oyama 1985, 2000; Oyama et al. 2001; Griffiths and Gray 1994, 2001, 2004; Griffiths and Stotz 2000), niche-construction theory (Odling-Smee et al. 2003), and neuroconstructivism (Mareschal et al. 2007a,b; Quartz and Sejnowski 1997). Developmental systems theory (Griffiths et al. 2010; Griffiths and Stotz 2000; Oyama et al. 2001; Griffiths and Gray 2004), for instance, has long recognized that the developmental trajectory of an organism is not a fixed genetic program but a matrix of internal and external resources. Evolution is not just change in gene frequencies; it is change in the entire spectrum of available developmental resources, and in the many causal pathways by which resources come to be deployed in development. All elements of the developmental matrix matter by way of an "interactive construction" whereby the effect of each resource depends on its interaction with many others. Neuroconstructivism has been especially helpful in this connection, offering a developmental account of the neural system as heavily constrained by multiple interacting factors, some intrinsic to the developing organism and some extrinsic to it. Similarly to developmental systems theory, these flexible and interacting constraints span multiple levels of analysis, from genes and the individual cell to the physical and social environment. Therefore, cognitive development is explained as the emergent product of the interplay of these constraints. In this context, the view of brain and cognitive development known as *probabilistic epigenesis* (Gottlieb 2002, 2003), which emphasizes the interactions between experience and gene expression (Gottlieb 2007), is of special interest. The unidirectional formula (prevalent in molecular biology) by which genes drive and determine behavior is replaced with a new scheme that explicitly recognizes the bidirectionality of influences between the genetic, behavioral, environmental, and socio-cultural levels of analysis. (The formula is illustrated in figure 3.1.) Genetic causality gives way to what has been termed "developmental-relational causality" (Gottlieb and Halpern

(a)

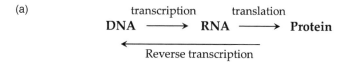

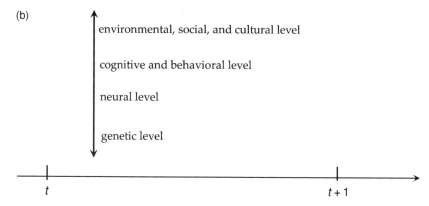

Figure 3.1
New theoretical frameworks such as that of "neuroconstructivism" and "probabilistic epigenesis" provide us with a new nonlinear and interactive model for understanding the relationship among genes, the brain, and behavior that characterizes
human cognitive becoming (b). Cognitive development is no longer seen as the
progressive unfolding of information that is laid out in the genome (a). The traditional view of a one-directional flow of cause and effect from genes (DNA) to RNA
to the structure of proteins they encode gives way to a subtler picture in which
physical, social, and cultural aspects of environment a behavior play fundamental
roles in triggering the expression of genes.

2002). As summarized by Gottlieb (2007, 1), probabilistic epigenesis
"emphasizes the reciprocity of influences within and between levels of an
organism's developmental manifold (genetic activity, neural activity,
behavior, and the physical, social, and cultural influences of the external
environment) and the ubiquity of gene-environment interaction in the
realization of all phenotypes." Put simply, this means that, owing to socially,
environmentally, and culturally caused differences and variations in life
and learning experiences, individuals of the same genotype can have different neural, cognitive, and behavioral outcomes. It also implies that one
cannot correlate a particular genotype and a certain neural or behavioral
outcome without taking "external" mediational properties and experiential

factors into consideration. This unpredictability of the phenotypes of similar genotypes when confronted with novel or different developmental trajectories and circumstances indicates that epigenetic outcomes are probabilistic rather than predetermined.

This emerging "post-genomic view" of behavioral biology (for a recent review see Charney forthcoming) showing that even gene expression can be influenced in very specific ways by environmental and experiential factors stands in clear contrast to many ideas that are well established in evolutionary psychology. (For examples of the latter, see Barkow et al. 1992 or Pinker 1997.) The brain, far from a hard-wired modular organ adapted to a specific ancestral lifestyle, emerges as a dynamic product of a co-evolutionary process that is still ongoing. A consequence of this co-evolutionary process is that culture can no longer be seen as a mere epiphenomenal influence on a biologically predetermined and universally shared set of capacities or features of human cognition. Perhaps, then, as Griffiths and Stotz suggest, we should recognize that "what individuals inherit from their ancestors is not a mind, but the ability to develop a mind" (2000, 31). (See also Karmiloff-Smith 1992; Chiao and Ambady 2007; Jordan 2008.) I will argue in this book that Material Engagement Theory may provide a useful framework in which to understand the long-term dynamics behind this "ability" and the ways it becomes realized. As the theory of "niche construction" points out, the defining feature of this ability to grow our minds may be found by looking at the systematic changes in the developmental niche brought about by humans as they alter their social and technological environments (Sterelny 2004; Laland and Sterelny 2006). This constructive process often results in unusual evolutionary dynamics (Day et al. 2003). Of course, such alterations in humans go well beyond what we observe when spiders make webs, when birds build nests, or when beavers construct dams. Archaeology may well testify that significant parts and episodes of the long developmental trajectory of the human mind appear relatively recently and can certainly be seen as the emergent products of various culturally instantiated social and technological processes rather than of innate biological capacities.

In approaching the questions set forth above, it is important that we try to incorporate in our explanations the inherently plastic and changing nature of the human brain. Nonetheless, the brain is only a part of the story. And that part of the story can easily mislead us to a sterile "neurocentric" attitude that has no place in cognitive archaeology, and that in fact stands in contrast to the grounding principles of MET. Thus, it is important to note that this empirical opening into the neural substrates of the human mind does not aim to reduce change, difference, and variability to some innate biological universals. The aim is, rather, to understand the nature and the meaning of cognitive difference and variation across the different levels and temporal scales of human experience, and to explain how the one level affects, interacts with, and helps explain the other. MET aims to accomplish that by framing research questions that focus on dynamic relationships or linkages that remain relatively undertheorized from the viewpoint of cognitive and brain sciences—that is, on the interactions among brains, bodies, and things.

The last point brings us to a final major differentiating feature of MET: The quest for establishing culturally sensitive and philosophically informed links between the brain's functional structure and material culture calls for a methodology that, among other things, is able to integrate different temporalities. Unlike other archaeological theories, MET is concerned to provide a framework that establishes some clear connections between micro-scale cognitive and neuroscientific theories and macro-scale material realities of the archaeological record. The notion of metaplasticity nicely exemplifies the above synergy, signifying the point of intersection between cognition and material culture. (See also Malafouris 2010a.) It also offers a widely applicable analytic unit that is especially useful for doing away with some deeply misconceived assumptions about the mind's function, ontology, and location.

"Vital materiality": How to take material culture seriously

As Bjørnar Olsen says in his book *In Defense of Things*, archaeology is "first and foremost a concern" with everyday things (2010, 2; see also Olsen et al. 2012). Those things, nonetheless, are inextricably bound with humans. This ongoing dialectic of our creating things which in turn create us has long been recognized in archaeology and in studies of material culture. Beyond archaeology and anthropology, the sociologists Bruno Latour and John Law were among the first influential voices to recognize that "there is no sense in which the notion of a human can be disentangled from the nonhumans into whose fate it has woven more and more intimately over the ages" (Latour 1994, 794). But precisely what do we mean when we say that things make us just as much as we make things? (See, e.g., Miller 1998.) Although in recent years it has become commonplace to say that archaeologists, anthropologists, and sociologists "take things seriously" (see, e.g., Hodder 2011a; Webmoor 2007; Webmoor and Witmore 2008), the precise meaning and the implications of this phrase remain rather unclear.

In the context of MET, the phrase "take things seriously" can be understood in two different ways. It can be understood as referring to the importance of understanding *how to take material culture seriously*. (For instance, what are the precise theoretical, methodological, and empirical commitments of such a conviction?) It also can be understood as referring to MET's contention that to understand human cognition *we must take material culture seriously* (more specifically, that without taking material culture seriously we cannot understand what makes a process cognitive). These two projects and senses of taking material culture seriously, although intimately related, are not identical and will unfold in a parallel fashion in the course of the following chapters. I should also point out that in both cases the word 'seriously' refers to a systematic concern with figuring out the causal and the affective efficacy of things in the *enactment* and the *constitution* of a cognitive system or operation. In Malafouris and Renfrew 2010, I dubbed this "the cognitive life of things." MET takes the transformational power of things to a new level that goes beyond the descriptive biographical dimension of their life histories. The cognitive life of things is not exhausted by their possible causal role in shaping some aspect of human intelligent behavior; the cognitive life of things also embodies a crucial enactive and constitutive role.

It must be obvious from the preceding discussion that for MET material culture is not merely the backdrop against which human cognition takes shape. Things mediate, actively shape, and constitute our ways of being in the world and of making sense of the world. Things also bring people together and provide channels of interaction. Things envelop our minds; they become us. As Timothy Webmoor and Christopher Witmore (2008) put it, "Things are us!" Following Michael Wheeler (2010b), I call this the element of "vital materiality." But, as I have already mentioned, in spite of our deep immersion in this material medium (Schiffer and Miller 1999, 4), or perhaps because of it, the cognitive life of things remains poorly understood. Thus, in one sense it can be argued that things are to human intelligence as the eye is to sight: constitutive and yet invisible. Is there a way we could proceed to explore and visualize this hidden aspect of our cognitive universe in concrete philosophical and empirical terms?

Metaplasticity

The image of the brain as an inherently plastic and environmentally contextualized adaptive organ is not new in developmental neuroscience. (See, e.g., Wexler 2006.) What has changed drastically in the past 20 years, however, is our understanding of the different types of plastic changes (functional, structural, and anatomical) and of what those changes imply for human development. Moreover, the rapid development of new imaging technologies offered new means of exploring the effects of culture on the human brain and of understanding the mechanisms of activity-dependent plasticity (Poldrack 2000; Kelly and Garavan 2005; Quartz and Sejnowski 1997) and "environmental enrichment" (Nithianantharajah and Hannan 2006). Social and developmental neuroscience can now confirm that our minds and brains are potentially subject to constant change and alteration throughout the human life span (Blakemore 2008; Blakemore and Choudhury 2006; Sowell et al. 2003)—change and alteration caused by our ordinary engagement with cultural practices and the material world.

There is little doubt, then, that the human brain is as much a cultural artifact as a biological entity, or that it is "both an artefact of culture and a cultural artefact" (Mithen and Parsons 2008). Like a piece of clay thrown on the wheel of culture, the human brain is subject to continuous reshaping, rewiring, and remodeling. On this view, the brain, far from a hardwired modular organ, emerges as a dynamic co-evolutionary process of deep enculturation and material engagement. The traditional neo-evolutionary view (also prevalent in archaeology) that takes the brain as a biological constant after the appearance of *Homo sapiens* needs to be revised. (See, e.g., Evans et al. 2005.) The possibility of ongoing evolution, with significant human genetic changes happening during historic time, continues to gain support. (See, e.g., Cochran and Harpending 2010.) It is precisely for these reasons that the focus of this book is not restricted to early prehistory but extends into more recent periods of human development. Grounded on a neural-constructivist (e.g., Westerman et al. 2007) developmental framework, MET recognizes that the hallmark of human brain evolution is not to be found in the ever-increasing sophistication or specialization of a modular mind, but in an ever-increasing projective flexibility that allows for environmentally and culturally derived changes in the structure and the functional architecture of the brain's circuitry.

The mind's extraordinary plasticity and its reciprocal openness to cultural influence and variation through active engagement with the material world are, according to MET, the keys to understanding the distinctive features of human cognition and how it changes. Of course, neural plasticity, as a property we obviously share with other species, may not constitute, in itself, a signature of human uniqueness. Nonetheless, what I call *metaplasticity*—the fact that we have a plastic mind which is embedded and inextricably enfolded with a plastic culture—might well be the locus of human uniqueness *par excellence*. Indeed, I propose that metaplasticity may be what makes change and alterability the natural state of a human intelligence that is unlike anything we see in other animals. This truly distinctive feature of the human cognitive system, I suggest, more than anything else, should be the focus of research in cognitive archaeology.

The term 'metaplasticity' was coined in neuroscience to refer to the emergent higher-order properties of synaptic plasticity and to their modification (Zhang and Linden 2003, 896). In the context of MET, the term is used, much more broadly, to characterize the emergent properties of the enactive constitutive intertwining between brain and culture (Malafouris 2009, 2010; Malafouris and Renfrew 2008).

The emergent higher-order properties of synaptic plasticity provide the substrate for experience-dependent brain development, learning, and memory (Abraham and Bear 1996; Abraham 2008; Zhang and Linden 2003, 896). In this context, 'metaplasticity' refers to plasticity at a higher level. It is a higher-order form of synaptic plasticity (Abraham and Bear 1996), or the plasticity of synaptic plasticity—including long-term potentiation and long-term depression. Essentially, 'metaplasticity' describes an activity-dependent change in the plastic state of neurons and the development of neural circuits. In other words, it refers to a change in the capability of neurons to generate plastic changes—that is, to modify the effectiveness or "strength" of synaptic transmission—and the level of changes that can be expressed. In particular, it describes the ways in which the activity-dependent synaptic plasticity that underlies learning and memory is affected by previous patterns of pre-synaptic and post-synaptic activity (Sheng-zhi and Huizhong 2009; Mockett and Hulme 2008). Professional musicians provide a good example (Ragert et al. 2004). Several studies comparing musicians with non-musicians clearly indicate important structural and functional changes in the brains of the former as a result of intense sensory and motor training associated with musical expertise (Elbert et al. 1995; Schlaug et al. 1995; Jancke et al. 2000; Munte et al. 2002; Haslinger et al. 2004; Ragert et al. 2004; Bengtsson et al. 2005). Characteristic examples can be seen in the study of Gaser and Schlaug (2003), which offers evidence for an increase in gray-matter volume in the sensorimotor cortex in musicians, and in the magneto-encephalographic study by Elbert et al. (1995), which provides evidence for enlarged cortical somatosensory representations of fingers for musicians. More relevant to the present discussion of metaplasticity is the finding that, depending on the age at which instrumental playing commenced and on the intensity of practicing, over the long term musical practicing seems to enhance excitability and plasticity in the motor system. For instance, tactile discrimination skills are more improved in musicians than in non-musicians (Ragert et al. 2004), whereas musicians who started musical training early in life (before the age of 7 years) learn a motor performance sequence task much better than musicians who started later and much better than non-musicians (Watanabe et al. 2007). It appears, then, not only that musicians have extraordinary motor and sensory skills, and better somatosensory discrimination abilities, but also that, relative to non-musicians, they have an increased ability to learn new tasks, and they show enhanced motor and sensory learning capabilities. For instance, Rosenkranz et al., using transcranial magnetic stimulation, were able to show that "basic neurophysiological measures of motor cortex excitability and synaptic plasticity in musicians are changed in such a way as to contribute to their enhanced motor skills and learning abilities" (2007, 5200). The musicians in that study showed increased susceptibility for synaptic plasticity (potentiation/depotentiation) and higher-than-normal sensitivity to changes of excitability. These changes can be seen as consequences of, or adaptations to, the learning demands of long-term musical practicing.

But how can all these findings be linked with MET? How can the notion of metaplasticity be understood at the level of human cultural practice, change, and situated cognition? At the micro scale of brain processes, it has been suggested, in order to understand how the brain is changed by practice, we need to integrate "analysis of changes in activity within specific regions and patterns of connectivity between regions" (Kelly and Garavan 2005). A preliminary conclusion that can easily be drawn from current findings in the context of practice-related neuroimaging would be that changes in the neural context of activity (that is, the interactivity between brain regions) may be far more significant than changes in regional activity when one is looking for plastic effects: "The important factor is not that a particular event occurred at a particular site, but rather under what neural context did that event occur—in other words, what was the rest of the brain doing?" (McIntosh 1998, 533) But in the case of macroscale processes of material engagement, I argue, simply to know what the rest of the brain was doing when a particular activation event occurred—that is, the "neural context" of activity (ibid.)—is not enough. Our concern here is to describe and understand the nature of plastic changes, not at the level of the individual, but in the broader systemic context of culture, social action, and "profound embodiment" (Clark 2007a, 2008b). At this higher level of human-nonhuman interaction, which underlies the constant and dynamic reorganization of human cognitive architecture, material culture competes, equally with any other brain region, for a place in the human cognitive system. There are, at present, no *a priori* reasons to believe that the mechanisms at play during cross-modal plasticity (i.e., the partial takeover of lost function by neighboring systems) differ from those involved in intra-modal plasticity (Bavelier and Neville 2002). From the perspective of archaeology and material-culture studies, it makes good sense to extend this point further and look at cultural change as a form of extra-neural or extra-modal plasticity. When that is done, the meaning and the scope of interactivity become more significant. Any decrease or increase of neural activation within any given brain region may then be also an effect of the engagement of that area with another extra-neural resource (bodily or artifactual) that, although located outside the brain, can be seen as complementary and continuous with the brain. In other words, the major difference can be expressed as follows: For neuroscience, interactivity is a process that happens between activity regions inside the individual brain as a consequence of practice or other interaction with the world. For MET, on the other hand, interactivity is not an "internal" consequence of practice or interaction with the material world but is continuous and co-extensive with it.

In the famous study of navigation-related changes in the hippocampi of London taxi drivers (Maguire et al. 2000), comparison of the structural MRI scans obtained from the taxi drivers and the control subjects showed two interesting findings: that the posterior hippocampi of taxi drivers were significantly larger and that hippocampal volume correlated with the amount of time spent as a taxi driver (positively in the posterior and negatively in the anterior hippocampus). Maguire's interpretation was that this structural change was clearly due to taxi drivers' extensive training and experience in navigating the streets of London.[1] How can we discern the basis, and account for the precise causes, of the changes recorded in taxi drivers? Note that hippocampus activation was observed both in taxi drivers and in control subjects. In addition, taxi drivers are, obviously, not the only successful navigators, and thus navigation accuracy cannot be the difference that made the difference in their case. Maguire et al. propose that, although our hippocampi are probably able to cope with our typical navigational needs without recourse to structural change, "there may be a threshold (either in terms of detail or duration of use) beyond which storage and elaboration of a large scale spatial representation induces hippocampal plasticity" (2003, 216). Although much remains to be understood about the developmental dynamics of neural plasticity, it becomes increasingly clear that it is these mediational thresholds, and the possible links between behavioral innovation, cultural practice, and brain architecture, that delineate the main "regions of interest" for a cognitive archaeology of the human mindscape. Of course, from the theoretical angle of MET, simply to ask how and why a London cab driver's "gray matter" enlarges to enable him or her to store a detailed mental map of London is not enough. It is necessary to ask how we should compare the plastic effects of different navigational practices, and how we should account for the transformative effects of the various mediational technologies and artifacts on these cultural practices (and, by extension, on the human brain). Since the introduction of GPS devices, a London taxi driver no longer has to expand his or her hippocampus in order to succeed in complex navigation tasks. The cognitive objective (navigating from one point to another) remains the same, but the process has changed. From a "systems view" (Norman 1991), no potential increase in "gray matter" is necessary. Not only have GPS devices amplified the drivers' biological memories; like many other cognitive artifacts and innovations, they have drastically reshaped or changed the nature of the cognitive operations involved in the navigation task and, as a consequence, the selective pressures placed on the hippocampus. MET is particularly concerned with the mechanisms that mediate those plastic changes, not at the level of the individual, but at the systemic level of enculturation and social practice.

Material engagement: The analytical nexus

Broadening our understanding of mind in the above manner suggests a much more radical rethinking of its character than that we can find in embodied and situated cognitive science. MET extends the properties of embodiment still further, drawing upon a nexus of radical ideas developed in particular under the rubric of extended and distributed cognition. There is also a clear parallel here between the material-engagement approach and the enactive approach. Enactivism sees cognition "as an embodied engagement in which the world is brought forth by the coherent activity of a cogniser in its environment" (Di Paolo 2009, 12). Moreover, thinking is something that we do rather than something that simply happen to us, or in us. (See, e.g., Noë 2004, 2009.) As was discussed in the preceding section, neurons and their intricate patterns of activation do not think and make sense; people do. For MET, as for the enactive approach, what goes on strictly inside the head (e.g., a brain state or representation) cannot be considered a cognitive process proper. Internal (that is, intra-cranial) processes can only count as constituents or participants in a broader cognitive process that exist as a relationship among brains, bodies, and things (Thompson and Stapleton 2008). Cognition belongs to, and occurs in, a "relational domain" (Maturana and Varela 1980; Varela et al. 1991; Thompson 2007; Di Paolo 2009). The challenge for MET, as was stated at the beginning of this chapter, then becomes one of penetrating the ontology of this "relational domain" from its own distinctive long-term archaeological perspective. To achieve this objective, MET incorporates three major working hypotheses, which can be summarized as follows:

the *hypothesis of the extended mind* (chapter 4), which explores the constitutive intertwining of cognition with material culture

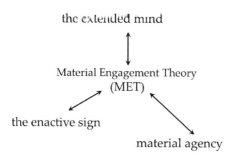

Figure 3.2
The nexus of Material Engagement Theory.

the *hypothesis of enactive signification* (chapter 5), which explores the nature of the material sign not as a representational mechanism but as a semiotic conflation and co-habitation through matter that enacts and brings forth the world

the *hypothesis of material agency* (chapter 6), which explores agency not as a human property but as the emergent product of situated activity asking not "What is an agent?" but "When is an agent?"

These three working hypotheses, although targeting different aspects of the process of material engagement—i.e., cognition, signification, and agency—are complementary and overlap as different facets of a common phenomenon. Taken together, the aim of these hypotheses is, in the words of Merleau-Ponty (1958), to get a "maximum grip" on the human condition. They are advanced in order to develop a fuller grasp of the phenomenon of mind as I search for the optimum point from which to perceive what at a shorter or greater distance, if not entirely invisible, is blurred through excess or deficiency. It is my hope that by advancing these three hypotheses this book will provide a new way of looking into the gray zone of material engagement.

An ontological recommendation

I end this chapter with a brief but necessary epistemological note: MET as a theoretical edifice should not be confused with positivistic scientific theories. *It is not a theory of such a kind.* Proof and support for MET will come primarily from the explanatory insights that this new perspective yields for the study of cognition and material culture. I do not mean to say that MET is not amenable to experimental research, or that it could not motivate rigorous empirical testing research of its major working hypothesis—far from it. I simply mean that, at its present stage and in its present formulation, MET is less a predictive theory than what we might, following Imre Lakatos (1980), call a "research program" based on a set of interdependent and largely exploratory postulates. In other words, MET is essentially an explanatory path—a path nonetheless, constructed for approaching phenomena and linking time scales beyond the conventional analytical units and constructs of behavioral and cognitive sciences.

Specifically from an archaeological perspective, to understand the epistemological position of MET it is necessary to draw an inductive lesson from the epistemic negotiations that recently took place in our field in the course of the "post-processual" debate between the extremes of objectivism and relativism. A careful look at this epistemic debate makes it possible to recognize immediately that archaeological thinking has gradually settled down to the medium position of what Ian Hodder (1991, 10) called "guarded objectivity," that is, the recognition that archaeological "data" are formed within a dialectical relationship. (See also Shanks and McGuire 1996.) This move, however, is not to be interpreted as an admission from both sides in this debate of failure to attain their original epistemic commitments. It should, rather, be perceived as a sign of accumulated experience and reflexive assessment on the basis of present-day archaeological reality and practice. Indeed, the point is not always to secure objectivity, but primarily to understand what objectivity means in the context of a specific scientific community. In this sense, it might well be suggested that archaeology, passing through this major epistemic negotiation, gradually came to recognize that the nature of archaeological knowledge is, was, and will be a dialectic historical symbiosis of the objective, the subjective, and the material.

From the standpoint of MET, objectivity is not seen as a single fixed position that gives you the best and true vision of things. Rather, it is seen as a constant search for the specific viewpoint that best enables you to perceive and understand the particularities of the phenomenon you investigate. Thus, for MET, objectivity involves recognition of the following paradox: When the phenomenon you seek to understand relates to the subjective character of human experience, it might well be that "any shift to greater objectivity—that is, less attachment to a specific viewpoint—does not take us nearer to the real nature of the phenomenon: it takes us further away from it" (Nagel 1979, 174).

Apparently, the principal aim of MET is not to compete for scientific "purity," but to articulate and bring into focus the intersection of people and things. To this end, MET subscribes to what might be called a hunter-gatherer analytic orientation. Like a hunter-gatherer, it enters into a relationship with the world with no intention to achieve mastery and control by slicing a continuous and hybrid reality into several distinct analytic domains. The aim is not to break things apart into a series of easily manipulated isolated entities, comprehensible in themselves yet incommensurable as a whole, but rather to understand how things are enmeshed and related, and to understand through what mechanisms those linkages are effected. MET aims to articulate the path to such an understanding, and to furnish the conceptual means for such an understanding, by replacing the categorical divisions of modernity with symbiotic relationships. In this sense, MET provides a new ontology of relatedness more than it provides a new way of demarcating between the inner domain and the outer domain. More than as an ontological *commitment* about how things are, it should be seen as an ontological *recommendation* that points to a new way of doing cognitive archaeology and a new way of thinking about the past, the present, and the future of human cognitive becoming.

II Outline of a Theory of Material Engagement

4 The Extended Mind

Beyond cognitivism: Thinking outside the brain

What is the stuff of which thoughts are made? On what general picture of the mind should the archaeology of mind rest? What are the meaning and the value of the concept of "mind" or "cognition" in archaeology anyway? Despite the many research breakthroughs in cognitive science and archaeology, we are still far from providing a coherent answer, let alone a unanimously accepted one. As a consequence, the Cartesian metaphysics of the discontinuity between what is "in" the mind and what is "outside of" the mind inevitably color perceptions of our species' distant past. Some archaeologists have gone so far as to suggest that we should eliminate the concept of mind altogether, replacing it with a more holistic conception that "stresses variable aspects of intelligence" (Gosden 2010, 39). I am very sympathetic, of course, with the essence of Gosden's critique, and with his suggestion for developing a notion of "social ontology" as a way of looking "at how human capabilities of mind and body are brought about through an interaction with the material world" (2008, 2003). However, I think the concept of mind is too important to throw out.

Notwithstanding these remarks, I believe that we are in a position to restate the question of how we can specify the "mark of the cognitive" in a more productive manner by focusing on some important questions that may have been marginalized and obscured in the process of thinking about the what and the where of human thinking. A number of new theoretical frameworks—including those of extended cognition (Clark 1997, 2001b, 2008a; Wheeler 2005; Rowlands 2009, 2010; Menary 2006, 2010; Manzotti 2006), distributed cognition (Kirsh 1995; Sutton 2008, 2010), embodied cognition (Shapiro 2010; Chemero 2009; Rowlands 1999; Anderson 2003;

Chiel and Beer 1997; Lakoff and Johnson 1980; Johnson 1987), embedded cognition (Rupert 2009), mediated cognition (Vygotsky 1978, 1986; Wertsch 1991, 1998; Cole 1985, 1996; Lave 1988), enactive cognition (Varela et al. 1991; Maturana and Varela 1980; Thompson and Stapelton 2009; Thompson 2007; Stewart et al. 2010; Noë 2009; Di Paolo 2009), dynamical (Beer 2003; Van Gelder 1995, 1999; Van Gelder and Port 1995a,b; Thelen and Smith 1994), and situated cognition (Clancey 1997, 2009; Wilson and Clark 2009; Suchman 1987)—emanate from such an awareness. As figure 4.1 illustrates, this conceptual network comprises a number of correlated yet in many cases independently developed and subtly different theoretical approaches to the study of mind. In a nutshell, the basic idea that unites all these new strands in moving the study of mind forward is that they break away from the mold of cognitivism and render problem-

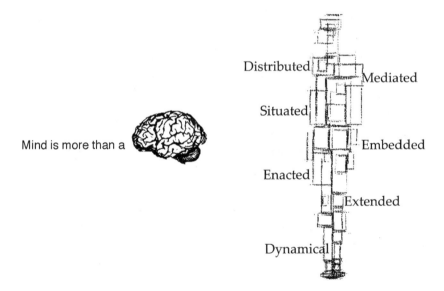

Figure 4.1
Mind beyond cognitivism. There are important differences among the above terms and their theoretical commitments especially relevant to the hard problems of mental extension, location, and representation (in the head or in the world). Still, underlying these differences, one can trace the emergence of a relatively stable set of postulates or tenets able to focus and reorient the study of human cognition setting important new research directions for a unified non-Cartesian cognitive science. (The drawing of a human figure was inspired by Antony Gormley's sculpture LIFT.)

allc any research procedure that artificially divorces thought from embodied action-taking and thus from its surrounding environment. Taken together, these closely related but not necessarily unified or homogeneous theoretical schemes collapse the conventional mind/brain tautology and mind-body dichotomy and challenge the representational "all in the head" view of human cognition. In that sense they can offer a firm conceptual foundation for my hypothesis of the constitutive intertwining of cognition with material culture. In fact, the proposed material-engagement approach would be of limited cross-disciplinary value and applicability were it not for the philosophical background of current theorizing and ongoing debate about human cognitive extension, or what, for convenience, I will call "the Extended Mind Hypothesis" or "the hypothesis of extended cognition." Exactly what, then, *is* the Extended Mind Hypothesis, and how precisely does it relate to archaeology, material culture, and the perspective of Material Engagement Theory?

The embodied mind

Since the time of Descartes the study of the human mind has involved an implicit choice between the two predetermined alternatives of the so-called mind-body problem. That is, either you adopt the dualism between an immaterial mind and a material body or you reject the dualism and reduce your two substances to one according to your ontological standing—body for materialists, mind or spirit for idealists. If you choose to reject the dualism, you end up either with a disembodied mind or with no mind at all. If you affirm the "official Cartesian doctrine," in the end you conceptualize the human person as a union of an inner mental entity (the mind) and a material external entity (the body).

It is hard to say whether what came to be known as the embodied-cognition paradigm has managed to solve this long-standing philosophical problem of human cognition. Yet it is safe to suggest that it has successfully resolved the mind-body question by placing it on a new foundation which recognizes that bodily features play a significant role in how or what an organism thinks and in how it makes sense of the world. Nevertheless, the exact status of the body in relation to human cognition remains a hotly debated topic. (See Shapiro 2004, 2010; Rowlands 1999; Chemero 2009; Wheeler 2005.)

The general idea of the embodied mind is quite simple: The body is not, as is conventionally held, a passive external container of the human mind; it is an integral component of the way we think. In other words, the mind does not inhabit the body; rather, the body inhabits the mind. The task is not to understand how the body contains the mind, but to understand how the body shapes the mind (Gallagher 2005; Goldin-Meadow 2003; Goldin-Meadow and Wagner 2005; Streeck 2009). A good example to consider in this respect is gesture. Recent studies don't simply show that gesture is tightly intertwined with speech in timing, meaning, and function; they suggest that gesturing reduces cognitive load and thus frees speakers' cognitive resources to perform other tasks (e.g., memory tasks) (Goldin-Meadow and Wagner 2005, 238; Goldin-Meadow 2003). Moreover, Michael Corballis (2003, 2009) has made a strong case for the evolution of language as a gestural system evolving from the so-called mirror system in the primate brain. According to Frank Wilson (1998, 7), the interdependence of hand and mind appears to be so strong that any theory of human intelligence that ignores "the historic origins of that relationship, or the impact of that history on developmental dynamics in modern humans" is "grossly misleading and sterile." (On the importance of manual concepts, see Cushing 1892.) Wilson's claim goes well beyond what Wilder Penfield probably had in mind when he developed the famous "motor homunculus" map showing the proportions of the human brain dedicated to various parts of the body (Penfield and Rasmussen 1950). Looking at Penfield's map, one is immediately struck by the enormous size of the part of the brain associated with the hand, which clearly shows the intimate linkage between hand and mind. Yet for the embodied-cognition paradigm the development of the five-fingered precision grip and the opposable thumb imply much more than simple evolutionary curiosities. In particular, the hand is not simply an instrument for manipulating an externally given objective world by carrying out the orders issued to it by the brain; it is instead one of the main perturbatory channels through which the world touches us, and it has a great deal to do with how this world is perceived and classified. Indeed, for embodied cognition, human conceptual categories, far from corresponding to inherent objective properties of an external reality, are to a large extent dependent on "the bodily nature of the people doing the categorizing" (Lakoff 1987, 371). In short, "the very structures on which reason is based emerge from our bodily sensorimotor experiences" (ibid., 386). The implications of such a position are far-reaching, shaking the objectivist foundation of traditional cognitive science, which is now replaced with a new ontological and epistemological basis that is named "experiential realism." And from the stance of "experiential realism" embodiment is the condition for meaningfulness (Lakoff and Johnson 1999). That is crucial for present purposes, and for that reason I will raise two further questions.

The first question concerns the exact nature of the pre-conceptual bodily experiences that define the way humans make sense of the world. The second concerns how abstract or higher-level cognitive operations can be explained in terms of this pre-conceptual bodily experiential structure. For example, we can easily see how an embodied account of human cognition can help us understand Colin Renfrew's (2001a) argument about weight as a meaningful experience that, in its substantive reality, precedes any notion of quantification and standardization, but what about other, more abstract notions and categories?

The embodied perspective suggests that the pre-conceptual structure consists mainly of directly meaningful universal schemata that exist prior to and independent of any conceptual categories and can, in Lakoff and Johnson's terminology, be divided in two major kinds: *basic-level structure* (which arises from our capacities for gestalt perception, mental imagery, and motor movement) and *image-schematic structure* (which comprises recurring patterns in our sensorimotor experiences and perceptual interactions, such as source-path-goal, center-periphery, experience of bounded interiors, the gravity vector, balance and equilibrium, and force dynamics).

In regard to the relationship between pre-conceptual structure and "higher-level" cognitive processing, the embodied perspective suggests that, in domains where no pre-conceptual structure is directly available on the basis of experience, we import such structure by way of metaphoric and integrative conceptual mappings:

Our brains are structured so as to project activation patterns from sensorimotor areas to higher cortical areas. . . . Projection of this kind allow us to conceptualize abstract concepts on the basis of inferential patterns used in sensorimotor processes that are directly tied to the body. (Lakoff and Johnson 1999, 77; also see Fauconnier 1997; Johnson 1987; Lakoff 1987; chapter 5 below)

In particular, as various experimental studies have revealed, an extensive system of metaphorical mappings underlies our thought processes, structuring some of the most basic categorizations we conventionally employ in conceptualizing the world. (For a neuroscientific view, see Gallese and Lakoff 2005.) On the basis of these observations, and in an attempt to demystify the deficient prevailing understanding of metaphoricity as a marginal instrument of poetic language, the proponents of embodied mind situate metaphor at the very center of the human cognitive landscape. In doing so, they differentiate—and in fact prioritize—the ontological nature of metaphor as a fundamentally cognitive phenomenon from its various surface linguistic or other manifestations, using the word 'metaphor' to refer to a cross-domain mapping in the conceptual system that constitutes the basis of understanding and meaning construction (Johnson 1987; Turner 1996).

A more specific example may help to illustrate the matter.

"Time events are things in space"

Consider the commonplace expressions "the day *before* yesterday," "in the *preceding* session," "the days *ahead* of us," "*back* in time," "in the *distant* future," "in the *remote* past," "the end is *near*," and "Christmas is *gone*." Each of these is in our ordinary vocabulary for speaking about time, and "they all serve to express ideas about *time* in terms of objects, positions and movements in *space*" (Núñez 1999, 42). More interesting, people seem to use these expressions in a natural and effortless manner. People never seem puzzled or confused about the meaning of "Christmas is gone." From a cognitive perspective, the following question can be raised: How is it that people can effortlessly and unconsciously make inferences about time while talking about space? Núñez puts it this way: "What does it mean to say that 'Christmas is gone'? . . . It does not move anywhere. So, gone where? In what space did it *move*? From where *to* where? Going through what locations?" (ibid., 44). A common-sense answer to these questions would be that we are merely dealing with figures of speech—ordinary features of our linguistic abilities and of conventional language use. But from the perspective of embodied cognition things appear rather different. Obviously, I am discussing metaphoric expressions here. However, as I have already pointed out, for embodied cognition a metaphor is not simply a figure of speech; it is a cognitive cross-domain mapping. It is such a conceptual mapping that enables us, in the examples cited above, to understand time in terms of motion in space. Thus, this mapping "does not

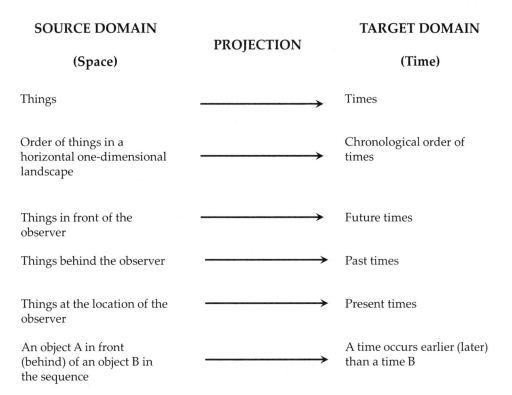

SOURCE DOMAIN	PROJECTION	TARGET DOMAIN
(Space)		(Time)
Things	⟶	Times
Order of things in a horizontal one-dimensional landscape	⟶	Chronological order of times
Things in front of the observer	⟶	Future times
Things behind the observer	⟶	Past times
Things at the location of the observer	⟶	Present times
An object A in front (behind) of an object B in the sequence	⟶	A time occurs earlier (later) than a time B

Figure 4.2
The main structure of the cross-domain mapping "Time events are things in space."

belong to the realm of words but to the realm of thought" (ibid., 45). Núñez uses the phrase "Time events are things in space" to refer to this general conceptual mapping, which enables us to understand "time" in terms of "things in a sequence" and "motion in space." The main structure of this cross-domain mapping is selectively illustrated in figure 4.2. Two particular points demand our attention in respect to this mapping.

The first point concerns the almost universal use of unidimensional space as a source domain of the mapping: As Núñez observes, although minor variations in the structure and form of the mapping have been observed in different languages and cultures, in every case that has been studied so far "time events" are mapped onto "space"—more specifically, onto "things in space." This indicates that such a conceptual mapping cannot be understood as merely a social or cultural convention. If it were merely such a convention, those studying it probably would have found additional experiential modalities (other than that of space) being used as source domains for generating inferences about time. But, Núñez notes,

We simply don't observe the conceptual structure of time flow based on domains of human experience such as tastes, flavours, or colours. Given this, the future can't taste purple. . . . *Human beings, no matter the culture, organize chronological experience and its conceptual structure in terms of a very specific family of experiences: the experience of things in space.* (ibid., 52)

The second point relates to the primacy of the inherent bodily orientation in the mapping. In every manifestation of the time-space mapping, the domain "objects in space being in front of the observer" is always mapped onto the domain "future," whereas the domain "objects in space being behind the observer" is always mapped onto the domain "past." More simply, "there is one bodily orientation that is predominant in a wide range of human cultures, namely, the future as being ahead of us and the past as being behind" (ibid., 53). If, as mainstream computational psychology has postulated for decades, cognition operates as an inherently abstract symbolic processing mechanism, why does the mind need a bodily orientation in order to make sense of time? More precisely, why does it need a particular bodily orientation (front/back) in order to do so? If human thought and reason is a matter of internal arbitrary representations with no direct bodily and experiential grounding, why does the future make no real sense as being above or below us, in our left or right, or indeed in our lower left rear? Strange as it might seem, when it comes to disembodied representations, any kind of bodily orientation could have served this function equally well. In fact, from a representational stance, there should have been no need to use bodily orientation or space to make sense of time. We should have been able to conceptualize time directly. From a representational stance, besides arbitrary convention, there is nothing else left to account for our preference to conceptualize the future as something that is ahead of us rather than as something that tastes purple. For the embodied-cognition paradigm, however, there are many other good reasons, and all of them are grounded upon a central observation: the primacy of bodily experience in the structuring of human conceptual processes.

Embodied cognition and material culture

Viewed from the perspective of Material Engagement Theory that I am developing here, the case of embodied mind, though promising as a model for the study of human cognition, has certain limitations. No doubt by grounding cognition in bodily experience we have taken a step toward resolving the traditional mind-body dichotomy. Nevertheless, as I have argued elsewhere in more detail (Malafouris 2008a), what this step essentially implies for the proponents of embodied-cognition approach is simply an expansion of the ontological boundaries of the *res cogitans* rather than the dissolution of those boundaries altogether. Transposing the conventional demarcation line of human conceptual architecture outside the brain but still inside the skin, the embodied-mind approach may have resolved the traditional "ghost in the machine" paradox by way of what Anderson (2003) calls the "physical grounding project," but it also has created a sort of embodied cognitivism in which the material reality remains external and epiphenomenal to the cognitive structure. Consequently, the traditional drawback of cognitivism remains, albeit in an embodied fashion. For example, it is a central premise of conceptual metaphor theory that metaphoric mappings present uniform properties. This means that "there is no formal difference between metaphor as revealed by linguistic expressions and metaphor as revealed by other forms of human action, including the production and use of material culture" (Ortman 2000, 616). I consider this premise mistaken in two major and related respects. First, such a claim fails to take into account the active role of material mediation in the enaction of metaphoric projection. Second (and correlated), such a claim homogenizes mediational means—language, artifact, gesture, ritual, and so on—that in reality present quite different properties and possibilities for metaphoric and integrative projections.

For example, materially enacted metaphors, unlike their linguistic expressions, present no text-like propositionality. They do not simply communicate meaning; rather, they communicate actively doing something. More specifically, material metaphors objectify sets of ontological correspondences, making possible the construction of powerful associative links among material things, bodies, and brains. If one accepts this logic of substantive participation, the most interesting questions have to do with how human cognition "becomes articulated to produce particular kinds of metaphorical links within historically determinant and determined social circumstances" (Tilley 1999, 35). Indeed, if metaphor is "as much a part of our functioning as our sense of touch" (Lakoff and Johnson 1980, 239), and if pre-conceptual structure is to be accepted as the experiential foundation of an embodied human mind, both metaphor and pre-conceptual structure have to be placed upon the concrete foundation of material culture. In fact, it can be argued that none of the kinesthetic image schemata discussed above can be experienced outside some context of material engagement. In such contexts of situated action, however, the boundaries of the embodied mind are determined not solely by the physiology of the body, but also by the constraints and affordances of the material reality with which it is constitutively intertwined.

The anthropologist Jean-Pierre Warnier asks

Is not material the indispensable and unavoidable mediation or correlate of all our motions and motor habits? Are not all our actions, without any exception whatsoever, propped up by or inscribed in a given materiality? (2001, 6)

The framework of distributed cognition has successfully shed new light on some of these matters.

The distributed-cognition approach

The distributed-cognition approach to the study of mind is a theoretical framework developed initially by Edwin Hutchins (1995, 2005, 2008, 2010a–c). Work by other anthropologists, including Charles Goodwin (1994, 2002, 2010), and by cognitive scientists, including David Kirsh (1995, 1996, 2010), has also been influential. What distinguishes this approach from other approaches to the study of human cognition can be nicely expressed by way of two basic theoretical commitments, which also characterize the Extended Mind Hypothesis.

What is outside the brain is not necessarily outside the mind

The first theoretical commitment pertains to the boundaries of the unit of analysis for the study of human cognition. It relates, in other words, to the crucial methodological question "Where do we look for the mind?" As has already been discussed, the standard reply to this question according to the traditional "all in the head" view of human cognition is, basically, "What is outside the head is outside the mind." As I noted earlier, this conviction was partially challenged when the embodied-cognition paradigm brought the body into the cognitive fold.

However, a final demarcation line remains to be crossed, and this is precisely the task that the distributed-cognition approach has set out to accomplish. To start with, the distributed-cognition approach recognizes that there can never be a full account of human cognitive operations based solely on internal states of the brain. A cognitive process is not simply what happens inside a brain; a cognitive process can be what happens in the interaction between a brain and a thing. The traditional boundaries of the unit of analysis for cognition must be extended beyond the individual in order to accommodate broader cognitive events that include interactions among people, artifacts, space, and time.

Another important feature of interactions between human and material agents is that they take place in real space and time. In having a body, humans are spatially located creatures. Embodied cognitive science has made a strong case for the fundamental role of bodily sensorimotor experiences in the structure of our thinking. Thus, for distributed cognition, space is not simply the passive background against which the activity unfolds; it is something that can be used as a cognitive artifact.

Cognition is not simply a matter of internal representation

This drastic expansion of the unit of analysis for the study of cognitive phenomena, now pursued "in the wild" (Hutchins 1995), leads directly to the second and correlated theoretical commitment of the distributed-cognition approach, which now pertains to the range of processes that can be assumed to participate in and characterize the nature of our mental machinery. Obviously the traditional computational image of the mind as a storehouse of internal representational structures and computational procedures is no longer sufficient once you expand the territory of the human mind beyond the skin and skull of the individual. From the perspective of distributed cognition, our mental machinery is essentially an extended functional system that does not simply involve internal representational states but also involves the transformation and propagation of such states across external media. This means that, although mental states can be "internal" in the traditional sense of inter-cranial representation, they can also be outside the individual (e.g., maps, charts, tools) and thus "external" to the biological confines of the individual. In other words, for distributed cognition "a cognitive process is delimited by the functional relationships among the elements that participate in it, rather than by the spatial co-location of the elements" (Hollan et al. 2000, 176). No proper understanding of our mental machinery can be achieved either by leaving those "external" cognitive events outside the cognitive equation proper or by reducing them to some "internal" neuronal activity or brain process. For example, rather than asking who is responsible for steering a ship into a harbor, one should ask how the necessary knowledge is enacted and propagated across people, artifacts, and time (Hutchins 1995).

Let us explore that issue using as an example one of the earliest writing systems: the Mycenaean Linear B script. My argument is that if we seek to understand the Linear B system as a technique of memory, focusing only on what is written on the surface of the Mycenaean clay tablets (that is, the representational content) or on the internal structure of the script, we will see only part of the picture. Instead of using the Linear B tablets as a medium for getting inside the Mycenaean head, I will show that a great deal of Mycenaean cognition lies out there in the world and it is enacted *through*, rather than written *upon*, the Mycenaean tablets.

Remembering through, or how a Linear B tablet helps you forget

By way of basic background, I will begin with a few broad remarks concerning the archaeology of the tablets. The system of writing we call the Mycenaean Linear B script originated around the fifteenth century BC to serve the administrative (record keeping and accounting) demands of the gradually emerging Mycenaean palatial system (Chadwick 1987; Palaima 1988; Shelmerdine 1997). The script, which comprised 89 syllabic signs and more than 100 ideograms, was adapted from the earlier Linear A Minoan writing system. Two major textual forms have been recovered; they come exclusively from the major palatial centers of the Greek mainland and Minoan Crete. The first, the dominant one, consists of tablets of unbaked clay. The second consists of painted inscriptions on large stirrup jars. It is important to note that the use of the Mycenaean script was strictly confined to record keeping in the context of palatial administration. In contrast with the situation in the Near East, there are no historical documents (annals, diplomatic correspondence, treaties, or religious texts). As John Chadwick correctly observes (1976, 27), "It cannot be too strongly emphasized that what mattered most to the users of these documents was the numerals. The numbers and quantities are important details which cannot be confided to the memory; the remainder of the text is simply a brief note of what the numerals refer to, heading to enable the reader to identify the person or place associated with the quantity recorded."

Une obvious way to look at this corpus of artifacts, and to study the Mycenaean Linear B tablets from the perspective of cognitive archaeology, would be, very simply, to try and read the messages inscribed on clay. Indeed, thanks to the efforts of Michael Ventris and John Chadwick (1973), who managed to break the code of the Mycenaean script, a great deal of information about the Mycenaean society and the Mycenaean economy has been deduced in recent decades through the systematic efforts of scholars specializing in the study of Mycenaean documents. (See, e.g., Chadwick 1976; Palaima 1988; Shelmerdine 1997; Bendall 2007.) However, for the purposes of this chapter I propose that we resist the temptation to read something of the content of Mycenaean thought as it may have been encoded on the tablets, and that instead we look at the process of Mycenaean thought and at the role Linear B might have played in shaping that process. In other words, I want to use the example of Linear B tablets to raise the question of how, rather than what, the Mycenaeans were thinking. To that end, it is necessary first to understand the Linear B system as a cognitive resource and artifact. How we do that? Let us consider how a distributed-cognition (Dcog) approach to the study of the Linear B system can help.

The intelligent use of clay

In physical morphology, Linear B tablets can be divided into two major types: small, elongated "leaf-shaped" tablets and large "page-shaped" tablets (figure 4.3). A "leaf-shaped" tablet usually is one part of a larger set; a "page-shaped" tablet usually is a complete document in itself. This functional differentiation, far from trivial, embodies the solution to a very important problem imposed on the writing process and the memory of the Mycenaean scribe by the very materiality of the tablets: once something was written on the surface of the wet clay, it dried rapidly (in a few hours, or perhaps a day at most). No additions or corrections could be made after the clay dried. As an implication, if a tablet were to contain a large number of entries, all the relevant information about those entries should have been available within the mentioned time limits. If this was not possible and the information required came in pieces at different times, or even from different persons, then the use of small individual tablets for each piece would have been necessary for storing the incoming information.

Figure 4.3
Linear B tablets from Knossos recording (a) women, probably textile workers, and
what appear to be their sons (kouroi) and daughters (korai); (b) chariot wheels listed
by form and type of material, including "of elm," "of willow," and "bound with
bronze"; and (c) swords: to-sa / pa-ka-na PUG 50 [so many swords (sword ideogram)
50 (at least)] (courtesy of Ashmolean Museum, University of Oxford).

These small tablets could then be filed in order, like cards in an index. And
once a file was complete it could be recopied onto large tablets. Archaeologically it is not always easy to recover those files and the sets or groups
of tablets that were intended to be read as a single document. However, in
a few cases direct evidence about this practice has been preserved in the
archaeological record. An excellent example can be seen in the case of the
Pp series recovered *in situ* by Arthur Evans in the course of his excavation
at the palace at Knossos (figure 4.4); it shows not "merely the set but the
order in which the tablets were filed" (Chadwick 1976, 22).[1]

From a classical cognitive science perspective, the cognitive processes
involved in the use and manipulation of those files could certainly be classified as instances of memory and information processing. But it would be

Figure 4.4
The Pp series file recovered *in situ* by Arthur Evans (after Evans 1935, figure 655).

very difficult to draw the boundary between the internal and the external parts of the cognitive system involved, even if one were able to locate precisely where these cognitive processes were enacted.

It is clear that in this case the cognitive process does not simply involve the internal representation of symbols via the Linear B code in order to produce the outcome that we see inscribed in the tablets. The cognitive process of producing the file also involves physical manipulation of the properties of the representational medium as a material object in real time and space. And the file, seen as a material spatial arrangement, is not simply amplifying the problem-solving process by reducing the complexity of the cognitive task—for example, directing attention so as to reduce the cost of visual search and to make it easier to notice, identify, and remember the items. The file, I want to suggest, is also transforming the physical boundaries of the problem's space, and thereby restructuring the problem-solving process. Indeed, any particular task space or context affords only certain possibilities of action. That means that by changing the physical properties of activity space one can restrict the freedom of the agent. However, the fewer degrees of freedom in a given context that an agent has, the simpler is the cognitive task.

In distributed cognition, space is not simply the passive background against which the activity unfolds; it is something that can be used as a cognitive artifact. Indeed, according to David Kirsh (1995, 1996), spatial arrangements form an important part of the functional architecture of any distributed cognitive system in at least three important and correlated respects: by supporting *choice*, by supporting *perception*, and by supporting *problem solving*. For example, space can be used to simplify choices either by constraining what is feasible in a given situation (that is, hiding affordances) or by drawing attention to what is feasible (that is, highlighting affordances). Moreover, spatial properties can be used to facilitate perception by directing attention and by offering visual cues for action. Two obvious examples are size and color, which can be used as attention-getting features. Indeed, a number of such epistemic features are evident in the Linear B script. To facilitate identification and perception of the information that would later be inscribed, several transverse lines running the full width of a tablets usually were drawn by hand. Especially on elongated tablets, the first word of the text was written in large signs, and paragraphs were separated by one or two blank lines (Chadwick 1987, 16).

The "epistemic features" of the Linear B system mentioned above, and many other features—e.g., repetition of standard formulae within set spatial formats, careful spatial separation of individual entries, stoichedon formatting of lexical and ideographic items within successive entries, and in general the systematic use of ideograms as tool for reference and retrieval (Palaima 1988, 330–332)—may seem trivial from the perspective of a fully literate present-day Western individual. Yet in the context of Mycenaean prehistory they amount to "a noticeable development" of recording and retrieval techniques, moving from Cretan Hieroglyphic and Linear A to the

Mycenaean Linear B (ibid., 331). More important in the context of the present discussion is that these "epistemic features" exemplify an important class of events that may serve to remind us that, in the case of Linear B, understanding the mind behind the artifact is not simply a matter of postulating the putative representational states or events being created inside the head of a Mycenaean when he or she is reading or writing a tablet. It is also a matter of postulating the dynamic interaction between that person and the physical properties of the medium of representation as a material thing—that is, a clay tablet.[2]

This takes us to the heart of the general hypothesis of extended cognition.

Were it to happen in the head: From "parity" to "complementarity" and beyond

As the Linear B tablets exemplify, the engagement between cognition and material culture, even in paradigmatic cases in which it can be conceptualized as involving the manipulation of abstract symbols (e.g., signs of names, places, and numerals), is not simply a matter of independent mental representation; it is also a matter of meaningful enculturation and enaction—processes that are dependent on and inseparable from their physical realization, bodily or material. Contrary, then, to the expectations of the orthodox view in cognitive science about the whereabouts of Mycenaean memories and their mental representations, the examples presented in the preceding section demonstrate that the Mycenaeans showed little respect for the boundaries between mental and physical domains. How do we account for that? Exactly where did explanation of Mycenaean memory depart from the traditional idea of "external symbolic storage" (Donald 1991, 2010) and enter the field of extended cognition? The answer is fairly simple: The shift happened the moment we recognized that in the case of the Linear B it was not simply information that was externalized but also the actual processing of that information. This statement has a number of important implications.

A useful way to explicate the Extended Mind (EM) Hypothesis is to consider the divide between internalism and externalism in philosophy of mind. (See, e.g., Wilson 2004; Wheeler 2005; Clark 1997, 2001a, 2008a; Clark and Chalmers 1998; Adams and Aizawa 2008.) Internalism claims that the contents of mental states are determined by features of the individual biological subject without recourse to "external" or "non-biological" conditions. Externalism argues for the opposite, recognizing that the content of a mental state is in part determined by elements of the external world, and thus that human cognitive skills cannot be studied independent of the external environment (social or technological). The extended-mind view should not be confused with the latter assumption about the externality of mental content, originally advocated by Hilary Putnam (1975) and Tyler Burge (1979), now widely accepted, and more recently known as "vehicle externalism" (Hurley 1998)—that is, the view that the vehicles of mental content need not be restricted to the inner biological realm. The extended-mind thesis, though rooted in externalism, took the externalist outlook a step further by arguing that not only the mental content but also the mental process (or at least part of it) can be external to the subject. This perspective became known as "active externalism" (Clark and Chalmers 1998). Whereas mainstream externalism (or the idea of external symbolic storage) implies externalization of cognitive *content*, active externalism implies externalization of cognitive *states and processes* (figure 4.5). For active externalism, marks made with a pen on paper are not an ongoing external record of the contents of mental states; they are an extension of those states. Cognition and action arise together, dialectically forming each other. There is a huge ontological distance between a mind able to externalize its contents to material structures and a mind whose states and processes aren't limited by the skin.

At the nub of this premise lies the famous and much debated "parity principle":

If, as we confront some task, a part of the world functions as a process which, were it to go on in the head, we would have no hesitation in accepting as part of the cognitive process, then that part of the world is (for that time) part of the cognitive process. (Clark and Chalmers 1998, 8)

To illustrate this principle, I return to the issue of memory using Clark and Chalmers' famous example of Otto and Inga. Inga and Otto both want to visit the Museum of Modern Art in New York, but they forget where the museum is. Inga stops, consults her memory, after a moment or two remembers the museum's location and goes on her way there. But Otto, who has Alzheimer's Disease, keeps important information such as the museum's address in a notebook, which he always carries. Otto has to

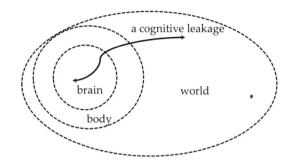

the extended mind

The actual local operations that realize certain forms
of human cognizing include inextricable tangles of
feedback, feed-forward, and feed-around loops: loops
that promiscuously criss-cross the boundaries of
brain, body, and world. The local mechanisms of
mind, if this is correct, are not all in the head.
Cognition leaks out into body and world.

—Andy Clark, *Supersizing the Mind* (2008a, xxviii)

Figure 4.5
A cognitive leakage.

consult his notebook, rather than his biological memory, to find the
museum's address. How can we interpret this difference? From a functional
perspective, it can be argued that the information stored in Otto's notebook and the information stored in Inga's biological memory appear to
resemble one another in at least one significant respect: They enable, albeit
in different media, the physical implementation of Otto's and Inga's dis-
positional beliefs about the museum's location. As we have seen, in the
case of the Linear B tablets a physical artifact, like Otto's notebook, makes
it possible for the system to remember something even if an isolated individual cannot. There is nothing special or strange in saying, then, that
Otto's notebook plays a special role in his ability to remember. But what,
more specifically, might this role be? Should we see Otto's notebook as an
instrument of or a substitute for his biological memory, or should we see
it as, literally, a constitutive "part" of Otto's mind and self (Clark and
Chalmers 1998)? To put it another way, what is the difference between
Otto and Inga so far as the function of memory as a cognitive process is
concerned?

There are many different ways to answer this question, and any attempt
to spread the operations of mind beyond skin and skull is subject to many

potential pitfalls. The philosopher Michael Wheeler (2010b) has addressed the question of deciding "what the benchmarks are by which parity of causal contribution is to be judged." Wheeler suggests that the wrong way to answer this question is to first "fix the benchmarks for what it is to count as a proper part of a cognitive system" and then "look to see if any external elements meet those benchmarks"—in other words, to first take the properties of the brain as the yardstick for the cognitive and then see whether there are things that manifest those properties. This strategy, though useful in some respects, must be wrong, because it deprives us of the ability to discover whatever unique properties might differentiate the cognitive life of things from the cognitive life of, let's say, neurons.

To understand this problem better, let us again consider memory. But this time, instead of thinking about Otto's notebook, let us return to the example of the Mycenaean Linear B tablets. Seen as a cognitive artifact, a Linear B clay tablet provides a prototypical "exographic" device and technology of memory. One way to read the parity principle, then, is as follows: If "exograms" (e.g., Linear B tablets) *act* as "engrams" do, then "exograms" count as parts of memory. At a certain level this might appear to be precisely the point that the extended-mind approach and the material-engagement approach take. But such a simplistic isomorphic reading of the parity principle is far from what I advocate, and can be considered to embody a number of serious drawbacks. For instance, what if what we call an "engram" was first described as something analogous to what we now identify as an "exogram'? Or, more important for present purposes, what if "exograms," though they are active and constitutive parts of memory, are different in important respects from what we know concerning the function of the engrams? What if, in other words, clay tablets and brains store information in radically different ways? I should clarify that Material Engagement Theory subscribes to a locationally neutral account of cognition but *not* to a substrate-neutral account of cognition. Contrary to what often appears to be a mere functional and isomorphic interpretation of the parity principle in the extended-mind literature, I argue that what minds are made of—that is, the stuff of mind—matters as much as how minds are functionally organized. I will return to this. Notice for now that the important question is not simply "Does a Linear B tablet extend the operations of Mycenaean memory beyond the boundaries of the body and brain?"; it is "Exactly how does it do so?" Similarly, although we can be sure that memory is a cognitive process, we need not assume that we know (exactly) what makes it a cognitive process. Indeed, what makes a process a cognitive process?

The hypothesis of the constitutive intertwining of cognition with material culture

Having given this conceptual background, I can now proceed to spell out what I call *the hypothesis of the constitutive intertwining of cognition with material culture*. The main postulate of this hypothesis can be expressed as follows: If we accept that the mind evolves and exists in the *relational domain* as our most fundamental means of *engaging* with the world, then *material culture is potentially co-extensive and consubstantial with mind*.

What are the ontological commitments of this? What does it mean to say that minds and things are *co-constituted* in situated action? Put simply, the principal contention here is that minds and things, more than merely being causally linked, are constitutively interdependent—that is, that the one cannot exist without the other. How can this be? Admittedly, brains and things are different sorts of stuff, yet the ontological compound we call human cognition needs both in order to operate. The parity of "outer" and "inner" cognitive elements advocated here does imply a "functional isomorphy" or "identity"; it implies a constitutive intertwining of brains, bodies, and things in a specific cultural setting. In the context of Material Engagement Theory, the parity principle does not require or imply an identity of mental causal contribution. It is introduced, instead, as a measure to ensure what Andy Clark (2007, 167) calls "equality of opportunity," or, to put it differently, a "non-anthropocentric" (Knappett and Malafouris 2008), "symmetric" (Latour 1999, 2005; Shanks 2007; Witmore 2007) view of mind, self, and agency.

Human thinking is, first and above all, thinking *through*, *with*, and *about* things, bodies, and others. In fact, one of my contentions in this book will be that, from a developmental and evolutionary perspective, only after that basic stage is achieved can metacognition (thinking about thinking) emerge. Indeed, what is meant by collapsing the distinction between the internal and the external aspects of human cognition is that neither the internal nor the external aspects are sufficient in themselves to contain the operations of the human mind. Thinking is not something that happens "inside" brains, bodies, or things; rather, it emerges from contextualized processes that take place "between" brains, bodies, and things.

These are strong claims, and it can be argued that so far proponents of the Extended Mind Hypothesis have failed to provide a coherent argument for why should we treat any of these integrated external structures as parts of the mind (that is, as constitutive parts of externally realized mental states and processes) rather than merely as tools or as influences on those processes. To bring all this into better view, I return to the example of the Linear B tablets. Chadwick's description of the processes that may have taken place in the main Archive room at the Mycenaean palace at Pylos offers a good starting point for trying to focus on the specific details of the cognitive ecology surrounding the Mycenaean clay tablets:

The scribe sits on a stool (*thranus* on the tablets) in the Main Archive Room; through the door at the back we can see through into the Annex, where most of the tablets were found. The written tablets are tidily filed in their labeled baskets; a few lie exposed drying before being put away. The scribe holds the tablet he is working on in his left hand; it is quite often possible to see the fingerprints on the reverse where the tablet was held, and large tablets have sometimes here depressions corresponding to the positions of the thumb and fingers. Next to him stands an official who has returned from a tour of inspection and is dictating the details he wishes to record; he has brought with him a tally-stick to remind him of the correct figures—a gratuitous invention, but it is certain that some form of temporary mnemonic would have been needed to ensure that the official got his figure right. In the foreground a small boy is kneading clay ready to make the next tablet for the scribe. (1976, 20)

This informed reconstruction offers only a small part of the complex interactions that characterize the usage and processing of the tablets. The operational sequence can easily be extended to incorporate further elements, materials, and practices. One example can be seen in the case of small blobs of wet clay (labels) that were pressed onto the outside of the baskets used for the storage of the tablets to facilitate the identification of the tablets after their storage (ibid., 18–19). Yet I believe that Chadwick's description illustrates an important point for the present discussion: In approaching Mycenaean memory through the material remains of the Linear B script, we are not simply looking at a disembodied system of signs. We are looking, instead, at a temporal sequence of relationally constituted embodied processes encompassing reciprocal and culturally orchestrated interactions among humans, situated tool use, and space.

When speaking about interaction, I do not simply refer to the process in which several individuals are bringing together their isolated and decontextualized bits of knowledge. The focus is, rather, on how those bits of knowledge are acquired, coordinated, and distributed in action. Also important to keep in mind is that the interactions that define a distributed cognitive system do not occur only among individual human agents but also occur among humans, objects, and materials of various sorts. The common idea about space and the environment as a static external recourse devoid of agency comes under question. (For other examples, see Knappett and Malafouris 2008.) I will be discussing the issue of material agency in detail later in the book. For now, the critical assumption is that a cognitive system that involves more than one individual has cognitive properties that differ from the cognitive properties of the individuals who participate in the system taken in isolation. This also means that no matter how detailed the knowledge of the cognitive properties of those individual agents in isolation might be, it is not in itself sufficient to account for the operations of the system as a whole. (See also Hutchins 1995.) Instead, we should be focusing on the interactions among human and material actors seeking to discern the properties, emergent or otherwise, that are relevant to the working space and the social setting. Focusing on the distribution of labor, or on the factors that determine the size of a clay tablet, or even on the various communicative pathways that define the flow of information across the different representational states and modes of the system (e.g., from verbal to inscribed) may be more important for understanding the cognitive operations involved than any isolated observation about the representational content of the tablets.

This change in perspective, which the archaeological preoccupation with things and cultural practices embodies, brings with it, with some elaboration, a whole new set of possibilities to the study of mind and memory. The new approach involves a change of analytic unit and a shift in the level of description from the micro level of semantics to the macro level of practice. As I will explain below, an important implication follows from that holistic relational outlook: Linear B is no longer seen as a disembodied abstract code; now it is seen as a situated technology instantiating a new way of remembering and a new way of forgetting. The Mycenaean simply reads what the Linear B tablet remembers. In fact, being able to read, that person no longer needs to remember.

Surely skeptics will think I am pushing the boundary of cognition too far here. Things and technologies (e.g., clay tablets and notebooks) are simply aids to cognition; they are not cognition itself. Things do not constitute our memories, nor do they have memories of their own; they simply help us remember. Adams and Aizawa (2008, 2010) probably would contend that in much of what I have said so far I have mistaken a mere and rather epiphenomenal causal influence of the tablet on the human memory system for something more substantial. Although it is certainly acceptable to claim that the Mycenaean is interacting with or using a Linear B tablet to store information outside the head, to say that a clay tablet actually instantiates memory or participates in the cognitive processes responsible for how the Mycenaean remembers is an entirely different claim—a claim that Adams and Aizawa (2008) would probably consider metaphysically suspect. In the latter case, the critique goes, we have conflated the ontologically important distinction between "causation" and "constitution"—that is, between "mere interaction" and "participation."

Though one could see the reasons for it, I believe that this worry fundamentally misrepresents the cognitive life of things, as I will try to illustrate below. The "coupling-constitution fallacy" (Aizawa 2010; Rupert 2004, 2010a,b) and what might be called "the locational fallacy" (Wheeler 2010a,b), I believe, illustrate, on the one hand, the intellectual uncertainty and residual cognitivism that one could still trace among extended-mind theorists, and, on the other hand, the inability of modern philosophy to make sense of the most significant attribute of the cognitive life of things: their ability to be, at the same time, mental and physical.

In chapter 3, I attempted to take a first step toward reconciling these fallacies by exposing the shortcomings of conventional boundaries and analytical units in the study of mind and by developing the notion of metaplasticity. Here I want to expand on those arguments, focusing on some issues that I believe are responsible for the worries mentioned above and which I think have not received the attention they deserve in the ongoing debate over the Extended Mind Hypothesis. Those issues are, of course, *materiality*, *time*, and *transformation*. I will argue that the current criticisms of extended-mind theory emanate principally from a deeply entrenched "I-centric" bias in philosophical thinking that defines the temporal scale and the ontological configuration of the human mind (extended or not). Essentially, this "I-centric" view implies that the mind is a property or a possession of the individual (which also means that the temporality of mind is constrained and determined by the temporality of the individual), that the individual has an ontological and agentive priority in the enaction of any particular cognitive process, and that the location of mind is coextensive with the organismic boundaries of the individual.

Things matter: The coupling-constitution fallacy

As I have already discussed, according to extended-mind theory the relationship that characterizes the interaction between cognition and material culture is usually described as that of "continuous reciprocal causation" between "functionally isomorphic" internal and external structures (Clark 1997, 163–166). The central assumption behind the coupling-constitution fallacy is that, although in the case of the Linear B tablet one could recognize the presence of "a causal connection" between mind and clay, this "causal connection" or "coupling" is not sufficient to warrant the argument for cognitive extension. "Real" cognitive processing necessitates the presence of what Adams and Aizawa define as "non-derived representations" (2008). The Linear B tablet, an artificial inscriptive device involving derived (humanly assigned) rather than non-derived content or representations, fails to make the grade. On this construal, technologies such as the Linear B tablets are merely memory aids that do not participate, in any important sense, in "real" cognitive processing.

I want to argue that this view, which sees the Linear B tablet simply as an "external" amplifier or storage device that serves to lighten the "internal" cognitive load, is mistaken. It is mistaken because it leaves out the element that matters most: the extended reorganization of the cognitive system. Contrary to what many people seem to believe, a Linear B tablet, more than simply amplifying memory, brings about some radical changes in the nature of the cognitive operations involved and in the functional structure of the system as a whole (Norman 1988, 1991, 1993). The difference that makes the difference in the case of Linear B is that a different set of skills and affordances[3] is introduced, and those skills and affordances radically reconfigure the cognitive ecology and the dynamics (including boundaries and connectivity) of the Mycenaean memory field. As an implication of that, the individual using the tablets now engages in a different sort of cognitive behavior. A different cognitive operation—reading—now emerges and becomes available in the system. As Merlin Donald correctly remarks (2001, 314),

The external memory field is not just another sector of working memory. It taps directly into the neural networks of literacy, located in brain regions that are distinct from those of working memory. Working memory and the external memory field thus complement each other, and this allows the brain to exploit their distinct storage and retrieval properties.

To put it simply, the numerals and iconographic signs that constitute the mnemonic component *par excellence* of the Linear B system did not simply *help* Mycenaeans to remember the precise quantities of the recorded commodities; rather, *they were part of the process by which the Linear B system remembered.* From the system's viewpoint, it is not the individual scribe that remembers; it is the Linear B tablet. The Linear B tablets, by "being there" in the "outside" world, enable the Mycenaean scribe to substitute visual recognition for recall, thereby transforming a difficult "internal" memory problem into an easier "external" perceptual one. Information, once inscribed on the clay tablet, transcends the biological limitations of the individual person and becomes available "out there" for other people to use, comment on, transform, or incorporate. It is important to note, however, that the mnemonic properties of the Linear B system are not the sum of the biological capacities of the Mycenaean scribe and the mnemonic affordances and storage capacity of a Linear B tablet. Rather, a hybrid historical synergy or cognitive assembly brings about a new ecology of memory. This new ecology cannot be reduced to any of its constitutive elements (biological or artificial) and thus cannot be accounted for by looking at the isolated properties of persons or things. The challenge for archaeology, in this respect, is to reveal and articulate the variety of forms that cognitive extension can take and the diversity of feedback relationships between objects and the embodied brain as they become realized in different periods and cultural settings (Sutton 2010, 2008; Sutton et al. 2010).

Being where? The locational fallacy

Earlier in this chapter I discussed Wheeler's question about how to decide "what the benchmarks are by which parity of causal contribution is to be judged" (2010b). I said that taking the brain and its properties as the unquestioned natural locus and yardstick for the cognitive must be the wrong way to think of "parity." The claim for functional isomorphism that such a reading of the parity principle embodies cannot do justice to the constitutive intertwining of mind with the material world. There are two particular problems that I wish to discuss in this connection.

1. Any isomorphism between cognition and material culture homogenizes the different roles that brains, bodies, and things might play within the cognitive system and thus deprives them of their peculiar features and properties. Paradoxically, it is those very properties that define the functions of brains, bodies, and things within the cognitive system and make them significant for what they are. Indeed, it cannot be emphasized too strongly that a Linear B tablet, like many other technologies of remembrance or forgetting, when seen as an "external" memory resource, differs a great deal from what we know about the workings of biological memory. (For more detailed discussions, see Malafouris 2004 and Malafouris forthcoming.) For one thing, as Merlin Donald was one of the first to point out, "unlike the constantly moving and fading contents of biological working memory, the contents of this externally driven processor can be frozen in time, reviewed, refined, and reformatted" (1991, 308–319; also see Donald 2010). The reformattable nature of exograms allows for information to be altered and then reentered into storage in ways that an engram clearly cannot afford. Meanwhile, whereas in the case of exographic storage recall is determined primarily by the nature of the stored representation, in the case of engrams the context of recollection is as important as the nature of the encoded traces.[4] (See Malafouris forthcoming.) Finally, although we can assume that whatever properties an engram might have will remain much the same between different individuals, in the case of exograms there is great cultural diversity in their properties and in how these properties become actualized in the social construction of memory. For instance, knots, stelae, rituals, monuments, and khipu strings differ greatly in how they activate human memory, and thus in the possibilities of cultural transmission that they offer. (See, e.g., Connerton 1989; Jones 2007; Kwint et al. 1999; Mack 2003.) Understanding how external resources matter (causally and ontologically) for memory in their own specific ways emerges as a major challenge for cognitive archaeology and for material-culture studies. Hence the need to explain the materiality of the objects, dwelling on the mundane qualities they possess (Miller 1998, 9).

2. Although the "parity principle" collapses the functional boundaries between the "inner" and the "outer," it essentially keeps the ontological boundaries of the "mental" and "physical" intact, as it implicitly prioritizes the traditional properties of the former over the latter. Using an analogy, Ezequiel Di Paolo nicely points out what "the absurd equivalent" of such a reading of the "parity principle" might be: "Isn't this the absurd equivalent of 'Even though in the past several cases of mental illness were erroneously diagnosed as cases of demonic possession, in modern days, in order to determine whether you have a case of mental illness you must always consult an exorcist first'?" (2009, 11) Is there any way that such question-begging can be avoided? Wheeler proposes that first, and independent of location, we define what elements, entities, or properties should count as proper parts of a cognitive system, and that we then look to see where these cognitive components happen to be located with respect to the internal/external boundary. My proposal here goes a step further. The basic idea I want to advance is very simple: Although a Linear B tablet, as a material entity, is certainly external to the Mycenaean brain, it may also be conceived as internal to the cognitive process we call memory. What ought to count as part of the mind is not to be found either by looking inside the head or by trying to find those "outside" processes or material structures that resemble the "inner" process of the human brain. Instead of seeing the Linear B tablet or Otto's notebook as the artificial cultural equivalent of a hippocampus, we should look at them as cognitive assemblies or compounds and seek their peculiar emergent properties. Taken in isolation in their well-confined and neatly articulated environments of brain and culture, both engrams (seen as internal ensembles of neurons) and exograms (seen as external ensembles of material structures and scaffoldings) are lifeless. The cognitive life of things, like the cognitive life of brains, can be found where engrams and exograms begin spiking, interacting, and complementing one another in such a way that memory emerges.

When we shift our attention from "passive" entities and organisms to "active" cognitive processes, performances, and assemblies, conventional organismic boundaries, surfaces, and interfaces no longer apply. This implies that what is to be considered "internal" or "external" to these cognitive assemblies is determined by the dynamics of interaction among the components (neural, bodily, social, or material) that bring forth a given cognitive operation. And as long as a cognitive process involves the dynamic configuration and coordination of both internal and external resources and structures, those should be conceived as being at the same time mental and physical. That means that any appropriate metabolically generated or artificially incorporated recourse can be, potentially, an important and indistinguishable part of a given cognitive process.

In a very important sense, then, from the perspective of material engagement, *cognition has no location*. The active mind cannot be contained. Cognition is not a "within" property; it is a "between" property.

The affect of engagement

As I have already noted, extended-mind theorists have, to varying degrees, expanded the territory of mind into the material world, but it can be argued that they have generally failed, or that they remain unwilling, to break completely from representationalism and move beyond its computational heritage. As a consequence, although it has now been more than 20 years since the human mind was reconfigured as a dynamic embodied sense-making machine, it remains largely a *problem-solving* machine. The cognitive system is now "wide" and extends beyond the limits of "the organismic boundary" (Wilson 1994, 2004), but it remains a computational system. Things emerge as "genuine" parts of extended but nonetheless problem-solving regimes and computational routines (see Clark 2008a, 47; Wheeler 2005). Material culture, when discussed at all, is simply viewed as an external information channel that transfers, stores, and sometimes even processes information outside the head.

I will be arguing that such a narrow focus on the power of non-neural structures to transform the human problem-solving and representational capacities is deeply problematic from an archaeological perspective and from an anthropological perspective. As Chris Gosden rightly points out, a notion of mind, even when extended, is not helpful if it does not take the sensual, affective, and emotional aspects of human intelligent behavior seriously by considering how things put novel demands on the bodies and brains of people experiencing and appreciating their aesthetic qualities (2008, 2010). Proponents of the enactive approach have also identified this shortcoming of the extended-mind theory, noting that it neglects emotion and that it treats cognition "as if it were largely affectless problem solving or information processing." Thompson and Stapleton point out that "sense-making comprises emotion as much as cognition" (2008, 26).

To an important extent, I hope that the focus on things will help us to reduce the blind spots of traditional cognitivist accounts of mind. However, in order to overcome this residual cognitivism, a temporal, agentive and affective dimension must be added to the initial spatial metaphor of an inner mind that is being extended in the outside world. We need to look at how things inhabit space, and we need to explore inter-artifactual relations and communities of things and objects (Knappett 2010, 2011).

Things have a strong affective response that has never been given serious consideration in the extended-mind literature. *Evocative Objects* (Turkle 2007), a recent collection of autobiographical stories on the evocative nature of things, nicely illustrates that the true power of everyday objects and things lies in their ability to become our emotional companions as much as they become our intellectual anchors. The same principles of extension and reorganization that enable a Linear B tablet to transform memory into forgetting can be seen to be active in numerous other contexts of our everyday emotional coping. Similarly to the way a Linear B tablet creates a specific location for remembrance, transforming an "internal" invisible cognitive happening into an "external" perceptual "event," objects can be transformed into powerful "emotional anchors." When it comes to object relations and material engagement, thought and feeling are inseparable companions in life experience that can take multiple and fluid roles (ibid., 5–6).

The centrality of material culture is also demonstrated in Daniel Miller's 2008 book *The Comfort of Things*, which is based on material derived from an ethnographic study of households on a single street in South London. Miller concludes that material culture matters because everyday objects help people to construct a material order of emotions and feelings that gradually forms an ecology of relationships and expectations about the self and others.[5] In a 2009 article based on the same fieldwork, Miller and Fiona Parrott describe how people use things in dealing with various experiences of separation and episodes of loss. When dealing with a death or with the ending of a relationship, people use objects to create an economy of memory. Miller and Parrott discuss, in particular, how mourning may entail either accumulation of objects or divestment of objects. As they observe, we have no control over "the way a person is taken away from us in death," but we "can control the way we separate from the material objects that were associated with the dead." Furthermore, "things may come to haunt us, however hard we try to banish them." One example Miller and Parrott use to illustrate the latter is that of Mrs. Stone, an immigrant from Jamaica who, after losing a daughter, devoted herself to accumulating memories of the daughter in the form of objects, photographs, and other things the daughter had possessed. Mrs. Stone's description of a gold heart on a chain that her daughter gave her just before her death is revealing:

She gave me this pretty little heart and I said: "What have I to put this away for?" I said: "I am going to be wearing this from now on." I sleep in it, I bathe in it, I do everything in it. She's gone and I'm wearing it. So I've been wearing it every day of my life. I don't take it off. (Miller and Parrott 2009, 509–510)

Archaeology and anthropology amply testify that things are not simply tokens or surrogates in some "external" or "internal" problem-solving activity. Things have also a strong affective response, and it has never been given serious consideration in the extended-mind literature. Things are made to be seen, exchanged, deposited, owned, valued, priced, manipulated, feared, fetishized, revered, ridiculed, and so on. The sensual properties of things and the aesthetic experience of things permeate every aspect of our cognitive activities and permeate our social and emotional relationships (Gosden 2001, 2004, 2005; Jones 2007; Thomas and Pinney 2001; Forty and Küchler 1999). These important elements in the cognitive lives of persons and things should be foregrounded and studied for what they are rather than subsumed under information processing. If we are to understand the idiosyncratic abilities of objects, past or present, to make us forget and remember, to guide our everyday action, to channel and signify social experience, and to sustain our embodied routines, we should resist or bypass our modern representational or computational preoccupations and allow a truly meaningful sense of how the material world constitutes our existence as human beings to emerge.

5 The Enactive Sign

If I could tell you what it meant, there would be no point in dancing it.
—Isadora Duncan, as quoted by Gregory Bateson (1973, 137)

In chapter 4, I argued against the dominant representational-computational view of mind. In this chapter, I want to explore the implications of that critique from a semiotic perspective. Underpinning the suggested constitutive intertwining of cognition with material culture is the capacity of material things to operate as signs. And indeed, insofar as all material culture has a semiotic dimension, understanding signification is important not only for how we study the symbols of the past but also for how we practice archaeology at all (Hodder and Hutson 2003, 4). For these reasons, my focus in this chapter will be on the semiotic dimension of Material Engagement Theory.

Moving beyond representation

Representation is the phenomenon that most semioticians see as the essence of symbolism. And for many people symbolism or signification is the crucial anthropological property that, more than anything else, defines what it means to be human. Generally speaking, there are two major types of representations: the internal or mental type and the external or public type. Mental representations can be understood as what philosophers call the representational content of a certain intention or belief about the world; public or external representations are those material signs or sign systems that are publicly available in the world.

Obviously, my proposal in this chapter to move beyond representation is not meant to deny the important role that this precious ability of our mental machinery plays in the case of signification in general. It is, instead, meant to challenge the role of representation specifically in relation to the material sign and the semiotic dimensions of material engagement. To this end, in what follows I will shift my focus from the traditional question of *what* a material sign means to the question of *how* it means.

What I am seeking to understand is, essentially, the semiotic basis of the relationship between cognition and material culture. Certainly representation is one dimension of this relationship, and indeed it is characteristic of our linguistic abilities. However, what may be central for language need not be central for non-linguistic semiotic systems. The fact that language seems to be based on representation should not be projected into the realm of material engagement. I do not dispute that the material sign can be seen to operate as a form of external representation or as a part of a larger representational structure. What I want to suggest in this chapter is that the exclusive focus on the representational properties of such structures that preoccupies archaeological interpretation of past material culture can seriously distort our understanding of how such semiotic entities or structures operate in various processes of material engagement. The argument I intend to develop is not simply that in the case of material culture the idea of the arbitrary signifier should be replaced with the idea of a motivated index or icon. More important, I want to suggest that the temporal and ontological priority of the signified over the signifier that most semiotic frameworks reiterate cannot be sustained in the case of the material sign. The principal underlying assumption of my analysis is that, from a semiotic perspective, language and material culture differ substantially in respect of the cognitive mechanisms that support their semiotic function. More specifically, my suggestion will be that the material sign does not primarily embody a "communicative" or representational logic but an *enactive* one. For material semiosis,[1] meaning is not the product of representation but the product of a process of "conceptual integration" between material and conceptual domains.

I will begin by articulating what I see as the principal problem of conventional semiotic accounts of materiality.

The fallacy of the linguistic sign

The lions in Trafalgar Square could have been eagles or bulldogs and still have carried the same (or similar) messages about empire and about the cultural premises of

nineteenth-century England. And yet, how different might their message have been had they been made of wood!
—Gregory Bateson (1973, 130)

By "the fallacy of the linguistic sign" I mean, essentially, the commonly practiced implicit or explicit reduction of the material sign under the general category of the linguistic sign.[2] Technically speaking, to commit this fallacy is to conflate semiotic ontologies. That means, put very simply, that you assume that a real ceramic vase and the word 'vase' possess the same semiotic properties and affordances. In other words, you presuppose that both the vase as a material entity and 'vase' as a word mean, or signify, in the same manner. When the issue is viewed from a methodological perspective, what this fallacy implies is that you have adopted the analogy of *material culture as language or text*. The problem with this analogy is that often it becomes a metaphor: Material culture *is* language or text. When that happens, it has a major implication for the understanding of material culture that can be deconstructed as follows: Once the arbitrary logic that characterizes the source domain of your metaphor as a semiotic system— i.e., language—is projected onto the domain of material culture, you are left with no means to discover what extra semiotic properties there might be that characterize your target domain as significant for what it is—i.e., a material thing rather than language.

Specifically for archaeology and anthropology, the suggested linguistic-sign fallacy translates into an implicit or an explicit grounding of symbolic approaches to past material culture on Saussurian (1966) semiology. According to this Saussurian conceptualization, which underlies both processual and post-processual theories, symbolic action is essentially a form of arbitrary representational or referential action. More specifically, signification is construed as a "stands for" or "means" relationship between a signified and a signifier that implies what the anthropologist Edmund Leach (1976) termed a "communication event"—that is, the transmission of a message between a sender and a receiver. Thus, from a structural perspective we have Leach's contention that "it is as meaningful to talk about the grammatical rules which govern the wearing of clothes as it is to talk about the grammatical rules which govern speech utterances" (1976, 10), and from a post-structural hermeneutic perspective there is the recent emphasis on textual approaches in which the meaning of the material sign equals the contextual *reading* of the sign (Tilley 1991; Hodder 1991). In other words, material symbols are construed primarily as media for the communication of information among agents, and symbolic archaeology is construed primarily as an exegetical procedure aiming to decode and interpret the information stored in those vehicles on the basis of their contextual associations.

A few clarifications concerning the principal features of Saussurian semiology seem necessary. First, the Saussurian position emanates from a "nominalist" rather than a "realist" ontological basis. The sign is defined as a disembodied and disengaged relationship between a "signifier" (acoustic or visual form) and a "signified" (concept). In other words, the linguistic sign exists as a "two sided-psychological entity" in the human mind, completely dissociated from and unaffected by the external reality. Thus, material culture *per se* has no place in that system. This brings us to the second point, which is that this internal bond between the signifier and the signified is postulated as "arbitrary." The linguistic sign, lacking any empirical motivation, is entirely a product of human convention. In one sentence, Saussure (1966, 66) asserts that semiosis takes place on a separate linguistic plane, entirely removed from substantive reality in an arbitrary manner:

The means by which the sign is produced is completely unimportant, for it does not affect the system. Whether I make the letters in white or black, raised or engraved, with pen or chisel—all of this is of no importance with respect to the signification.

This is not the place to evaluate Saussurian semiology in the context of language. My aim here is to expose the roots of an important archaeological problem. This problem, as mentioned, concerns the nature of the material sign and, more specifically, the extent to which that nature has anything to do with language in the first place.

Imagine a person signing a document. Approaching that common activity from a semiotic perspective, we can easily recognize a signified-signifier relationship between the person and the signature. Accepting Saussure's suggestion that by what means a sign is produced doesn't matter implies that whether the signature is handwritten, photocopied, or otherwise artificially produced (e.g., stamped) has no effect on its meaning. The message on the paper should remain the same. But is that really the case? Ethnographies of the workplace environment—and common sense—show that it is not. (See, e.g., Pellegram 1998.) For example, in the case of an artificially produced signature, although the explicit message reads the same as a handwritten signature, the implicit message has changed. By that I mean that the affective impact of the signature is no longer the same, and that, contrary to Saussure's contention, the change seems to have a direct effect on the meaning of the actual message. The artificially produced signature, not being consubstantial with the signified person, has lost the element of sympathy. It has been transformed into a kind of commodity that no longer bears any personal imprint. From the perspective of Peircean (1955, 1991) semiotics, it has changed in status from an index to a symbol. A letter that bears an artificially produced signature isn't perceived as a direct extended part of a signer, or as one of a kind. Although in terms of explicit communication the message or meaning of the signature remains the same, in terms of pragmatics the power of this signature to represent the person has changed. The letter, and thus the message or statement of the person, will be given less attention than one with a handwritten signature would have been given, or may even be disregarded. Strangely enough, in the case of this example, it appears as if "the resistance of the pen on paper is also the precondition for the inscription of the personality into the message" (Shore 1996, 140).

It is precisely through those subtle, mundane, often unconscious affective channels that material culture manifests its dynamic character and its semiotic force. Indeed, when it comes to material signs—and in direct opposition to the Saussurian contention concerning the arbitrariness of signification—to make the letters "black or white, raised or engraved, with pen or chisel" is in most cases the defining feature of the signification process. Moreover, not only the physical form of the letters but also the physical properties of the medium upon which they are inscribed are being dynamically implicated in the semiotic process. As Andrea Pellegram has shown (1998, 106), not only are business letters "dressed in fine inks and textures to reflect well on their authors," and not only are letterheads "designed to leave a unique mark on memory"; in addition, the nature of the paper has much to do with the message a letter conveys:

Letterhead paper is high quality bond that is slightly closer to the colour of cream than white: it is thicker than the paper used for the photocopier and has tiny bumps and ridges along the surface. Everything about it says "special purpose": it does not flop around as much as other papers and the little ridges make it feel rough between the fingertips that hold it.

Very simply, under normal conditions you do not send an official letter written on a Post-it. This is not, however, because such a message cannot actually be written on a Post-it. It is, rather, because you know that using the small yellow piece of paper probably would have a negative effect on how your official message would be interpreted. If materiality can be seen to affect the meaning of a message, even in a case where the message is clearly articulated through the use of written language, one can easily imagine the impact of materiality on the vast majority of cases where the message is not explicitly inscribed on matter but rather is embodied and objectified *through* matter. Obviously, for material culture, the means by which a sign is produced and the physical properties that define the sign for what it is as a physical object can be argued to have a direct bearing on the nature of the semiotic process. Contrary to what appears to be. the case in the context of language, the relationship between the signified and the signifier in the context of material semiosis is far from arbitrary. Saussure was probably aware of this when he stated that a pair of scales that operates as a symbol of justice cannot be replaced by just any other symbol. Yet it is a point that clearly falls outside the domain proper of his semiology (i.e., language), and as such it seems to have posed no real challenge to his thesis of arbitrariness. For Saussure, it is precisely the inherent conventionality and arbitrariness of language that makes it possible for it to realize "the ideal of the semiological process" better than any other sign system and thus to become the "master pattern for all branches of semiology" (1966, 68). However, in the context of material semiosis it is precisely the absence of this arbitrariness that we must take as our point of initiation for developing a systematic account of the material sign.

Searching for the properties of the material sign

It follows from the above that no isomorphic projection of linguistic models can be accepted[3] for the case of the material sign. From a more pragmatic perspective, I believe the best we can do has been cogently expressed by Christopher Tilley in the epilogue of his *Ethnography of the Neolithic* (1996, 337):

any theory of material culture cannot avoid the problem of language, indeed it has to start from language, but must modify linguistic analogies and go beyond them.

The durable nature of the material sign clearly contrasts with the ephemeral nature of the linguistic sign. A physical sign can be touched, carried, worn, possessed, exchanged, stored, transfigured, or destroyed. Things act most powerfully at the non-discursive level, incorporating qualities (such as color, texture, and smell) that affect human cognition in ways that are rarely explicitly conceptualized. These are properties not afforded by the nature of the linguistic sign. Moreover, what would be the starting point from which to read a constellation of material signs? Language is linear and sequential. In contrast, material culture, even when it can be seen as a spatial arrangement, preserves no obvious point of commencement.

Thus, it emerges that the material sign is not the isomorphic substitute for the linguistic sign. From a semiotic perspective they should be rather understood as independent yet complementary. The distinctive properties of the material world bring about meaning in ways that language cannot, and vice versa. This is the point where the functional/symbolic dichotomy breaks down, and this is the reason why the strong tendency inherited from traditional semiotics to reduce signification to a kind of contextual encoding and decoding of fixed meanings should be avoided in the case of the material sign. As I shall argue in the next section, materiality objectifies a different semiotic path.

The call for the disentanglement of material culture from the conventional linguistic idiom echoes in a number of recent discourses on the semiotics of material culture (e.g., Keane 2003; Gottdiener 1995; Riggins 1994; Byers 1992, 1999a,b; Gell 1998; Boivin 2008; Preucel 2006). Despite this gradually expanding reaction against the equation of the material and linguistic sign, a systematic alternative semiotic treatment of the material sign is currently lacking. The work of the philosopher and semiotician Charles Sanders Peirce (1955; also see Hoopes 1991) is often introduced to counterbalance the arbitrariness of the Saussurian model. Indeed, Peirce, being concerned in particular with the nature of non-linguistic signs, developed a basic tripartite classification of signs that offers an excellent entrance point for approaching the meaning of things. (See, e.g., Riggins 1994; Knappett 2002.) This classification distinguishes three major types of signs:

icons: signs that signify through some sort of visual resemblance or similarity, as when a portrait signifies its subject or "when a restaurant uses a pot symbolically to advertise the traditional or 'home-cooked' nature of their meals" (Hodder and Hutson 2003, 60)

indexes: signs that signify by being physically connected with their referent in some causal spatio-temporal sense of contiguity—for example, a footprint, the barometer, the symptoms of a disease or simply the smoke caused by the fire

symbols: signs that, as we know from Saussure, signify in an arbitrary manner, as when a word refers to a concept or a letter stands for a sound.

Peirce's major contribution to the understanding of the material sign lies in his recognition that meaning is not solely a matter of "arbitrary" symbols but also—and this is especially the case for non-verbal communication and non-linguistic sign systems—a matter of "motivated" icons and indexes.[4]

However, an important problem remains. No doubt a Peirce-inspired semiotic approach to the study of material culture can help us tackle the question of meaning with an eye to the physical properties of the sign and to the non-representational attributes of signification. Unfortunately, the same cannot be suggested with respect to the question of how a sign emerges and acquires symbolic force—that is, the question of the becoming of the material sign, first as a real substantive entity and only secondarily as a representation or index. It is precisely this becoming that characterizes material engagement as a semiotic procedure.

The enactive logic of the material sign

A useful starting point for articulating what an enactive sign is really about would be the distinction between the *expressive* and the *designative or denotative* meaning of signs (Taylor 1985; see also Byers 1999a). A designative or denotative sign is one that refers to something that exists independent of the sign itself. For example, when we ask about the meaning of an unknown word (a linguistic sign, spoken or written) we essentially seek the concept that the word signifies, which exists independent of the specific word that is used as its signifier in a particular language. Once such a concept is revealed to us by way of a definition capable of identifying and distinguishing this concept from others, the unknown word is immediately transformed from a meaningless sound or letter arrangement into a meaningful entity. The reason for that is quite simple: The linguistic sign, being denotative, operates on the principle of equation. The word, by convention, equates to a definition. However, in the case of the material sign such an equivalency is rarely the case. If we ask for the meaning of an artifact (a material sign), the questions evoked will far exceed the above-mentioned definitional realm. The predicates that have to be brought to bear on these questions, and the inferential processes that such a sign evokes, are far more complicated than those we see in the case of words. The questions evoked may include questions of being and substance, questions of what is and is not, questions of quantity and quality, questions of relation and becoming, questions of place and time, questions of position and state, and questions of potentiality and actuality. Contrary to my discussion of the linguistic sign, the meaning of the material sign is *expressive*. That means that the material sign, in most cases, does not stand for a concept but rather substantiates a concept. This is what in philosophy of mind is called *instantiation*. The material sign instantiates rather than symbolizes. It brings forth the concept as a concrete exemplar and a substantiating instance. It is what we might call, following Colin Renfrew, a "constitutive symbol." The material reality takes precedence, and "the concept is meaningless without the actual substance" (Renfrew 2001a, 130). Indeed, a material sign as an expressive sign does not refer to something existing separately from it, but is a constitutive part of what it expresses and which otherwise cannot be known. It operates on the principle of participation rather than that of symbolic equivalency.

Thus, to approach a material sign or an assemblage of material signs as the symbolic materialization of a given concept or social abstraction (e.g., status) is to assume that the concept or social abstraction is temporally and also ontologically prior to its actual objectification. Temporal priority poses no real problems, but ontological priority violates all the properties of material semiosis discussed above. Thus, I consider such a violation to be inherently problematic. It implies an idea similar to that of considering the concept or property of whiteness as existing independently, outside of and prior to the concrete things that it serves to express. A piece of white A4 paper and a white flower are concrete relational instantiations of whiteness and not simply representations of some pre-existent Platonic world of ideas. Reality, at least for Material Engagement Theory, is neither *post* nor *ante res*; it is *in res*. Material signs are not simply message carriers in some pre-ordered social universe. Material signs are the actual physical forces that shape the social and cognitive universe.

Indeed, as the archaeologist Martin Byers (1999a) suggests, material signs can be seen also to operate as action warrants. They possess a "warranting capacity" like that of police badges and uniforms. People bearing these symbolic warrants are endowed with action capacities, and people denied access to these symbols are denied these capacities. For example, a passport allows one to travel in a different country, a visa allows one to dwell or work somewhere, money allows one to purchase things, and a driving license allows one to drive on public roads. Such a form of modern documentation is not simply a reflection of the social reality it documents; it is "a symbolic pragmatic constituent element of that reality" akin to that of a court warrant. Indeed, the reality that a passport represents does not exist independent of the user but is embodied and constituted in action. Furthermore, warranting, far from being a by-product of literacy, is equally if not more pervasive in non-literate societies, and arguably is generally most effective when objectified in concrete material symbols. Consequently, for Byers (1992, 415), material culture should be understood in "action-constitutive terms":

In action-constitutive terms, all material cultural items have action-constitutive force. Just as the judge's 'ermine' is a constituent element of her/his judicial speech action by endowing the wearer with institutional authority which simultaneously transforms the utterance of specific words into a legal declaration, so the (utilitarian) axe is also a constituent element of the user's material action, endowing its user with institutional or virtual property, e.g., that of being a peasant, thereby transforming the physical labour into the material action of discharging feudal dues, etc.

Developing his "warranting model" of pragmatic signification, Byers explicitly argues against the general tendency of symbolic archaeology to collapse the meaning of material culture into a kind of referential or designative meaning. Such an assumption, Byers suggests (1999b, 31), contradicts the "active" nature of material culture since it reduces the material sign to a passive means of referencing rather than an active means of constituting reality.

Renfrew follows a similar line of reasoning in his exposition of the constitutive symbol. More specifically, he defines the constitutive symbol as a sign "where the symbolic or cognitive element and the material element co-exist, are in a sense immanent, and where the one does not make sense without the other" (2001b, 98). To illustrate that better, let us use Renfrew's example of weight (2001a, 133):

|W|eight can have no meaning in a disembodied sense. Only material things have weight and the concept has no meaning without experience of these. The substantive reality precedes any notion of quantifying it or standardising it by balancing a standard object (the "weight") against other objects.

Indeed, weights and measures can be used as an excellent example for illustrating the dense structural coupling between the supposedly internal and external domains of the human conceptual map. If weight has a meaning, it is a meaning that can be grasped primarily through the mind's body rather than through the mind's brain. To speak about weight in a disembodied sense is to speak about numerical relationships, not about weight as a meaningful experience. These relationships, however, are possible only after weight has emerged as a symbol in the context of praxis— that is, as an embodied meaningful experience. This is why in this case, as Renfrew proposes (2001a), symbol comes before concept.

What we are still lacking, however, is some precise cognitive mechanism able to account for the emergence of this hypostatic unity between mind and matter, or between signified and signifier in the case of the material sign. In the case of language, this crucial role was played by representation. But how does matter become a sign in our case? In an attempt to answer that question, I propose the following premises:

(1) I define the *material sign* as a semiotic conflation and co-habitation through matter that enacts and brings forth the world.

(2) I define *enactive signification* as a process of embodied "conceptual integration" responsible for the co-substantial symbiosis and simultaneous emergence of the signifier and the signified that brings forth the material sign.

(3) I propose *enactive signification* as the crux of material semiosis and thus of the meaningful engagement of cognition with matter.

Projections through matter

My concern in this section is to exemplify and illustrate the notion and the cognitive basis of enactive signification as defined above. To do so, I will first develop the notion of *cognitive projection*, drawing on the general principles of embodied cognition discussed in relation to the Extended Mind Hypothesis. I will then introduce the *conceptual integration* or *blending* theory (Fauconnier 1997; Fauconnier and Turner 1998, 2002) as a useful cognitive mechanism for approaching the semiotic dimensions of material engagement.

To begin with, I would like provisionally to define *cognitive projection* as the pervasive and (in most cases) unconscious capacity of the cognitive agent to establish direct implicit ontological correspondences between domains of experience. In this sense a cognitive projection can be understood as a conceptual mapping. It is thus important that projection not be confused with representation. A projection between a phenomenal domain A and phenomenal domain B (mental or physical) is not the representation of domain A through B; it is the establishment of an ontological correspondence between A and B. More specifically, these ontological correspondences primarily involve connections of identity, analogy, similarity, causality, change, time, intentionality, space, role, and part-whole, and in some cases also of representation. Thus, cognitive projections offer us a basic non-representational conceptual mechanism through which the "dense structural coupling" between mind and matter that was discussed in the preceding chapter becomes possible. They constitute the basic cognitive mechanism by which we make sense of things, often without being able to explain why and how. As in the case of the "pre-intentional background" that I will be discussing in the following chapter, these cognitive projections are automatic and transparent. Nonetheless, one important difference in my use of the term 'projection' should be made clear from the start: Although it usually (especially in cognitive linguistics) refers to internal mappings between mental spaces or domains, I shall—following the hypothesis of extended cognition—be using it to refer also (indeed primarily) to projections or mappings between internal and external domains. (See figures 5.1 and 5.2.)

Recent work by David Kirsh may be relevant here. Although his proposal is grounded in the language of computationalism, Kirsh's concern is with interactivity and distributed cognition. He asks how, when, and why people interact with their environment as part of sense-making actions. According to Kirsh, projection is a special human capacity that provides the basis for sense making (2009). He defines projection as "a way of 'seeing' something extra in the thing present" and "a way of *augmenting* the observed thing, of projecting onto it" (ibid., 2310). It is similar and complementary to

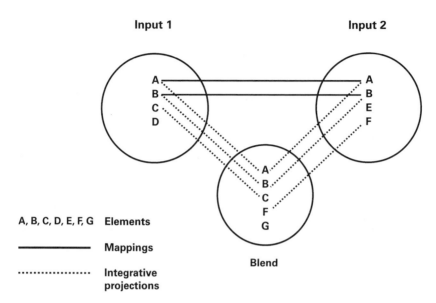

Figure 5.1
A conventional conceptual blend between mental spaces.

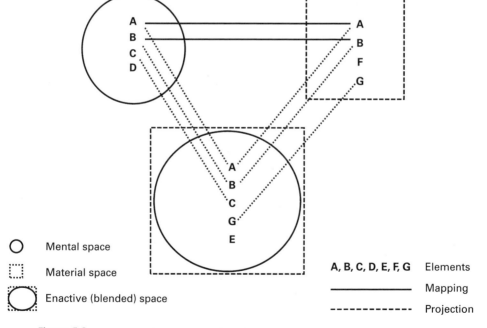

Figure 5.2
A conceptual blend with a material anchor.

perception and imagery, but also different from both processes in important respects. For instance, whereas perception is tied to and tightly coupled to what is in the outside environment (normally we cannot see what is not there), projection appears to be less so. Projection goes beyond what is immediately perceived. More than "seeing what is present," projection "is concerned with seeing what is not present but might be" (ibid., 2310). It "offers a peek into the possible, into what could be there, or what might be useful if it were there, but is not" (ibid., 2312), although, as Kirsh also recognizes, enactive theories of perception (O'Regan and Noë 2001; Noë 2004) contain a projective component of "seeing the future." Similarly, unlike imagery, which is usually defined as "a mental representation of a nonpresent object or event" (Solso 1991, 267, cited in Kirsh 2009, 2312), projection requires "material anchoring" (Hutchins 2005a, 2010) and scaffolding to which it adds mental structure and builds upon. Some form of external manipulable structure, persistent or ephemeral, must be present to trigger and support projection (repeated or momentary). According to Kirsh this is precisely what distinguishes projection from pure imagery.

Metaphoric projections

As discussed in the context of embodied cognition, a metaphoric projection is, essentially, the conceptual mapping between a familiar or concrete and an unfamiliar or abstract phenomenal domain primarily for the purpose of explication. A good example of this can be found in the case of the so-called Container schema. The Container schema is one of the most significant image schemata, with a topological structure that comprises an Interior, a Boundary, and an Exterior. What a metaphoric projection actually does is project the spatial logic of this image schema—as this is meaningfully experienced in our everyday concrete interactions with physical containers, such as a glass of water—to other abstract conceptual domains that are not inherently meaningful in themselves. Thus, categories can be understood as containers of ideas, and bodies as containers of souls; indeed, even mathematical relations such as those of Venn diagrams become meaningful in this sense (Lakoff and Núñez 2000). Obviously, the crucial function of metaphoric mappings is to project—and not represent—the structure (spatial, perceptual, or other) of a concrete and directly meaningful domain of experience (e.g., the embodied experience of weight) upon a meaningless abstract conceptual one (e.g., the concept of weight).

Material anchors and integrative projections

The directionality of metaphoric projection from a familiar domain to an unfamiliar domain cannot be argued to be the case for many of the non-metaphoric mappings that characterize the complex ways in which phenomenal domains and entities become engaged and interact. The aim of conceptual integration or blending theory (Fauconnier 1997; Fauconnier and Turner 1998, 2002) is precisely to accommodate and account for non-metaphoric mappings. Indeed, for conceptual blending theory, an integrative projection essentially refers to a cross-domain mapping in the conceptual system that constructs a new hybrid or blended phenomenal domain. The difference in this case is that the mapping receives structure from various input spaces or domains that cannot be differentiated in terms of a source (familiar or concrete) and a target (unfamiliar or abstract).

From a technical perspective, the basic structure of conceptual integration can be presented schematically by way of a minimal network that comprises at least three mental spaces: two input mental spaces (though there can be any number of influencing spaces projecting to a blend) and the blending space. The input spaces contribute structure selectively via projection to the blended space, which as a result develops a new structure ("emergent" structure) not initially available from the separate inputs. Thus, conceptual integration constructs a new hybrid assembly with "emergent" meaning (figure 5.1). The structure of this emergent conceptual space is identical to none of the contributing input spaces but is instead constructed according to a set of uniform structural and dynamic principles defined by Fauconnier (1997) as composition, completion, and elaboration. It is precisely this process of conceptual integration that I want to foreground as the main mechanism behind the constitution of the material sign and the semiotic dimension of material engagement.

Indeed, conceptual integration theory offers the basic outline of an extended cognitive process that can account for the consubstantial interaction between cognition and material culture, in all the different manifestations of material engagement. Although the input spaces are usually construed as "internal" or "mental" in the traditional computational sense of the term, there is no need that they be so construed. In recent years, experimentation with this model from various perspectives has made that clear, adding extra support to the general hypothesis of extended cognition.

Central in this respect has been the work of Edwin Hutchins (2005), who, using various case studies, has nicely illustrated that material culture may provide a direct input to the conceptual blending process (figure 5.2). Hutchins' argument, more specifically, is that often material structure is directly projected into the blended space in order to stabilize the conceptual blend. Hutchins calls this direct projection of material structure into the blend "material anchoring."

A complementary proposal recently advanced by Andy Clark (2010) focuses on the idea of "surrogacy" or of "surrogate situations." In particular, Clark introduces the term "surrogate material structures," referring to any kind of real-world structure, artifact, or material assemblage that is used to stand in for, or take the place of, some aspect of some target situation, thereby allowing human reason to reach out to that which is absent, distant, or otherwise unavailable. Clark points out two interesting and often unnoticed properties of many surrogate situations: the way they highlight important features by suppressing concrete detail and the way they relax temporal constraints on reasoning. It is these properties of surrogate material structures, Clark argues, that make it possible for the human mind to come to believe things that it would never otherwise come to believe or imagine. Religious artifacts, for example, enable us to use basic biological skills of perception and manipulation to penetrate absent, abstract, or non-existent cognitive domains that we would otherwise find very hard to conceive. According to Clark, this is how "mere things" come to participate richly in our cognitive life as parts of the extended circuitry of human thought.

My suggestion is that anchoring blends—via a dynamic network of integrative projections—may be seen as the prime operation of material engagement, by which conceptual and material structure is integrated in material objects. This blending of conceptual and material structure may also explain how material signs emerge and are constituted in action. In these cases, conceptual integration incorporates both physical and mental spaces. As Hutchins (2010a, 2005) shows, physical relations can become proxies for conceptual relations, or what he calls "material anchors for conceptual blends" (2005). In particular, physical objects become material anchors, thereby enhancing and tightening conceptual blends in a memorable and durable manner. Through this process, the material sign is constituted as a meaningful entity not for what it represents but for what it brings forth: the possibility of meaningful engagement. What essentially happens in those cases, put in very simple terms, is that the vague structure of a flexible and inherently meaningless conceptual process (e.g., counting), by being integrated via projection with some stable material structure or thing, is transformed into a perceptual or physical process. However, perceptual operations embody a spatial logic and thus can be directly manipulated and explored in real time and space. Thus, the process becomes meaningful, and I want to suggest that meaningful engagement of material signs is the precondition for the emergence of symbolism. These physical relations and interactions between the body and cultural artifacts should not be taken as mere "indications" of "internal" and invisible mental processes; they should, rather, be taken as an important form of thinking. These embodied engagements, not the isolated brain, create mechanisms for reasoning, for imagination, for "Aha!" insight, and for abstraction (Hutchins 2010a; Goodwin 2010). Cultural things provide the mediational means to domesticate the embodied imagination.

To highlight and illustrate the significance of the above observations, particularly from the perspective of cognitive archaeology, I will now place them against the background of current research in the domain of numerical cognition. In this area of cognitive research, the accumulation of new experimental data has set the crucial question "Where does arithmetic come from?" on a whole new basis. The traditional idea that for many years recognized the cognitive foundation of arithmetic in the recursive character of the human language faculty is gradually giving way to a subtler differentiation between "approximate" arithmetic that relies on nonverbal visuo-spatial cerebral networks (subjects engaged in approximate numerical tasks recruit bilateral areas of the parietal lobes implicated in visuo-spatial reasoning) and "exact" arithmetic that is dependent on language (subjects engaged in exact numerical tasks display significant activity in the speech-related areas of the left frontal lobe). More specific, approximate arithmetic is considered as the innate biological competence, shared by adult humans with human infants and other animals, that involves a basic appreciation of changes in quantity and a simple number sense (oneness, twoness, and threeness) (Dehaene et al. 1999). On the other hand, exact arithmetic should be understood as a product of subsequently elaborated numeration systems associated with our representational linguistic abilities. The crucial question for cognitive archaeology can thus be put as follows: Could *Homo sapiens* alone—that is, in the absence of external material support—have ever have moved beyond approximation (Dehaene 1997, 91)? From the perspective of Material Engagement Theory and the theory of conceptual integration discussed earlier in this chapter, this seems to be a rather remote possibility. But let us take one step at a time.

Making numbers out of clay

What you see in figure 5.3 is a small group of clay objects. I shall be saying more about their specific use and function as material signs and cognitive artifacts later. For now, I just want you to look at them, and to try—without bothering too much about their meaning, use, and archaeological context— to answer a simple question: How many objects do you see in this image?

The interesting part of my question does not pertain to the answer itself. In fact, you probably intuitively identified the number before I even asked the question. The interesting part of the question concerns the nature of the cognitive process that enables us to intuitively identify the number. What is that process or ability? What is it that makes it possible for us, without any particular effort, to perceive the number of these objects at a glance?

A broad consensus in many disciplines claims that we appear to possess an evolved cognitive capacity for nonsymbolic numerical intuition. We share this basic cognitive and perceptual ability, also known as "number sense," with pre-verbal infants, and apparently also with many other animal species. This nonsymbolic numerical intuition enables us to iden-

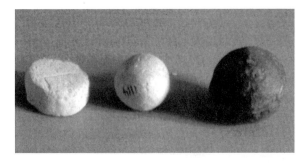

Figure 5.3
How many?

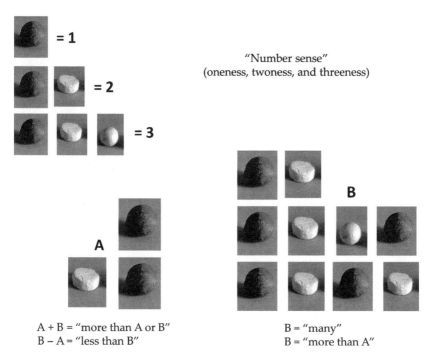

"Number sense"
(oneness, twoness, and threeness)

A + B = "more than A or B"
B – A = "less than B"

B = "many"
B = "more than A"

Figure 5.4
Basic number sense.

tify the exact numerosity or cardinality of up to three or four individual objects, to approximate and compare how many objects are present in a scene, and to discriminate basic changes in quantity by way of addition and subtraction (Dehaene 2009; Feigenson et al. 2004).

This basic "number sense" appears to be independent of language. Our intuitions concerning the cardinality of small sets of objects are available even in the absence of formal education and a sophisticated mathematical language. In other words, we can identify the number of clay objects even if we don't have a word to express the number (Dehaene 2009, 235). We also can identify the number of up to four objects without having to count them. We simply look at them. In other words, we do not have to count their number; we perceive it. The importance of these points will become more obvious later.

Now look at figure 5.5. The question remains the same as it was in the case of figure 5.3, but the number of objects has changed slightly. Interestingly, if we try to identify the number of objects shown in this image, I

$$1, 2, 3, \ldots, \mathbf{6}, \ldots, 9, 10, 11, \ldots$$

Figure 5.5
"Exact numerosity" beyond the subitizing range of three or four.

am sure that most of us will immediately sense that something in our thinking process has changed. It feels as if something that before was immediate and automatic now demands more of our attention. To answer the question "How many clay objects do we see here?" it is no longer enough simply to look at the objects, as in figure 5.3. Instead, we have to count them. And counting may appear natural and easy to us, but it presupposes the ability to manipulate large *exact numerosities* beyond the range of three or four—something that took us years to learn as children, and something that people in different cultures may perform in different ways or may even lack altogether (as appears to be the case in some recently studied Amazonian tribes). (See Tang et al. 2006.)

Indeed, a huge mental leap is required to go from approximate arithmetic to making sense of an exact, large cardinal value, and it is this mental leap that distinguishes the capabilities of the human mind from those of all the other number-competent species, which apparently fail to make that leap even after years of training.

How did we make that leap, overcoming the limits of approximate numerical thinking? I will try to tackle this question in the following sections, looking at the intersection of brains, bodies, and things and crisscrossing epistemic domains, units, and scales of human experience that are usually kept separate. First I will explore what each epistemic domain or "scape" has to offer in isolation; then I will try to uncover some hidden connections; finally I will try to build a joint integrative explanation that avoids reducing one domain to the other.

I will begin with the neurological foundation of numerosity the brainscape, if you prefer. I will only summarize very briefly what seems to be the current consensus about the functional anatomy of the areas involved in quantity processing in humans and monkeys. (For more detailed recent reviews, see Dehaene 2009 and Neider 2005.) Brain imaging of various number-processing tasks reveals a clear cerebral substrate in the form of neuronal networks primarily located in the parietal lobe, particularly in a small subregion in the depth of the horizontal segment of the intraparietal sulcus (HIPS). This brain region presents consistent activation patterns when subjects discriminate numerosities in estimation and approximation tasks and can be clearly differentiated from the brain areas more active in exact calculation tasks, such as the left angular gyrus and areas of the prefrontal cortex (Dehaene et al. 1999). With that in mind, let us return to the main question I identified earlier. I said that basic numerosity is an evolved biological competence, shared with preverbal infants and nonhuman animals. Yet moving beyond this "basic number sense" (Dehaene 1997) of subitization and magnitude appreciation presupposes a mental leap of which no other animal seems capable. (See, e.g., Biro and Matsuzawa 2001.) What is it that drives the human mind beyond the limits of this core system?

Trying to answer that, most researchers have claimed that language (the presence of number words and verbal counting routines) enabled humans to move beyond the threshold of approximation. (For a good review, see Gelman and Gallistel 2004.) In fact, two major hypotheses about the role of language in the origin of numerical concepts are currently entertained by most researchers working in this field. The first hypothesis, which derives from the strong form of the classical Whorfian thesis, is that language determines thought and thus arithmetic thinking. More simply, the argument is that counting words are necessary for developing concepts for numbers larger than three or four. The implication of such a view would be that children growing up in cultures where there are few or no counting words will not develop "true" or "exact" understanding of the concept of number. For most proponents of this strong view this is precisely what happens in the case of the well-studied Amazonian tribes of Pirahã (Gordon 2004; Frank et al. 2008) and Mundurukú (Pica et al. 2004), which lack exact number words.

There is, however, a less deterministic way to look at the relationship between language and number. Broadly, this view claims that, although the possession of an elaborate number vocabulary may be helpful in learning to count and in advancing arithmetic abilities and their ontogenetic realization, such a vocabulary is not necessary for the development and possession of true numerical concepts (Gelman and Butterworth 2005, 9). From such an angle, one could argue that, for instance, the observed deficits in the numerical capacities of the Pirahã and the Mundurukú may derive from the fact that "numbers are not culturally important and receive little attention in everyday life" (ibid., 9). Daniel Everett (2005) has argued convincingly that the Pirahã lack numbers of any kind, a concept of counting, and any terms for quantification in their language because their culture constrains communication by emphasizing the value of immediate experience. Another interesting possibility is that it isn't the lack of number names but the lack of a "counting routine" or a "technology for counting" that keeps the Pirahã from developing exact numerical thinking.

Indeed, language may not be the only way to grasp the concept of number. Where the aforementioned Amazonian tribes have failed, other societies have succeeded not through the medium of some elaborate numerical lexicon but through the material affordances of their bodies or the agency of material culture and innovation. (For examples, see Ifrah 1985.) This is not, of course, to deny the evident association between language and exact arithmetic. However, I would like to argue that, especially from a long-term archaeological perspective, language cannot account for the emergence of exact numerical thinking in those early contexts where *no* such verbal numerical competence and counting routine could have existed.

The signification process I am talking about here should not be confused with how children nowadays map the meaning of available number words onto their nonverbal representations of numbers. My concern is not with the semantic mapping process by which a child learns number words or learns to associate, for instance, the word 'ten' with the quantity 10. My question, instead, is about how humans conceive or grasp the quantity of 10 when no linguistic quantifier, and no symbol to express it, is yet available.

This ability that enables humans to conceptualize the quantity 10 in the absence of language or symbol does not refer to a process of learning but to a process of *enactive discovery and signification*. I suggest that, despite the evident association between language and exact arithmetic, language lacks in itself the necessary "representational stability" (Hutchins 2005) that would have made such a transition possible. How did humans move beyond approximation, then? How did they develop the concept of number? If language, the human cognitive artifact *par excellence*, is not sufficient to account for that development, what is sufficient? It is now time to put brain, body, and world back together and see how the archaeological record can help us answer that question.

Learning to count in the Neolithic

In this section I will focus on the case of the Neolithic Near East system of counting, drawing on the work of the archaeologist Denise Schmandt-Besserat (1992, 1996). I will explore the enactive effect of different types of material signs, operating through a long sequence of integrative projections unfolded in time and according to the situational affordances of a specific socio-cultural matrix, and on how they might help us understand the long-term human developmental passage from approximate to exact arithmetic. Indeed, a first indication for the long-term implications of such processes can be seen in Peter Damerow's examination of the historical development of numerical concepts and operations in Babylonian culture (1988, 1998; also see Nicolopoulou 1997). Examining arithmetic operations as they are manifest initially in the use of clay tokens in the preliterate period, and later in the proto-literate texts from Uruk, Damerow argued that the initial emergence of the concept of conservation of quantity is tied to the substantive reality and concrete use of clay tokens and not to any pre-existing cognitive skills of an arithmetical nature. Moreover, he contends that the physical qualities of the material signs as well as the forms of social interaction mediated by those signs influence this process by marking the horizon of possibilities for their ontogenetic realization. He supports this claim by showing how the system of numerical signs present in the archaic texts of Uruk is in fact a semi-abstract system that represents an intermediate stage between the absence and the full presence of the number concept. Furthermore, he asserts that the real impetus behind this transition to proto-arithmetic operations comes from the change in the medium of representation (i.e., clay tablets) and the social conditions that surround it, and not from any antecedent change in cognitive structure.

Let me explore some of these claims in more detail. I will begin with a brief summary of the major developmental stages in the evolution of the

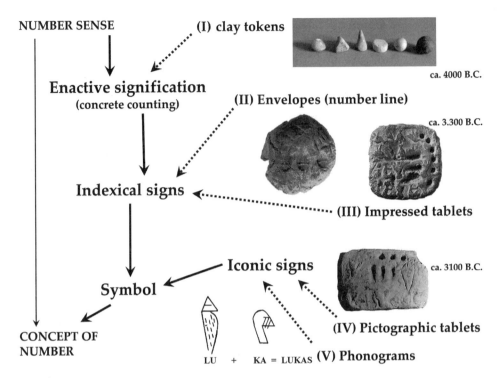

Figure 5.6
The emergence of number out of clay.

Near Eastern accounting system used to record and compute entries and expenditures of goods (7000–3000 B.C.). (For a more detailed discussion of the archaeological material presented below, see Schmandt-Besserat 2010.) The roman numerals here correspond to those in figure 5.6.

(I) The clay tokens represent the earliest stage. Modeled in multiple shapes, they were used mainly to record the type and quantity of commodities. In our example, the cone and the sphere signified different quantities of grain (a "small" and a "large" basket of grain), the ovoid with a circular incision signified a jar of oil, and the tetrahedron signified a unit of labor. Tokens, which dealt only with approximate quantities, recorded the number of units of goods in one-to-one correspondence (for instance, two cones stood for two small units of grain, three cones for three small units of grain, and so on).

(II) The so-called envelopes represent the second major stage. An envelope was a hollow clay ball that contained a certain number of clay tokens. The precise amount and type of tokens was also visible on the outside, as the accountants created markings by impressing the tokens on the wet clay surface before enclosing them. For instance, the envelope in the figure (from Habuba Kabira, Syria, ca. 3300 B.C.) shows the imprints of three ovoid tokens, and incised lines represent jars of oil.

(III) Around 3200 B.C. the envelopes were replaced by solid clay tablets, which continued the system of signs impressed with tokens. The tablet in figure 5.6 (from Susa, Iran, ca. 3300 B.C.) shows impressions of spheres and cones associated with measures of grain.

(IV) With the formation of city-states (ca. 3200–3100 B.C.), the practice of impressing token-signs on clay tablets was changed to that of inscribing schematic "icons" (i.e., pictographs) of the most intricate tokens. The sign for oil, for example, clearly reproduced the outline of the ovoid token with a circular line. More important, plurality was no longer indicated by one-to-one correspondence. Numbers of jars of oil were not shown by repeating the sign for "jar of oil" as many times as the number of units to record. The sign for "jar of oil" was preceded by numerals—signs indicating numbers. The tablet in figure 5.6 (from Godin Tepe, Iran, ca. 3100 B.C.) features an account of 33 measures of oil (circular = 10, wedges = 1).

(V) Around 3000 B.C., the recording of the names of the recipients or donors of the goods listed on the tablets became necessary. A new type of sign—the phonogram—was created. Phonograms were sketches of things that stood for the sounds of the words they evoked. In our example, the drawing of a man stood for the sound "lu" and that of the mouth for "ka," the sounds of the words for "man" and "mouth" in the Sumerian language. For example, the modern name Lucas could have been written with the two signs mentioned above: "lu - ka."

What might be the causal role of this long-term process of material engagement in the development of exact numerical thinking? How can this causal role be understood against the neurological background of numerosity?

In relation to the first question, my suggestion, very briefly, is that the process of material signification responsible for the emergence of symbolic numerical thinking, in the particular context I am discussing, begins with the invention of the clay-token system. The clay tokens provided a material anchor that enabled a double metaphorical projection between the mental and physical domains of basic numerical thinking as an embodied experience.

On the one hand, basic numerosity was objectified through the materiality of the clay token by way of one-to-one correspondence (concrete counting). On the other hand, approximate quantity became associated with the shape of the token. Remember that the tokens were linked, according to their shape (cylinders, cones, spheres, and so on), with approximate quantities of particular agricultural commodities (e.g., the ovoid with a jar of oil). For the purpose of understanding the developmental spiral of innovation, it is important to note that at this early stage of concrete counting the concept of number had not yet emerged. The clay tokens did not stand for numbers. The tokens did not represent numbers (e.g., two, three, four). For instance, there was no token representing "two" or "three" jars of oil (even if two and three were certainly numerosities within the range of their basic "number sense"). Moreover, each token type counted exclusively a specific category of items (for example, ovoids could only count jars of oil, and jars of oil could only be counted with ovoids).The tokens were not symbols (in the sense of arbitrary signifiers) but enactive material proto-signs. When the envelope was invented, however, and enactive material proto-signs (tokens) were pressed onto an envelope's surface to make their shape and number visible from outside, two additional semiotic properties became active within this extended cognitive system. The first of these properties was indexicality. The impressions of the tokens on the outside were physically connected with the actual tokens on the inside of the envelope. Moreover, since the three-dimensional tokens were reduced to two-dimensional markings that resembled the original shape of the token a second semiotic property, iconicity also emerged. The co-emergence of indexicality and iconicity provided a semiotic basis and a powerful perceptual stimulus for abductive thinking. The pictographs that mark the momentous event when the concept of number was abstracted from that of the items counted probably were products of such abduction. Thus, returning to our question about the causal role of this long-term process of material engagement in the development of exact numerical thinking, one could argue that essentially what happened was that the vague structure of a very difficult and inherently meaningless conceptual problem (counting), by being integrated via projection with the stable material structure of the clay tokens, was gradually transformed into an easier perceptual and semiotic problem. However, perceptual problems can be directly manipulated and manually resolved in real time and space. Thus, the process of counting, as an embodied and mediated act, became meaningful. The clay tokens brought forth the numbers by making the manipulation of their properties visible and tangible.

How can all these developments be understood against the neurological background of numerosity? How does the neurological substrate of our evolved "number sense," which we appear to share with other species, interact with this complex, extended system of "extra-neural" numerical thinking? How can the intraparietal networks of neuronal interaction, necessary for the emergence of true numerosity, be grounded upon a clay foundation? As I have already said, neither brain nor culture, in isolation, will ever answer those questions. Instead we should explore the possible links and bridges between embodied cognition and material culture that may have caused the critical integration of the different intraparietal areas associated with numerical thinking.

Of course, such a topic demands a far more detailed treatment than I can offer here. But the general outline of my working hypothesis can be put as follows: I propose that the process of engaging and grasping the number as a clay token may have effected an extended *reorganization* (Kelly and Garavan 2005, 1090; Poldrack 2000) in the neural connectivity of the intraparietal area. The crucial neurological link in this respect, I suggest, should be seen between the anterior intraparietal area (AIP) (an area that is crucial for the manual tasks of pointing, reaching, and grasping three-dimensional objects and tools, as a number of imaging studies have demonstrated), the horizontal segment of the intraparietal sulcus (hIPS) (which helps to establish semantic associations between numerical concepts and signs, thus providing an important basis for connecting the world of sense-perception to the domain of symbolic concepts), and the angular gyrus (AG) (an area associated with semantic properties and with our abilities for metaphorical thinking). (For a more detailed discussion, and for references, see Malafouris 2010c.)

Making sense of the above interactions demands more than a simple translation from a cultural to a biological realm. Enactive signification does not work that way. For one thing, none of the above processes would have taken place without the necessary social context. For another, I believe that what the archaeological evidence from the Near East shows us is *not* some gradual representational process by which our inherited approximate numerical mental engine was externalized and amplified through a series of linear steps, first to a kind of symbolic token-manipulating representational system and then to some sort of computational numerical device. The dynamics of material signification should be interpreted from an enactive rather than a representational angle. The agency of clay, in all its different manifestations, is not to be found in the way it represents number but instead in the way it *brings forth* the concept of number. The clay token as enactive sign is a constitutive part of what it expresses, which otherwise cannot be known. The discussed process of extended reorganization could not have been achieved by the naked biological brain. In other words, the tangible material reality of the clay token as an "epistemic" artifact enabled the already evolved parietal system to support approximate numerosity, by getting reorganized, and thus partially "recycled," to support also the representation of exact number. (See also Piazza and Izard 2009.) No doubt the representational properties of neural networks, like those that subserve numerical thinking, become realized inside the head, but in this case the systemic properties of the cognitive structures from which they derive extend beyond skin and skull.

These clay objects, however, should not be understood as a series of perceptual stimuli that activate the right neural network. Instead, they should be viewed as constituting a new numerical "habitus"—an embodied semiotic field for the engagement, if not the direct physical grasping, of number. Cultural knowledge and innovation are not intracranial processes; they are, rather, infused and diffused into settings of practical activity, and thus they are constituted by experience within these settings through the development of specific sensibilities and dispositions, leading people to orient and think about themselves within their environment in specific and often unexpected ways. This is why a simple Neolithic token can drive the sapient mind beyond approximation. It does the trick by transforming and simplifying the problem of number, thereby enabling the building of neural connections that otherwise couldn't have been built. It also does an even more important thing: It takes care of a part of the problem by itself, thus becoming an inseparable part of what is now an extended system of numerical cognition reaching beyond the brain and into the world.

The material sign and the meaning of engagement

In this chapter I have attempted to highlight some problems associated with the representational approach to the meaning of material culture. I have suggested that the most important deficiency of this dominant line of thinking about symbolism is that it misconstrues the nature of the material sign in two important respects: by neglecting to explore the becoming of the material sign (that is, how a material sign emerges and is constituted in different contexts and on different time scales of engagement) and by failing to take into account how the physical properties of the medium of representation affect the semiotic process.

Attempting to overcome those problems, I have approached the issue of material semiosis from a different angle. I have suggested that the material sign is more than a thing that stands for something else, or the passive conduit of a message—that it provides the substantive basis for the enaction of a given semiotic process, at the same time defining the phenomenological contours of this process. It does not primarily possess a meaning to be interpreted or carry a message to be decoded; rather, it provides the stimulus and simultaneously constitutes the technology for meaning or communication. In the context of material engagement, a material sign can be seen to operate simultaneously as a signifier and a signified. It can be used both as something in itself and as a representation of something other than itself. However, we will have to explore both properties of the material sign in order to gain a proper understanding of material semiosis. What is important in this respect is not to differentiate between the possibility that a figurine may be used as an iconic representation of some deity and the possibility that the figurine itself may operate as the concrete embodiment of the deity itself. What is important, rather, is to recognize that both possibilities are equally afforded and can be seen as active even in the context of the same ritual process. It is those huge and often unconscious ontological shifts in how material signs can be engaged in real time and space that render their attributes so difficult to discern from a representational or linguistic idiom. Meaning does not reside in the material sign; it emerges from the various parameters of its performance and usage as these are actualized in the process of engagement. That means that the material sign engages us primarily in "pragmatic-epistemic actions" (Kirsh and Maglio 1994) rather than hermeneutic circles. There is no meaning inherent in past or present material signs; there is only the capacity for meaning. Meaning is the temporally emergent property of material engagement, the ongoing blending between the mental and the physical. In the case of material signs, we do not read meaningful symbols; we meaningfully engage meaningless symbols. Material signs have no meaning in themselves; they merely afford the possibility of meaning, as a door affords the possibility of being opened. In real life, to interpret a material sign is not to provide a verbal substitute for it; rather, it is to become habituated with the interactive possibilities and consequences of its performance in context without bothering about exegetical questions. Material signs do not represent; they enact. They do not stand for reality; they bring forth reality. As long as archaeology fails to recognize that, it will remain a prisoner of its Cartesian genealogy, endlessly protesting with no real chance of escaping.

6   Material Agency

When a problem is debated for too long and an agreed solution is not reached, it is often the case that the problem, as stated, does not afford a solution. In such cases, reformulating the problem might be the only thing left to do—that is, if abandoning the problem altogether is not an option. In chapters 4 and 5 we crossed the boundary between persons and things from a cognitive and semiotic perspective. It is now time to do the same from a different angle. The question to be pursued now is that of agency, and the ensuing problem to be reformulated is that of the dualism between agents and things. For those reasons, my focus in this chapter will be on the third and last major dimension of Material Engagement Theory: *material agency*. The term 'material agency' is, to some extent, a misnomer, yet I believe it serves well my basic intention in this chapter, which can be expressed very simply: *If there is such a thing as human agency, then there is material agency; there is no way human and material agency can be disentangled.* Or else, while agency and intentionality may not be properties of things, they are not properties of humans either; they are the properties of material engagement.

I will begin developing my thesis by discussing the deficiencies of the concept of agency and exposing the anthropocentric basis of its conventional usage. Then, adopting a non-anthropocentric perspective, I will discuss *methodological fetishism* as a conceptual apparatus for studying the agency of things. I will conclude the chapter by advancing the argument for material agency.

Material culture and agency

With the advent of post-processualism, the concept of agency became a central component of archaeological interpretation. The notion of agency is mostly conceptualized through the lenses of practice theory and so is closely associated with issues of power and individuality. In view of the inherent ambiguity of the meaning of agency, it is not surprising that a whole book can be written—and indeed one has been written—on the nuances and the archaeological conceptualizations of the notion. Let me summarize its opening statement:

[A]gency has become the buzzword of contemporary archaeological theory . . . a lingua franca—an ambiguous platitude meaning everything and nothing. . . . there is little consensus about what "agency" actually means . . . nor has there been sustained consideration of basic methodological and epistemological issues as to make it applicable and appropriate to the premodern past. (Dobres and Robb 2000, 3)

Despite the pessimism of the above remarks, Marcia-Anne Dobres and John Robb conclude their introductory chapter in a quite different spirit. Archaeologists "deal with material culture far more seriously and innovatively than do most social scientists, and material culture is clearly central to creating agents and expressing agency" (ibid., 14). No dispute about the first part. It is no exaggeration to argue that no other discipline has ever engaged with material culture from as wide a variety of perspectives—not to mention temporal depth—as archaeology. Philosophy has never attempted a systematic account of the nature of this overwhelming category of human experience. The category of material culture, with its inextricably enfolded social and cognitive implications, remains neglected and theoretically marginalized even within philosophical frameworks (e.g., phenomenology) that claim a direct relationship with materiality and the human embodiment. (See also Miller 1987.) At the same time, putting Bourdieu's exposition of practice theory and his notion of *habitus* aside, a similar lacuna is evident in the domain of sociology. Only very recently, in a desperate attempt to discover the "missing masses" (Latour 1992, 227) that will bring a balance in the fabric of social theory, has sociology begun to think about the role of materiality in the social nexus. Finally, anthropology (with the brilliant exception of the recently formalized domain of material-culture studies), under the fear of fetishism, continues to prioritize the human informant and to approach material culture "for what it means rather than for what it does" (Warnier 2001, 20).

Obviously, mundane artifacts that (in the words of Bruno Latour) "knock at the door of sociology" and "beg us for understanding" (1992,

227) have been archaeology's main focus of study since it was first formalized as a discipline. Despite the unique relationship between archaeology
and material culture, I remain skeptical toward the second part of the
previously quoted remark by Dobres and Robb—that is, about the extent
to which, in current archaeological theorizing, material culture is "clearly
central" to the expression of agency. Strange as it might seem for a discipline that seems to have reached an agreement about the so-called active
nature of material culture at least 20 years ago, I believe that archaeology
remains attached to an anthropocentric view of the world and, by extension, of agency. (See Knappett and Malafouris 2008.) A possible reason for
that might be that archaeology, by adopting a passive attitude of theory
consumer and by extensively borrowing theoretical frameworks from other
disciplines, has inherited their shortcomings without having the power or
the will to act back. No doubt the above intellectual loans have made a
substantial contribution to the archaeological "loss of innocence" (Clarke
1973). However, since this has been accomplished they have simply proved
inadequate to tackle the new complex emerging personality of the archaeological object. As a result, although with the recognition of the active
nature of material culture the artifact has gained a portion of the ontological status it deserves, the conceptual metaphors that followed this break-
through failed to realize its full potential. Indeed, on closer inspection the
much-celebrated post-processual passage from the passive to the active
artifact was essentially a reevaluation of the human rather than the material agent. What the active nature of material culture in its common usage
seems to imply is, essentially, the recognition that *humans*, far from passively adapting to external systemic forces, are *actively using* material
culture as an expressive symbolic medium for their social strategies and
negotiations (Hodder 1982, 1986). In other words, the essence of the argument is that material culture may not simply reflect but also actively
construct or challenge social reality, *on the necessary condition*, however, of
human agency and intentionality. The above sounds too obvious to be
wrong, and indeed this is precisely how material culture operates in many
cases. However, this is only a part of the picture, and I am afraid it is a
part that, once you embrace it, leaves you with few chances to discover
what the active nature of material culture really means.

The point I am trying to make here is that, although the concept of
agency is much contested, it is contested within the theoretical margins

of a narrow anthropocentric perspective. This anthropocentric view of agency, though it incorporates a variety of nuances, is based on a general agreement about a single undisputable fact: that agency, in the real sense of the word, is a human property, and "the only true agents in history are human individuals" (Giddens and Pierson 1998, 89). Whether this individual is conceived through a Cartesian or an existential lens makes no important difference. What is important is that when we speak about agents proper we are referring to human individuals, and preferably to human individuals of the modern Western type. In short, agency is an attribute of the human substance.

It is this deeply entrenched anthropocentric idea of agency that I intend to challenge in what follows.

Toward a non-anthropocentric conception

A gradually developing suspicion of the humanistic determinations of agency can be traced back to Marcel Mauss (1954) and Martin Heidegger (1977). In *The Gift*, Mauss illustrated the fluidity of the boundaries between persons and things and the capacity of the latter to embody and to objectify as well as to produce social consequences. The same point is found also in Nancy Munn's observations on the Kula exchange system, in which "shells and men are reciprocally agents of each other's value definition" (1983, 284). But it was probably in Arjun Appadurai's 1986 book *The Social Life of Things* that we saw the first explicit attempt to battle the prevailing tendency to limit conceptions of the social to the space of human interaction. Appadurai's book introducing the biographical dimension of artifacts and indicating the various unnoticed ways in which things, like persons, have social lives (Kopytoff 1986; Gosden and Marshall 1999; Hoskins 1998, 2006) was followed by a number of other influential works on the archaeology (Buchli 2004; DeMarrais et al. 2004; Gosden 1994, 2004, 2005; Jones 2004; Knappett 2002, 2005; Meskell 2005; Miller 2005, 2010; Olsen 2003; Preucel 2006; Renfrew and Scarre 1998; Tilley 1994; Thomas 1996, 2004, 2007; Wylie 2002) and the anthropology (Hutchins 1995; Hoskins 1998; Henare et al. 2007; Ingold 2007, 2008) of material culture. Soon it became obvious that the *enframing* that according to Heidegger (1977) characterized the attitude of the Western individual toward the world as a "standing reserve"—a passive recourse to be controlled and manipulated for human ends—had no place and no meaning in a number of ethnographic contexts with a very different understanding of what it is like to be a person and what it means to engage the world. What could be, for example, the meaning of agency for the "partible," "composite," and relationally constituted Melanesian person (Strathern 1988)? Clearly the idea of the isolated agent who acts upon the world, imposing shape and meaning upon inert matter, can hardly be accommodated or make sense in a Melanesian context where the categories of persons and things are inseparably distributed over biographical time and space. In recent years the idea of decentralized agency has gained increased momentum. The work of Alfred Gell and that of Bruno Latour has been central in this, albeit for different reasons and from different disciplinary perspectives. I shall discuss some of Gell's reasons for regarding his car as "a body-part" but "also the locus of an 'autonomous' agency of its own" (1998, 18) in a later section. First, however, I will discuss Latour's work (1991, 1992, 1993, 1999) and the general framework of so-called Actor-Network Theory. (See also Law 1999.)

Actor-Network Theory

Actor-Network Theory (ANT) can be defined as a semiotics of materiality that is symmetrical with respect to human and non-human agents (Law 1999, 4). Conceptualizing agency as variously distributed and possessed in relational networks of persons and things, ANT proposes that all entities participating in those networks should be treated analytically as of equal importance. In other words, for ANT what we call actors or agents are essentially products or effects of networks. That means that no primacy of the human actor—individual or collective—over the non-human actor can be accepted on *a priori* grounds. This may seem to be yet another attempt to reconcile the two traditional oppositional poles of social theory (agency and structure), but in reality it is something quite different. In drawing material things into the sociological fold, the aim of ANT was not to overcome this contradiction, but to ignore it and develop what Latour calls a "bypassing strategy" (1999, 16–17).

For example, to answer the question whether people or guns kill we have to move beyond what is acceptable in either the materialist or the sociological account of activity (Latour 1999, 180; see also chapter 9 below). Both accounts start with essences, and essences result in antinomies, and antinomies are the reason that modernist theories fail to capture practice.

A speed bump, to use another example, does more than simply remind drivers to slow down. In addition to being a passive speed-controlling device, the speed bump is at the same time a sign and a moral agent. Contrary to what appears to be the case with conventional traffic and warning signs, in the case of the speed bump the primary intention is not indirect communication but direct physical action. The primary role of a traffic sign—usually iconic—is to communicate, clearly and on the basis of well-established conventions, a visible message to which the driver may or may not conform—at least the sign itself has no such direct enforcing capacity. The speed bump, however, embodies no such communicative purpose. In this case, we leave the negotiable representational realm and enter into the territory of brute yet meaningful material relations. In this realm, the medium is the message, and to ignore or misinterpret the sign has immediate and direct physical consequences. Enactive material signs are often non-negotiable. Very simply, and indeed advisably, under normal conditions we do not engage a speed bump from a hermeneutic perspective, and certainly not from a "death of the author" viewpoint. However, this shift in the kind of signification—delegation, as Latour calls it—is not without cost. The initial altruistic statement "slow down so as not to endanger other people," when expressed in concrete, becomes something new. Being objectified, the statement takes on a new meaning. It now can be seen to embody a different and rather selfish morality that can be expressed as "Pass over me at a speed that will allow your back and your car's suspension not to suffer any damage."

To illustrate the implications of this point further, I will discuss a different example, this one from Latour's essay "Technology is society made durable" (1991, 104):

Consider a tiny innovation commonly found in European hotels: attaching large cumbersome weights to room keys in order to remind customers that they should leave their key at the front desk every time they leave the hotel instead of taking it along on a tour of the city. An imperative statement inscribed on a sign—"Please leave your room key at the front desk before you go out"—appears to be not enough to make customers behave according to the speaker's wishes. . . . But if the innovator, called to the rescue, *displaces* the inscription by introducing a large metal weight, the hotel manager no longer has to rely on his customer's sense of moral obligation. Customers suddenly become only too happy to rid themselves of this annoying object which makes their pockets bulge and weighs down their handbags: they go to the front desk on their own accord to get rid of it. Where the sign, the inscription, the imperative, discipline, or moral obligation all failed, the hotel manager, the innovator, and the metal weight succeeded. And yet, obtaining such a discipline has a price: the hotel manager had to ally himself with an innovator, and the innovator had to ally herself with various metal weights and their manufacturing processes.

The example Latour discusses here may appear trivial, yet I believe it offers an excellent illustration of how the notions of agency, intentionality, power, and innovation can be understood through the lens of Actor-Network Theory.

Figure 6.1 is an attempt to visually deconstruct the complex dynamic transformations and interactions that every socio-technical trajectory

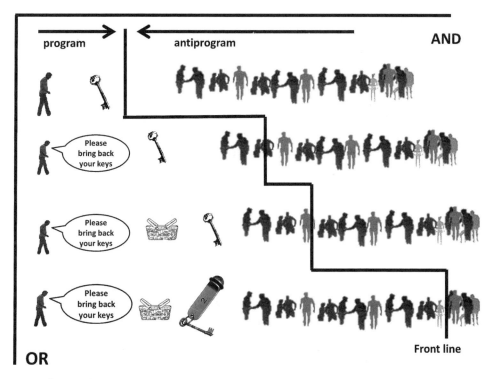

Figure 6.1
Latour's view of a socio-technical trajectory.

embodies. In the case of our example, this trajectory has been divided into four major stages that, according to Latour, define the dialectics of power involved in this particular case. The actor network is presented along a vertical axis and a horizontal axis. These two axes correspond respectively to two dimensions that characterize the successive transformations of the hotel manager's initial intention or statement: "Please leave your room key at the front desk before you go out." In particular, the horizontal axis, referred to as "association" or (AND), corresponds to the number of actors that are being attached or added to this initial statement, whereas the vertical axis, referred to as (OR), corresponds to the number of "substitutions" that are being gradually introduced into the network in order to "power over" the customers' resistance to or neglect of that message. Each of the stages enumerated on the vertical axis is characterized by a novel substitution. In other words, in each stage a new mediation is added to support the intention of the hotel manager. Finally, the bold dividing line that cuts across the successive stages of the process separates those agents (human or material) that participate in the "action program" (on the left in the diagram) from those that resist the program (on the right).

For the purposes of this chapter, three major points exemplified by Latour's diagram should be discussed:

1. The medium is the message.

The objectification of a statement is not simply a more effective and successful transmission of that statement but instead a translation, a displacement, and an inevitable transformation of its initial state. The meaning of the statement (in this case initially expressed as a sentence uttered by the hotel manager), far from remaining stable, is constantly transformed along the way in accordance with the semiotic affordances of the apparatuses that are drawn into the system. This is why, in the context of ANT, the meaning of the word 'statement' does not refer to linguistics "but to the *gradient* that carries us from words to things and from things to words" (Latour 1991, 106). This also indicates why the meaning of the word 'network' in the context of ANT should not be confused with its meaning in common usage—for example, in relation to the Internet. As Latour himself points out (1999, 15–16), to understand the notion of network as a kind of circuitry that enables the instantaneous transport and communication of information without deformation—like electricity along a wire—would be "exactly the opposite" of what the notion meant to express in the context of ANT. Indeed, in the case of the material sign the medium matters and has a direct bearing on the message. By the same token, in the case study now under discussion the initial statement of the hotel manager may read the same but it is no longer the same:

Customers no longer leave their room keys: instead, they get rid of an unwieldy object that deforms their pockets. If they conform to the manager's wishes, it is not because they read the sign, nor because they are particularly well mannered. It is because they cannot do otherwise. They don't even think about it. The statement is no longer the same, the key is no longer the same-even the hotel is no longer quite exactly the same. (Latour 1991, 105)

2. The problem of closure: network before meaning.

As Carl Knappett comments (2002, 100), and as our present example illustrates, "agency comes to be distributed across a network, inhering in the associations and relationships between entities, rather than in the entities themselves." It can be argued that two crucial methodological questions follow if one accepts this claim: (a) Where do you draw the boundaries of your network? (b) How do you select which elements (actors) are significant in the structuring of your analysis? In the case of our hotel-key example, answering those questions was not difficult. But socio-technical networks—as archaeologists know well—are usually far more complicated. Indeed, perhaps the most important methodological limitation of any symmetrical or relational viewpoint is precisely what might be called the problem of closure.

That same problem, in a slightly different version, is already familiar from contextual archaeology as an interpretative procedure. More particularly, if we define context as the totality of what is relevant to the object environment (where "relevant refers to a relationship with the object which contributes towards its meaning" (Hodder 1987, 4–5)), it follows that the relevant environment (the context) is also determined by the meaning of the object. Indeed, this circularity is the essence of any relational viewpoint. The problem lies in the fact that the contextual approach has been advanced primarily as a "methodological procedure for reconstructing past symbolic meanings" (ibid., 1), which gives rise to a methodological paradox: How can you reconstruct the meaning of an artifact on the basis of its contextual associations when these contextual associations are determined by the meaning of the artifact? The point I am trying to underline here is not, of course, that I consider the basic assumption of contextual archaeology concerning the relationality between context and object to be wrong. My disagreement pertains, rather, to the general objective of contextual archaeology to be primarily a procedure for the reconstruction of past *meanings*. This implies that context is not the end of analysis but the means of interpretation. In contrast, I want to suggest that, as ANT and the present example illustrate, there are no meanings but only contexts, and more specifically networks of material engagement. The artificial separation that the analysis of such socio-technical networks often embodies between a descriptive level and a subsequent explanatory or interpretive level should be avoided as unproductive and in some cases misleading. As Latour points out, once a symmetric perspective is adopted this separation is no longer necessary. There is nothing to be found outside the network:

> If we display a socio-technical network—defining trajectories by actants' association and substitution, defining actants by all the trajectories in which they enter, by following translations and, finally, by varying the observer's point of view—we have no need to look for any additional causes. The explanation emerges once the description is saturated. . . . There is no need to go searching for mysterious or global causes outside networks. If something is missing it is because the description is not complete. (Latour 1991, 129–130)

3. The problem of the prime mover.

The last point I want to raise pertains to the arbitrariness of the choice to trace the starting point of any socio-technical network to the statement, intentionality, belief, or ideology of a certain human agent or institution. In the hotel-key example, the decision to choose the intention or statement of the hotel manager as the central point of reference for the sequence of events to follow may give us a starting point for our analysis, but it also embodies a serious drawback: Such a decision fails to question the starting point itself. That is, it fails to ask why the hotel manager needs or intends that the keys be returned, or why we need keys in the first place. In other words, the question about how a certain intention, belief, or ideology emerges remains unaddressed.

I believe that reducing the complex network of interactions that constitute a given socio-technical trajectory to a mental template or ideological disposition of a certain individual agent (the prime mover), or a certain group of individuals, does not count as a solution to the problem of change. Such a reduction is simply a transposition of the problem to a different realm—the realm of ideology. This transposition, far from providing an adequate explanation of change, poses a new problem: How did this ideology emerge in the first place, or how did those motivational impulses for materialization and the agentive power to actualize those intentions come about? Those questions remain unanswered. That is why I believe that, when processes of material engagement and their long-term trajectories are at issue, explanation of change cannot be reduced to some hypostasized abstraction, social or ideological. In such cases, change must be understood and articulated at the level of the concrete artifact. In short, abstract social or ideological structures—if such structures exist—are part of the problem, not a solution. These abstractions cannot explain anything before we account for how they emerge and how they are maintained, transformed, and transmitted. In other words, ideology is the result of analysis rather than its point of departure.

In real-world practice, we are never faced with isolated objects or abstract social relations and institutions; "we are faced with chains which are associations of human (H) and non-humans (NH)" (e.g., H-NH-H-NH-NH-NH-H-H-H-NH) (Latour 1991, 110). Power, intentionality, and agency are not properties of the isolated person or the isolated thing; they are properties of a chain of associations. The crux of the process lies specifically in the temporally unfolding causal coupling between the "program" and the "anti-program." More specifically, "the number of loads that one needs to attach to the statement"—the stages of the program—"depends on the customer's resistance"—anti-program. As long as this process of "accommodation and resistance" (Pickering 1995) continues, the overall structure of the system remains unpredictable. This means that "the force with which a speaker makes a statement is never enough, in the beginning, to predict the path that the statement will follow" (Latour 1991, 104). In other words, in our example, the power strategy (or, if you like, intention, belief, or ideology) of the hotel manager remains a socio-technical network, fluid and contested up to the point where the metal weight is introduced. Only then does the metal weight successfully (which in this case means also unconsciously) stabilize the dynamic of the system by forcing the customers to leave their keys at the front desk. Indeed, the stability of such a socio-technical chain depends primarily on the degree of attachment among its elements. However, this attachment is symmetrical and does not discriminate between physical linkages and affective or cognitive linkages:

"The key is strongly attached to the weight by a ring, just as the manager is very attached to his keys. It does not matter here that the first link is called 'physical' and the second 'emotional' or 'financial.'" (ibid., 108)

The argument for material agency

The sin of anthropomorphism

I have argued that once the symmetric perspective of ANT is adopted, the artifact is transformed from a passive instrumental mediation to an "actant"—that is, an actor-entity "that does things" (Latour 1992, 241; Akrich and Latour 1992). As the sociologist Andrew Pickering observes (1995, 13), "the most attractive feature of the actor-network approach is precisely that its acknowledgment of material agency can help us to escape from the spell of representation. It points a way to a thoroughgoing shift into the performative idiom." However, this methodological shift is not without its problems. Indeed, by adopting the symmetric approach we are immediately entering an unknown territory—the blind spot mentioned in my introductory chapter—where conventional boundaries between subjects and objects or persons and things are blurred. This blurring, however, causes some radical changes not only in the way an ordinary object can be perceived, but also in the type of language that is needed to express the changes. For example, a hydraulic door closer becomes "a well-trained butler" (Latour 1992, 233–234), a speed bump a "sleeping policeman," and an anti-personnel mine a "moral entity" (Gell 1998, 21). From the symmetric viewpoint, these expressions are not simply metaphors in the conventional sense of the word; they carry with them increased heuristic value. This is why the whole framework appears to succumb to the sin of anthropomorphism. Speaking about things as agents seems to imply a personification of the inanimate and thus an illegitimate ascription of human form and attributes to the non-human.

Insofar as my goal in this chapter is to advance my own argument for material agency from the perspective of Material Engagement Theory, I believe it is essential, before I proceed further, to clarify my position in relation to this important criticism. My overall argument, briefly, amounts to the following: I believe that the accusation of anthropomorphism is deeply flawed in two senses. First, it fails to recognize the important difference between anthropomorphism and anthropocentrism. Second, it begs the question of material agency—that is, it takes "human" agency for granted and denies material agency *a priori*.

Let me begin by clarifying the difference between anthropocentrism and anthropomorphism. To engage in anthropocentricism is to perceive humans as the center of reality; to engage in anthropomorphism is to perceive reality in human terms. Anthropocentrism is a bad intellectual habit, characteristic of Western modernity, that we need to overcome. Anthropomorphism is a biological necessity of the human condition that we need to embrace, or else we run a constant risk of removing the human subject from the center of the social universe only to place this subject in a god-like position on top and outside of it. Indeed, as the anthropologist Roy Ellen observes (1988, 226), "to say that non-human objects of all kinds are treated anthropomorphically is not, in itself, to say a lot, since human-kind has no option but to apprehend and represent its world in anthropomorphic terms." This is something that the embodied-cognition paradigm discussed in chapter 4 has illustrated beyond doubt. To understand what is at issue here, simply imagine what it would be like to live and think in the absence of such deeply anthropomorphic and basic metaphors as up/down, front/back, and interior/exterior. In fact, as Stewart Guthrie (1993) suggests, anthropomorphism, besides being an abiding feature of human cognition, can be seen to have a strong evolutionary significance. Guthrie's main argument, as summarized by Alfred Gell (1998, 121), is that "strategically, it is always safer to impute the highest degree of organization possible (such as animacy) to any given object of experience. It is better, [Guthrie] says, to presume that a boulder is a bear (and be wrong) than to presume that a bear is a boulder (and be wrong)." This statement may sound alien to present forms of being-in-the-world and to modern intellectual predispositions. Yet if my understanding of what Latour essentially implies in his 1993 book *We Have Never Been Modern* is correct, the failure of modernism to meet its ideals lies precisely in the fact that the old evolutionary strategy of which Guthrie is speaking in the passage quoted above remains a defining part of our lives and our scientific practices. In other words, despite the efforts of objectivism to overcome it, anthropomorphism is still with us. However, we need to understand that anthropomorphism remains a part of our thinking not as a problem that we failed to overcome, but as a central characteristic of human projection and material engagement that demands attention and understanding.

In other words, one might suggest (transforming the old saying of Protagorean sophistry) that, being humans, we certainly are the embodied measure of all things, yet we are certainly not the *center* of all things. This is not an anti-humanistic statement; it is simply a meta-humanistic one. The aim is not to devalue the importance of the role of human subjectivity in the drama of life for the sake of some neo-materialism or neo-determinism, but to understand the nature of this subjectivity from a new and symmetric point of view.

Thus, to give a specific example, my reply to Adam T. Smith when he argues, denouncing Gell's "vision of 'things' as social agents," that "such anthropomorphism tends to obscure the distinction between action and instrument, between subject and the apparatus of subjectivity" (2001, 167), would be simply the following: This is precisely the distinction that we need to dissolve, and if the element of anthropomorphism offers a helpful means to this end then it might be worth a try. Accusations of this type are simply begging the question of material agency. Obviously, the problem with material agency is not that it violates those categorical distinctions that Smith is referring to; this is precisely what the notion of material agency as a *modus operandi* is introduced to do. If there is a problem with material agency, it concerns the epistemic validity of such a stance. It concerns, in other words, whether the ascription of agency to things, seen as a method, is able to lead us closer to the reality of the phenomenon we seek to investigate, i.e., the causal efficacy (social or cognitive) of material culture. That is, however, a different issue. My intention here is simply to show that the element of anthropomorphism that the argument for material agency incorporates becomes problematic only when placed against the intellectual background of modernism. It is our deeply entrenched assumptions about persons and things as separate and independently defined entities that make any attempt to understand the one in terms of the other look problematic; it is not the projection itself.

Although I do not consider anthropomorphism in itself problematic, I have no intention of confining the notion of material agency to an instance of this order. The element of anthropomorphism is simply symptomatic of the non-anthropocentric orientation of this stance. The concept of material agency is much broader and more complicated than a kind of anthropomorphic stance for looking at things. In fact, if there is a notion that can be seen to resonate well with what material agency is really about, it would be fetishism, but this time fetishism of a slightly different kind—

one that we might, following Arjun Appadurai (1986, 5), call *methodological fetishism*: a return to the things themselves as socially alive and active in a primary sense. I believe that, if we are to develop a discourse able to penetrate the mutual constitution of persons and things, a kind of methodological fetishism may be a necessary precondition for undertaking the task of exploring the cognitive and social life of things beyond the limits of representation. But let me exemplify more precisely my intention of turning the customary anthropological accusation against the study of material culture into a method.

Methodological fetishism

The notion of fetishism is usually linked with two major intellectual traditions: that of anthropology, where it is associated primarily with the study of religion and animism, and that of Marxist theory and the "fetishism of commodities." To avoid the unwanted connotations of this term, I want to clarify that my use of it relates to neither of the above intellectual traditions. Instead, it relates to the underlying cognitive processes responsible for the generation of the objects or phenomena labeled as fetishes. These cognitive processes, which can be argued as being the same in any manifestation of the phenomenon of "fetishization," have been identified and articulated by Roy Ellen (1988, 219–229) as follows:

1. Concretization. Although any culturally modified or unmodified object can become a fetish, this becoming always involves a process of objectification. Whatever its physical form (stone, nail, relic, icon, etc.), the concretization of abstraction "is an intrinsic quality" of the fetish.

2. Animation or anthropomorphization. The second prominent feature of those things called fetishes is that they involve the attribution of qualities and properties of living organisms. In other words, they incorporate organic metaphors. This does not necessarily mean that a fetish has to resemble or look like a person; it simply means that interaction between persons and fetishes resembles interaction between persons rather than interaction between persons and things.

3. Conflation of signifier and signified. Where "fetishization" has occurred, the signified is treated as though it were embodied in the signifier. The process of concretization often results in material objects that operate as things signified. That is, it results in objects that operate as causative agents

in their own right rather than for what they might stand for—as with signifiers.

4. Ambiguous conceptualization of power. The process of "fetishization" involves an ambiguity of agency and is characterized by "an ambiguous relationship between control of object by people and of people by object."

Although I fully subscribe to the above differentiation, I emphasize that my major disagreement with it—a rather important one—is that, whereas Ellen identifies fetishes as "cultural representations," I construe them as *enactive signs* (chapter 5) and thus as products of conceptual integration rather than of representation. Apart from that, I fully subscribe to Ellen's claim about the universal character of fetish-like behavior. Fetishism as a process, far from a marginal and "primitive" mental condition that brings about a special category of exotic objects, is an ordinary feature of material engagement.

Concerning methodological fetishism, what I am proposing here is basically what in philosophy is referred to as *abduction*. Abduction, as we know from Peirce (1955, 1991; see also Gell 1998), is a process of hypothesis formation that draws on a metaphoric logic rather than on the usual inductive logic. Very simply, first you hypothesize some resemblance between a familiar phenomenon or domain of experience and something unfamiliar that you seek to explain, then you project the properties of the familiar onto the unfamiliar. If the abduction leads somewhere and affects your initial problem, it is worthy of being pursued further. I consider material agency to be the unknown domain of experience that we seek to explore, and I hypothesize the properties of fetishism as being the familiar domain to be abducted. In other words, the properties of fetishism are abducted and projected into the general domain of material culture and used as a comparative reference point for detecting the agency of things. Through this projection I want to explore the effect those properties might have in helping us understand the question of material agency—that is, how things matter. The basic idea is quite simple and embodies a spirit similar to that of "active externalism" (chapter 4): If the social and cognitive life of things is the phenomenon you seek to understand, then, methodologically speaking, it is more sensible and productive to treat material things as agents (and be wrong) than to deny their agency (and be wrong). There is, however, a further feature that distinguishes methodological fetishism from other approaches to the study of agency and material culture. This feature lies in the recognition that the closest parallel to the idea of a material agent that we have is not that of a person but rather that of a fetish. This important recognition of what methodological fetishism as a conceptual apparatus embodies can protect us against the danger of treating material agency as a homologous and isomorphic extension of human agency. As Chris Gosden points out (2001, 164), "objects can be seen to be active, but they are active in the manner of objects not in the manner of people." A failure to recognize that may create problems not dissimilar to those I discussed in chapter 5 under the banner "fallacy of the linguistic sign."

Although in principle to approach objects as active in their own manner may well be conceived as the ultimate objective of material-culture studies, it is an objective that in practice involves many potential pitfalls. Most important, being active (either in the manner of objects or in the manner of people) is to engage in activity. But in the context of activity, to speak of manners of objects and manners of people makes no real sense from a symmetric viewpoint. Activity obeys a strictly transactional logic whereby manners of people become manners of objects and vice versa. Hence the problem with anthropomorphism that I discussed earlier in this chapter.

The point I am trying to emphasize with the above quotation from Gosden is not that the active nature of material culture should be, or could ever be, understood in its own independent and objective terms. Such a claim would be inconsistent with the grounding principles of Material Engagement Theory in general and with the argument for material agency in particular. The point I am trying to make here, which I hope is similar to what Gosden meant to express, is that when we are approaching the agency of things we should be extremely cautious not to transform the "symmetry" into a mere isomorphic projection. Indeed, this seems to be precisely the problem that arises with Gell's differentiation between "primary" and "secondary" agents.

Intentionality and secondary agents

The position that Gell adopts in respect to the issue of agency is already clear from the first chapter of his influential treatise *Art and Agency* (1998). In the section titled "Paradox Elimination" (19–21), Gell gradually unfolds what may be seen as the strongest and the weakest part of his theory. Starting with the strongest part, we have his insightful definition of agency:

Because the attribution of agency rests on the detection of the effects of agency in the causal milieu, rather than an unmediated intuition, it is not paradoxical to understand agency as a factor of ambience as a whole, a global characteristic of the world of people and things in which we live, rather then as an attribute of the human psyche, exclusively. (20)

This definition is followed, 16 pages later, by an unnecessary and to my mind unfortunate differentiation between "primary" agents (defined as entities endowed with the capacity to initiate actions or events through will or intention) and "secondary" agents (defined as entities not endowed with will or intention by themselves but essential to the formation, the appearance, or the manifestation of intentional actions). This differentiation appears, at least to me, inconsistent with and contradictory to the crux of Gell's theory in two ways. On the one hand, it seems to imply that Gell accepts that intentionality is a criterion of agency attribution; on the other, it violates the above-mentioned symmetry between persons and things. Indeed, to call humans "primary agents" is to place human intentionality *before* material engagement—ontologically speaking—and thus outside what I will define later, following Searle, as the Background, whereas "to call objects secondary agents is make them look like people, but with certain deficiencies of intention" (Gosden 2001, 164).

Agency and intentionality

There is no doubt that intentionality is often perceived as the major diagnostic feature of agency and so presents a significant obstacle to any discussion of material agency in a proper sense. Consequently, it is important for present purposes that I tackle that issue with due care before it can be said that my proposal about material agency stands on a firm foundation. I intend to begin by clarifying the notion of intentionality as a philosophical problem.

First I should note that the notion of intentionality was originally introduced to provide a firm criterion for the distinction between the mental and the physical. Etymologically it derives from the Latin verb *intendo*, meaning to point (at) or aim (at) or extend toward. In present-day philosophy of mind it is usually seen as a fundamental property of human mental states to be "directed at, or about, or of objects and states of affairs in the world" (Searle 1983, 1; see also Dennett 1987 and Brentano 1995

[1874]). In other words, intentionality is construed as a strictly internal phenomenon of human consciousness with no counterpart in the realm of things.

Seen from this "internalist" philosophical perspective, the issue of intentionality appears to be pretty much straightforward—no room for "active externalism" here. Intentional states are essentially projections that aim at, point at, and extend toward objects or representations. Thus, it appears initially that, if we accept a close correlation between intentionality and agency, we have no option but to admit that, as long as the former is conceived as strictly a human property, the latter must be conceived the same way. In other words, if the nature of agency is intentional then it has to be a human property; things cannot exhibit intentional states. Indeed, the orthodox view, as Gell describes it (1998, 19), defines the agent according to the "capacity to initiate causal events in his/her vicinity, which cannot be ascribed to the current state of the physical cosmos, but only to a special category of mental states; that is, intentions."

In what follows, I want to show that none of the above claims necessarily follows—at least not in all cases. Without denying that agency and intentionality are intimately connected, I believe that our understanding of this relationship is based on a misunderstanding of the issues involved and thus has to be placed on a new foundation. My principal means of doing so would be by clarifying the important difference between *prior intention* and *intention in action*, drawing upon the work of the philosopher John Searle, and then exemplifying the notion of Background as the *sine qua non* of human intentionality.

Agency as "intention-in-action"

The philosopher John Searle defines the meaning of action as "a causal and Intentional transaction between mind and the world" (1983, 88). More specifically, Searle describes activity as composed of two essential parts: an intentional state in the mind and an external movement in the world. Based on that assumption, Searle differentiates between two types of intentional states. (See figure 6.2.) The first type of intentionality, called "prior intention," refers to premeditated or deliberate action in which the intention to act is presumably formed in advance of the action itself. The second type of intentionality, called "intention-in-action," refers to non-deliberate everyday activity in which no intentional state can be argued to have been

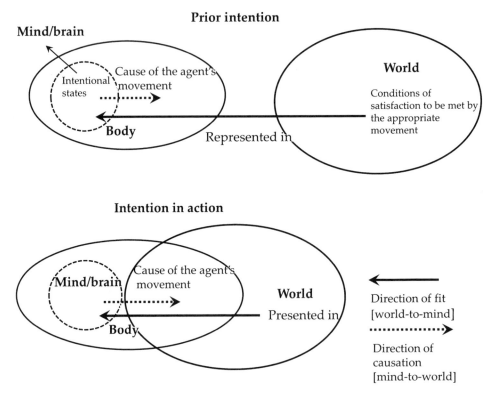

Figure 6.2
"Prior intention" and "intention in action."

formed in advance of the action itself. Moreover, Searle analyzes intentionality in terms of two basic properties. The first property is referred to as "direction of fit" and is specified as world-to-mind. What Searle means is that, in order for a certain intention to be successful, conditions *in the world* must conform to the conditions specified by the intentional state *in the mind*. The second property is referred to as "direction of causation" and is specified as mind-to-world. By that Searle is mainly expressing the fact that it is the intentional state *in the mind* that causes the movement of the agent *in the world*.

Despite their differences, for Searle both "prior intention" and "intention in action" are essentially representational phenomena. In both cases the intention (as an internal representational state) causes the agent's movement (as an external physical state in the world). The difference is

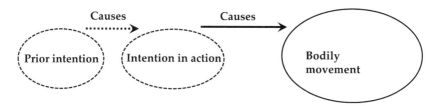

Figure 6.3
The causal relationship between "prior intention" and "intention in action" according to Searle.

that in the case of "intention in action" the internal intentional state and the external movement become indistinguishable. But this, according to Searle, doesn't mean that the intentional state isn't a representation; it simply means that in this case representation happens, one might say, on the wing. To highlight this difference, Searle suggests that "intention in action" presents, rather than represents, its relevant conditions of satisfaction. But this change of terminology from "representation" to "presentation" does not seem to imply much in essence. Presentations are simply "a special subclass of representations" (Searle 1983, 46).

Coming back to Searle's account of intentional activity, which he conceptualizes as a mind-world transaction, we can represent the relationship between the "prior intention" and the "intention in action" as in figure 6.3.

My suggestion is that if we accept that agency is about causal events in the physical world rather than about representational events in our mental world, it follows that, if an association between agency and intentionality can be made, it has to be with the type of intentionality I have called "intention-in-action." In the case of "prior intention" no such correlation can be made before this intention becomes realized in the world—that is, before it meets its relevant condition of satisfaction. This, I argue, is because "prior intention," as long as it is simply an internal representational state, has no pragmatic effect in the world. As I will discuss in more detail later, pragmatic effect (and thus agency) is not a matter of private thought and imagination but a matter of actual practice and being-in-the-world. However, once a "prior intention" is realized in the world and so acquires pragmatic effects, it is immediately transformed to "intention in action." One might suggest that in this case the "prior intention" can be seen as the cause of the "intention in action," but such is not necessarily the case. This I argue for the following reasons: First, in most cases "intention in action" is not preceded by a "prior intention." As Searle observes, "all intentional actions have intentions in action but not all intentional actions have prior intentions" (1983, 85). Second, even when such a "prior intention" exists, it does not necessarily cause or determine the nature and the form of a particular activity. For example, an agent may act differently or even in a manner contradictory to his prior intentions, or may simply fail to meet in action the conditions of satisfaction necessary for such an intentional state to be realized. Finally, even when a prior intention is successfully realized and thus can be argued to cause the intention in action, it is already itself being shaped by what I will discuss in a moment as the Background. I want to suggest that the observed association between agency and intentionality makes proper sense only if conceived as an association between agency and "intention in action." This minor shift in perspective has some important implications for the meaning of agency because in this case intention no longer comes before action but it is *in the action*. The activity and the intentional state are now inseparable. As I intend to show, the boundary between the mental and the physical collapses in this case. That means that "intention in action" is not an internal property but a component of extended cognition. Consequently, it constitutes and is constituted both by persons and things, and thus it cannot be used as a criterion for ascribing agency to the human component of material engagement.

The Background

Searle defines the Background as "a set of non-representational mental capacities that enable all representing to take place" (1983, 143). The Background is the reason that intentional states have the conditions of satisfaction that they do and the reason they are the states that they are. Let us consider the example Searle uses to illustrate this point (1983, 143):

Think of what is necessary, what must be the case, in order that I can now form the intention to go to the refrigerator and get a bottle of cold beer to drink. The biological and cultural resources that I must bring to bear on this task, even to form the intention to perform this task, are (considered in a certain light) truly staggering. But without these resources I could not form the intention at all: standing, walking, opening and closing doors, manipulating bottles, glass, refrigerators, opening, pouring and drinking. The activation of these capacities would normally involve presentations and representations, e.g., I have to see the door in order to open the door, but the ability to recognize the door and the ability to open the door are not themselves further representations. It is such nonrepresentational capacities that constitute the Background.

Indeed, it might also be suggested, from a developmental perspective, that engagement always precedes intentionality. A child will open a door and discover the affordances of the door before formulating an intention about the opening of the door. In this sense, the opening of a door is not in itself an intentional state but rather a part of what Searle calls "local Background" and distinguishes from the "deep Background." However, exactly what the notion of Background implies in terms of the mind-brain-world connection remains unclear. Here Searle, being trapped in an essentially internalist-representationalist view of human mind and intentionality, often appears to be puzzled about exactly where to draw the boundary of human cognition in respect to the Background and exactly how to conceptualize the nature of its properties. Searle settles the issue by calling the Background "preintentional," meaning something that is neither truly mental nor physical. The Background comprises the various kinds of "know-how"—rather than of "knowing that"—against which intentional states arise:

The Background, therefore is not a set of things nor a set of mysterious relations between ourselves and things, rather it is simply a set of skills, stances, preintentional assumptions and presuppositions, practices and habits. And all of these, as far as we know, are realized in human brains and bodies. (154)

That is an exposition not dissimilar to Bourdieu's (1977) version of *habitus*, only this time at a more substantive level as far as the interaction of cognition and matter is concerned. Yet a problem remains, and Searle seems to be well aware of it:

[T]here is a real difficulty in finding ordinary language terms to describe the Background: one speaks vaguely of "practices," "capacities," and "stances" or one speaks suggestively but misleadingly of "assumptions" and "presuppositions." These latter terms must be literally wrong, because they imply the apparatus of representation with its prepositional contents, logical relations, truth values, directions of fit, etc.; and that is why I normally preface "assumption" and "presumption" with the apparently oxymoronic "preintentional," since the sense of "assumption" and "presupposition" in question is not representational. My preferred expressions are "capacities" and "practices," since these can succeed or fail without being themselves representations. . . . Ordinary usage invites us to, and we can and do, treat elements of the Background as if they were representations, but it does not follow from that, nor it is the case that, when these elements are functioning they function as representations. The price we pay for deliberately going against ordinary language is metaphor, oxymoron, and outright neologism. (1983, 157)

It is precisely because of all these problems that I believe a much better understanding of the Background can be gained if we view the issue of intentionality from a phenomenological angle, focusing on the work of the philosopher Hubert Dreyfus (1991, 2002). From this angle the differentiation between "prior-intention" and "intention-in-action" is now replaced with that between "R-intentionality" (where R stands for representationally mediated) and "G-intentionality" (where G stands for gestalt). More specifically, for present purposes, the latter type of nondeliberate intentional state (the one that relates to agency) is described by Dreyfus as "an experienced causal connection" between the person and the world that involves direct physical responses rather than indirect representational ones. In other words, in the case of "G-intentionality" the Background is at the same time mental and physical. At least in the case of "intention-in-action," the boundary between the internal intentional state and the external preintentional state is dissolved.

Seen from the perspective of "active externalism," the Background becomes a part of the mind, or what might be called an *extended intentional state*. This implies that the objects and material structures that constitute this Background can be argued to project toward me as much as I project toward them. In other words,

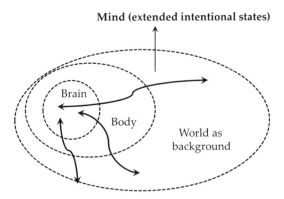

Figure 6.4
The background as an "extended intentional state."

The world is inseparable from the subject, but from a subject which is nothing but a project of the world, and the subject is inseparable from the world, but from a world which the subject itself projects. (Merleau-Ponty 1962, 430)

In the case of "G-intentionality" the line between human intention and material affordance becomes all the more difficult to draw. In fact, it might even be suggested that in certain cases human intentionality identifies with the physical affordance. In a quite significant way, the mediational potential of a certain artifact shapes (both in the positive and negative sense of enabling and constraining) the nature of human intentions. Taking as an example the relationship between a person and a car (which Gell also discusses), I suggest that there are many intentions that a person might have about a car, but certainly the formulation of an intentional state about eating the car does not appear to be one of them. That is so because such an intention is not afforded. A car might afford a variety of human intentions, some of them quite odd indeed, but at the same time it constrains and limits them:

I can, for example, intend to peel an orange, but I cannot in that way intend to peel a rock or a car; and that is not because I have an unconscious belief, "you can peel an orange but you cannot peel a rock or a car" but rather because the preintentional stance I take towards oranges (how things are) allows for a completely different range of possibilities (how to do things) from that which I take toward rocks or cars. (Searle 1983, 144)

Although at a purely internal imaginative level one may suggest that a person might be in a position to entertain a belief or formulate a mental image about eating or peeling a car, that is not relevant to the present discussion. What is at issue here is not the capabilities of the faculty of human imagination, but rather the relationship between intentionality and agency and to what extent intentionality can be considered as the principle of agency attribution. In other words, even if I may be capable of somehow imagining eating a car, that kind of internal mental activity— "prior intention" if you like—can never have any social effect or any pragmatic implications. Social effects arise from actual interaction between my car and me, not from the private thoughts I might be in a position to entertain about it by exercising the faculty of my imagination. Intentionality matters to agency only once the conditions of satisfaction relevant to the intentional state can be placed against some concrete Background. But in this case my car, as the primary objectification of this Background, has a great deal to say and do in the formulation of my intentional state. The intention belongs to both of us.

Indeed, as is the case with the general issue of human cognition, so it appears to be also in the case of intentionality that "some of our deeply felt assumptions about intentionality, at least as a property of individual minds alone, may be mistaken" (Gibbs 2001, 121). As with many other dimensions of the human mind, intentionality should be understood as a distributed, emergent, and interactive phenomenon rather than as a subjective mental state. The artifact should not be construed as the passive content or object of human intentionality, but as the concrete substantiating instance that brings forth the intentional state. The world of things elicits and actualizes intentionality according to the "situational affordances" (Gibson 1979) of a given context of engagement.

The Background, then, is where intentionality and the Extended Mind Hypothesis collide. Thus, as long as the Background is considered as the *sine qua non* of intentionality, intentionality cannot be considered as an internal and purely mental property. But if intentionality is not an internal property, it cannot be used as the criterion for the attribution of agency to humans. We are engaged in what Searle himself recognized as "Networks of Intentional states" (1983), but with the requirement that those networks should be better perceived as actor networks and, as such, not reducible to any of the constituent elements in isolation.

Let me now return to the starting point of my discussion of intentionality: Gell's distinction between primary (intentional) and secondary (nonintentional) agents. It is, I hope, obvious from the discussion above that such a differentiation does not hold. At least it does not hold without contradicting the crux of Gell's account of material agency. But was this really what Gell meant to imply when he introduced these terms?

Rethinking "things" as agents

My contention is that this inconsistency in Gell's theory can be understood in a different sense. I believe that his initial ontic distinction between "primary" and "secondary" agents was nothing but his analytic scaffolding toward discovering the dialectic between agency and patiency. In other words, it should be seen as a visible residue of the evolution of his framework, rather than as an integral part of its final form. I believe that to identify Gell's conception of material agency with the above-mentioned definition of "secondary agents" is to produce a quite distorted view of the idea that constitutes the heart of his theory. As Gell clearly states, the concept of agency is employed in his theory in a strictly relational rather than a categorical sense. The question of agency is raised in an attempt to underline the fluid dialectic between "agents" and "patients" as states to be acquired in practice and not as *a priori* categorical positions:

> My car is a (potential) agent with respect to me as a "patient," not in respect to itself, as a car. It is an agent in so far as I am a patient, and it is a "patient" (the counterpart of an agent) only in so far as I am an agent with respect to it. . . . All that is stipulated is that with respect to *any given transaction* between "agents" one agent is exercising "agency" while the other is (momentarily) a "patient." (Gell 1998, 22)

Thus, we need not allow ourselves to become trapped in the artificial dichotomy between "primary" and "secondary" agents, which would blind us to Gell's subsequent insight: that "primary agents" and "secondary agents" do not refer to persons and things as entities but instead refer to the states of agent and patient as ontological moments or ingredients that persons and things share.

This is precisely the point that methodological fetishism aims to illuminate by projecting the ambiguity of agency that characterizes the interaction between persons and things, as seen in the phenomenon of fetishism, into the general domain of material culture. This projection is not without a cost, and it is often the case that when the conventional boundaries collapse what is left seems to be an amorphous blend of categories.

Two ways of dealing with such a problem seem to be available. The first is to follow Latour's (1999) advice and "by-pass" instead of attempting to reconcile what is essentially an inescapable "language game." Though I agree with the essence of this "eliminative" argument, I disagree with the pragmatics of it. Rituals composed entirely of new elements are likely to fail to become established. As Latour himself has recognized in various instances, to abandon such deeply entrenched and from certain analytic perspectives even useful dichotomies and categorizations is not easy—if even possible—in the absence of some suggested alternative that can be seen to "have at least the same discriminating power as those just jettisoned" (1994, 795). It is specifically to smooth this conceptual passage that I am using the term 'material agency' instead of Latour's term, 'actantiality'.

The second way is to follow Gell and adopt an anthropological perspective. Whether or not they are ontologically autonomous agents, artifacts are often being treated by humans as such. The issue is not whether the notion of material agency is "philosophically defensible" (Gell 1998, 17) but to what extent it is cognitively, socially, and historically practicable. It is this anthropological perspective that I wish to adopt, first making it clear that such a perspective doesn't necessarily imply that I rest my case solely on the premises of cultural relativism. Material agency is not a figment of a particular cultural imagination that I seek to understand, but a real, philosophically and ontologically defensible aspect of reality. Thus, my conception of material agency is not to be grounded in the gray zone of Frazerian "contagious" and "sympathetic" magic where supernatural powers dwell and acquire material form and substance, but in the relational ontology of material engagement.

I believe that this is precisely what the notion of the Background contributes to the present discussion and the present analytic objectives. More specifically, it provides a well-accepted basis—at least as far as philosophy of mind is concerned—upon which we can ground and explore the non-human (or, if you prefer, non-standard) manifestations of agency that, as Gell has pointed out, no philosopher would be willing to defend. As Searle himself remarks, what makes the intention of a given person to "become President" meaningful and the intention of another to become "a coffee cup or a mountain" impossible and meaningless is not the truth of the propositions themselves. It is the degree to which those intentions can fit into the network of intentional states that is afforded by a given Background. That means that, once the relevant Background is given, both options may appear of equal validity, though in our example the suggested intentional states have very little chance of being satisfied. An equally puzzling intentional state is very familiar: the state, well attested historically and ethnographically, in which humans intend things to be animate and to have intentions. This is a scenario that is valid, real, meaningful, and certainly philosophical defensible once a Background that is able to provide the conditions of satisfaction for such a "bizarre" intentional state is present. Against the Background of those systems, to argue that a non-biologically-alive entity possesses intentionality, far from being a naive figment of cultural imagination, is the natural extension of the intentional stance.

Ask not "What is an agent?" but "When is an agent?"

It is against the conceptual background introduced above that the argument for material agency as a form of methodological fetishism is built. The argument is not for an either/or choice between human and material agency, nor is it for extending a human property to the realm of materiality. The argument is that agency is not a property but the emergent product of the "irreducible tension of mediated activity" (Wertsch 1998). Within this situated dialectic of activity, material or human predications of agency make sense only from the perspective of power relations. An agent is defined as "any element which bends space around itself, makes other elements dependent upon it self and translates their will into a language of its own" (Callon and Latour 1981, 286). This is a condition that, in any given process of material engagement, can be equally satisfied by persons and by things, the only difference being that in the case of things this process can be sealed in a "black box" and sink below the surface of our conscious horizon.

In the dynamic tension that characterizes the processes of material engagement, sometimes it is the thing that becomes the extension of the person. At other times, it is the person that becomes the extension of the material agent. There are no fixed agentive roles in this game; there is a constant struggle toward a "maximum grip." Agency as an emergent property cannot be reduced to any of the human or the nonhuman components of action. It can only be characterized according to that component that, at a given moment, has the upper hand in the ongoing phenomenological struggle. In the context of engagement, the antithetical poles of the *pour sui* and the *en sui* are positions rarely if ever acquired in any pure sense.

As is the case with most of the notions associated in one way or another with the realm of material engagement, agency should be approached as an "open" concept. That means that it cannot be framed as an essence but it can be framed as a process in need of continuous rethinking and amendment. We simply cannot step outside the realm of material engagement and define agency in terms of a fixed set of necessary and sufficient conditions. The important question is not "What is agency?" (as a universal property or substance). The important question is, rather, "When and how is agency constituted and manifest in the world?" To treat agency as the natural property of human beings is to adhere blindly to an image of personhood as seen through the distorting Cartesian lens of Western modernity, and to strip the notion of agency from any analytic value and significance. To approach agency as a fixed phenomenon it is to take as the starting point of analysis what should have been its end. The only available starting point and obligatory point of passage for the emergence and determination of agency is that of material engagement. As Andrew Pickering (one of the first sociologists of technology to use the term 'material agency') comments in his book *The Mangle of Practice*,

Just as the material contours and performativity of new machines have to be found out in the real time of practice, so too do the human skills, gestures, and practices that will envelop them. . . . Gestures, skills, and so on—all these aspects of disciplined human agency come together with the machines that they set in motion and exploit. . . . Just as material agency is temporally emergent in practice, so, necessarily, is disciplined human agency . . . they are intimately connected with one another, reciprocally and emergently defining and sustaining each other. (1995, 17)

With respect to agency, there is nothing to be found outside this tension of mediated activity, and this is precisely the area to which we should look for its manifestations—human or material. Agency is a property or possession neither of humans nor of nonhumans. Agency is the relational and emergent product of material engagement. It is not something given but something to become realized. In short, as far as the attribution of agency is concerned, what an entity (a car or a person) *is* in itself doesn't really matter; what does matter is what the entity becomes and where it stands in the network of material engagement.

A conceptual talisman

In this chapter I have suggested that a shift from asymmetric and anthropocentric conceptions of agency toward non-anthropocentric and symmetric ones will effect a radical change in the way we conceptualize material culture—a change that can bring us closer to an understanding of the ontology of the artifact and the active nature of material culture. In keeping with my discussion of extended cognition, I have proposed that agency should not be perceived as a fixed property of humans but as the emergent product of our engagement with the world. In engaging the world, the intentions of the human agent are subject to the mediational capabilities of the surrounding materiality that constitutes the intentional background through which the engagement is enacted. Thus, recognizing and examining the agency of things essentially means penetrating the dialectic of resistance and accommodation that emerges through, and is constitutive of, the processes of material engagement. To this end I have proposed the strategy of methodological fetishism. A prerequisite for the success of this process, however, is to move from the representational to the performative idiom (Pickering 1995). That means asking not what a thing stands for, but what a thing does and what reality it brings forth in the world.

As I mentioned at the beginning of this chapter, the concept of material agency is, to some extent, misnamed. Yet I hope to have shown that it serves well to arouse us from our deep humanistic slumber and to offer us a powerful talismanic—protective—device against the binding spells of modernity. Indeed, from a certain perspective the notion of material agency can be understood as a conceptual homeopathic amulet. It protect us by reminding us of the following:

In the human engagement with the material world, there are no fixed roles and clean ontological separations between agent entities and patient entities; rather, there is a constitutive intertwining between intentionality and affordance.

The artifact is not a piece of inert matter that you *act upon*, but something active with which you *engage* and *interact*.

We cannot bridge the Cartesian gap between persons and things without being willing to share a substantial part of our human agentive efficacy with the mediational means that made the exercise of such efficacy possible in the first place.

The social universe is not human-centered but activity-centered, and activity is a hybrid state of affairs.

Agency and intentionality may not be innate properties of things, but they are not innate properties of humans either; they are emergent properties of material engagement.

III Marking the Mental: Where Brain, Body, and Culture Conflate

7 Knapping Intentions and the Handmade Mind

Minds like ours were made for mergers. Tools-R-Us, and always have been.
—Andy Clark (2003, 7)

Homo faber: Prosthetic gestures

A fundamental theme that cognitive archaeology shares with philosophical anthropology when it comes to understanding what it is to be human is, of course, the theme of the tool-making and tool-using abilities of humans. Tool making, as the prototypical exemplar of what in this book I call the process of material engagement, provides a unique means of understanding how mental events relate to matter and project to the world. Beyond that, the beginning of early-hominin stone flaking, as documented in the archaeological record approximately 2.7 million to 2.5 million years ago (Semaw 2000), may have been an important threshold in the prehistory of mind. For many, this form of embodied mediated action and its products defines the genus *Homo*, the descent of "man the toolmaker." (See Ambrose 2001.)

No other species has been or can be defined *as a species* on the basis of its relationship with tools and material culture. We humans are precisely a species of this rather strange sort, i.e., *Homo faber*. In contrast to the prevalent cognitivist, intracranialist, executive, modernist, or sapient definition, I think that *Homo faber* still provides the best predicate for what it means to be human. We came to have a sapient mind because we are *Homo faber*. Of course, what distinguishes us from other animals is not so much that we make and use tools. Other animals seem to be capable of that to some degree. Yet, despite the famous feats of termite-fishing chimpanzees and hook-crafting crows (for a review of the evidence, see Seed and Byrne

2010 or Tomasello and Herrmann 2010), Henri-Louis Bergson's words in his book *Creative Evolution* remain largely unchallenged:

> If we could rid ourselves of all pride, if, to define our species, we kept strictly to what the historic and the prehistoric periods show us to be the constant characteristic of man and of intelligence, we should say not *Homo sapiens*, but *Homo faber*. In short, *intelligence, considered in what seems to be its original feature, is the faculty of manufacturing artificial objects, especially tools to make tools, and of indefinitely varying the manufacture*. (1998 [1911], 139)

I am not questioning that nonhuman animals and especially primates also use a variety of tools for a variety of purposes, including subsistence and display. (See, e.g., Boesch and Boesch 1984; Boesch et al. 1994; Goodall 1964; Whiten et al. 1999, 2009.) I am saying that—even if we look at the most sophisticated examples of animals' tool use, as in the putative scenario of the reuse of a stone hammer from one year to the next (Boesch and Boesch 1984)—the room for meaningful comparisons with humans is very limited. Even the most highly trained nonhuman nut crackers couldn't equal the abilities seen in the earliest hominin makers of stone tools (Davidson and McGrew 2005; Iriki and Sakura 2008).

There is more to the notion of *Homo faber*, however. It is not the sheer variety and sophistication of human technologies that matters the most, but rather the profound complexity of our engagement with tools and technologies. We humans alone define and shape ourselves by the tools we make and use. Inspired by the work of Bernard Stiegler (1998) and André Leroi-Gourhan (1963/1993), I would like to describe human tool use as the prosthetic gesture *par excellence*. Tools, I suggest, are enactive cognitive prostheses. My use of the term 'prostheses' here derives from the work of the philosopher Bernard Stiegler and refers not to a mere extension of the human body but to an essential characteristic that co-constitutes the world inhabited by humans. For Stiegler (1998, 152), humans are essentially defined as prosthetic beings: "The prosthesis is not a mere extension of the human body; it is the constitution of this body qua 'human.'" Had we not used the techniques we used, we would not have been the kind of beings we are. This central idea of Stiegler's "originary technicity"—that is, of the common origin of humans in technology and of technology in humans—is also what links prosthetics with the "exteriorization of memory" and, through that, with André Leroi-Gourhan. Leroi-Gourhan also believed that human beings evolved as a product of technics, and many of Stiegler's ideas are grounded in his early work on the "freeing" of hands and the importance of "gesture" and tools in the making of the human mind. Andy Clark (2003) has revived this old theme by using the concept of the "cyborg." Ontologically speaking, we humans are a "cyborg" species. It is "our total reliance on these objects" (Hollenback and Schiffer 2010) that truly stands out. This is a species-unique and self-transforming human predisposition that leaves very little space for valid relational comparisons with other animals (or so I wish to suggest).

I understand that those committed to the long-held evolutionary ideal of a cognitive "continuum" between human and nonhuman animals would probably object to my previous points as anti-Darwinian. However great the difference between humans' and animals' tool use, Darwin wrote (1871, 105), it must be "one of degree and not of kind." But I think Darwin's claim is rather misleading so far as the human entanglement with tools is concerned. What must have begun as a difference in degree soon became a difference in kind—that is, a difference that makes a difference.

We can, of course, learn a great deal by teaching nonhuman primates how to knap stone (Schick et al. 1999; Toth et al. 1993). And many important lessons about early-hominin tool use have been learned from looking at nonhuman primates' tool use in the wild and comparing the kinds of learning, memory, and skill required. (See, e.g., Davidson and McGrew 2005; Seed and Byrne 2010; Byrne 2005.) But although the comparative study of animals' tool use can be extremely useful in the study of human cognition, I doubt that it provides the best way to understand animal intelligence. Nonetheless, an important lesson can be learned by looking at animals' tool use—a lesson about the role tools can play in bringing about human forms of intelligence. The study of animals' tool use also reveals important information about the status of tools as cognitive artifacts. (For a contextualized discussion of tool use by animals, see Hansell and Ruxton 2008.)

In any case, what I wish to address in this chapter is not whether humans' and animals' tool-using abilities are different, but rather why they are different and how they became so different.

The tools of the Stone Age

The prehistory of mind begins with the tools of the Stone Age. A very simple way to classify those tools according to five main types or technological modes of production was developed by Grahame Clark (1969, 31). (See also Foley and Lahr 2003, 114. For a recent review of the problems and weaknesses of this framework, see Shea 2012.)

The earliest (Mode 1) stone tools, called the Oldowan or Oldowan Industrial Complex after the famous site of Olduvai Gorge in Tanzania, were common among some hominin groups in Africa between 2.6 million and 1.5 million years ago. The technology essentially consisted of sharp stone flakes struck from cobble "cores" by direct percussion with another

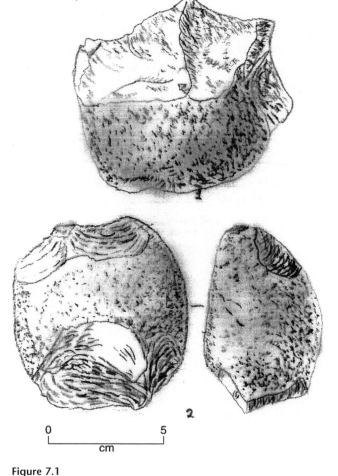

Figure 7.1
1.8-million-year-old stone tools from Olduvai Gorge, Tanzania. Redrawn by Odysseus Malafouris from figure 3 of Wynn 2002.

stone (the "hammerstone") (Stout 2011, 1051–1052). Recent experimentation with percussion-induced flaked stone technologies and ethnoarchaeological data from hunter-gatherer group suggests two possible reasons for the adoption of Oldowan technologies: creating sharp-edged cutting tools for use in animal butchery and creating chopping and scraping edges that could be used to produce wood implements such as digging sticks or spears (Whiten et al. 2009; Schick and Toth 1993).

The first Mode 2 industries emerged in Africa between 1.7 million and 1.5 million years ago in the form of crude handaxes and cleavers, although it often is difficult to draw a line between them and the developed Oldowan Mode 1 industries (Foley and Lahr 2003, 114–115). The advent of the Acheulean Industrial Complex is marked by the standardized bifacial shaping of cores (slab and cobbles) to form large cutting tools (typically about 10–17 centimeters long) (Ambrose 2001). Acheulean large cutting tools date back to between 1.5 million and 0.3 million years ago and were first manufactured by *Homo erectus*. Both cleavers and the more typical teardrop-shaped handaxes were probably multi-purpose tools used for butchery and woodworking. Three marking features characterize the Acheulean handaxe (figures 7.2, 7.3). The first is enormous geographical distribution, ranging across Africa, the Middle East, most of Europe, and large parts of Asia (Lycett 2008; Lycett and Gowlett 2008). The second is the wide temporal distribution of the Acheulean biface. The handaxe, despite regional variation, is probably the longest-lasting piece of material culture in the archaeological record, the oldest findings coming from sites in Africa at around 1.6 million years ago and the most recent at around 100,000 years ago (Lycett and Gowlett 2008, 295). The third feature, the symmetrical shape of these early bifaces, remains a subject of heated controversy. On one side of the debate, some archaeologists, among them Thomas Wynn (1995, 2002), identify "conscious intention" behind the symmetry of the handaxe, although they differ on the precise selective forces or mechanisms that they see as furnishing the main influences on handaxe morphology. (For a summary discussion, see Lycett 2008.) On the other side, many archaeologists would disagree with the above. Instead they will argue that the perceived symmetry in stone tools is simply a consequence of the manufacture technique, rather than a product of human intention (Noble and Davidson 1996; McPherron 2000). On this construal, symmetrical handaxes are simply seen as more effective cutting

Figure 7.2
An Acheulean handaxe. Photo by the author.

and chopping tools that do not involve any conscious choice on the part of Acheulean toolmakers (e.g., Ohel 1987; Mitchell 1996; Simao 2002).

Mode 3 industries represent a major shift in the technique of lithic production: The core is prepared before striking off a major flake as a means of having greater control over the shape and thickness of the flake. This distinctive refinement of the reduction process became the diagnostic feature of the so-called Levallois-style core preparation 300,000 years ago, during the European Middle Paleolithic and the African and Indian Middle Stone Age (Ambrose 2001, 1751; Foley and Lahr 2003, 114–115).

Mode 4, a blade-based lithic technology, continues and develops on the same technical process of core preparation used in Mode 3, only now the aim is to produce longer flakes; that results in cylindrical prismatic cores and fine, elongated blades (Ambrose 2001, 1752; Foley and Lahr 2003, 115). This substantially increases the number of usable sharp edges that can be obtained from a core.

Mode 5 involves microlithic technologies associated with later parts of prehistory (the African Later Stone Age, beginning approximately 30,000 years ago) and found more widely across Europe and Asia in the latest parts

Figure 7.3
Knapping intentions: symmetrical cores, or sharp blades? Image courtesy of Dietrich Stout.

of the Pleistocene and in the early Holocene. The term 'microlithic technologies' refers to "the production of very small flakes and blades that are retouched and worked into various shapes in some contexts or are used as composite unmodified tools in others" (Foley and Lahr 2003, 115).

What should we make of the above classification? If we are to look at early human prehistory in an attempt to understand what in chapter 4 I called the constitutive intertwining of mind with the material world, it is probably with these lithic assemblages that we should start asking our questions. But what questions should we ask? The possible role of these technocomplexes within the co-evolutionary processes that led to the emergence of our own species, *Homo sapiens*, and particularly in the emergence of language and the development of human sense of agency and self-awareness, poses a great challenge for the archaeology of mind. Detecting changes in the underlying cognitive skills has been difficult. How are we, then, to understand the cognitive life of those objects?

Few prehistorians would question that different lithic types or industries speak of differences at the level of technical sophistication. But do they also speak of possible differences at the cognitive level, and in what sense? For instance, does the presence of an early Oldowan stone tool assemblage demonstrate in itself, or reflect the presence of, a particular cognitive set-up that can be associated with the prehistoric hominins who made and used those tools? Probably not. What these formal typological classifications do reflect is, rather, the cognitive categories of the archaeologists who impose forms and identify patterns in order to make sense of the archaeological record and of the way in which archaeological analysis often forces the appearance of standardization. (See Chase and Dibble 1987, 266–271.) This taxonomic or typological neatness hides important complexity and variability at the level of praxis and material engagement. Indeed, one problem with the classical archaeological approaches to technological variation based on typology—a problem that today is widely recognized (Davidson 2009; Stout 2011; Whiten et al. 2009)—concerns their obvious tendency to focus on the form of tools rather than on the technical processes that brought them about. This oversimplified view presents technical evolution in terms of a linear progression from simple Oldowan stone choppers to the bifacially shaped Acheulean handaxes and cleavers, and from Levallois flakes and Mousterian scrapers to Upper Paleolithic blade-based end scrapers and projectile points (Stout et al. 2008; Lycett and Gowlett 2008). The archaeologist Iain Davidson (2009) has called this basic framework the OALMUP (Oldowan-Acheulean-Levallois-Mousterian-Upper Paleolithic) view of stone artifact sequence. Drawing an analogy with the QWERTY keyboard, I suggest that it exerts a similar "lock in" effect. (See Arthur 1989.)

One way archaeologists tried to cope with this problem was by shifting their focus away from the formal aspect of lithic assemblages and toward reconstructing the underlying processes. That shift was accomplished by focusing on the operational sequences and on what archaeologists have come to call "actualistic" studies of present-day knapping techniques of human and living nonhuman primates. (See, e.g., Whiten et al. 2009.) The French tradition of the *chaîne opératoire* approach (Bar-Yosef and Van Peer 2009; Delagnes and Roche 2005; Schlanger 1994; Pelegrin 1993) has been particularly influential in this context. Providing a powerful analytical means for reconstructing sequences of decisions and action "chains" made by ancient knappers, from procurement of raw material through every step of knapping, use, and discard, the *chaîne opératoire* approach provided a sequential temporal anatomy of tool making situated in time and space. Although Davidson's OALMUP typological sequence was not abandoned altogether, it was gradually replaced by an "action-oriented" typology, which has productively replaced the emphasis on static tool "types" and "forms" with an emphasis on active "reduction sequences," knapping skills, and procedures. More important for cognitive archaeology, the *chaîne opératoire* approach paved the way for a more dynamic and integrative approach to the study of Paleolithic tool production that combines insights gained from the experimental replication and refitting of flakes and cores left by the knappers and from "reading" of action scars left on tools with the possible cognitive and neural signatures associated with the sequential structure and flexibility of these behaviors. (See, e.g., Stout 2011.) Still, a number of problems remain. For instance, in most applications of the *chaîne opératoire* the distribution of cognitive labor remains unidirectional, teleological, and above all asymmetric. I think it helps if we remain unbiased by modern assumptions when we try to distribute cognitive labor in the early stages of human evolution. As Andy Clark reminds us (2003, 174), the "capacity to creatively distribute labor between biology and the designed environment is the very signature of our species." It is in this connection that the contribution of Material Engagement Theory may be particularly useful.

Where does the knapper end and the stone tool begin?

A good place to start would be where the making of stone tools starts: the process of "knapping," i.e., the striking of a flake off a core (Roux and Bril 2005). This elementary fracturing process, which, as testified by the early findings in Ethiopia (Semaw et al. 1997, 2003), has been practiced for more than 2.5 million years, defines the making of stone tools in spite of any differences in the *chaîne opératoire* of the technique employed.

But what is so special about knapping? I will argue here that the process of knapping is crucial not simply in the archaeological sense of what it can or can't tell us about the evolution of human skill, society, or technology, but also in a deeply philosophical sense. More specifically, it encapsulates two fundamental themes that run deeply and persistently through the history of philosophy of mind. On the one hand, it raises for archaeology the question of the boundaries of mind, which is akin to the mind-body problem in philosophy. On the other hand, knapping also relates to another profound metaphysical problem, indeed a metaphysical ambition: human intentionality. I will discuss the former problem first. I will begin by rephrasing the question to fit the context of the present discussion: Where does the knapper's mind end and the stone tool begin? The fact that this question has never been raised explicitly in the context of the making of stone tools can only mean one of two things. Either we archaeologists have a very clear idea of or a strong intuition about where the boundaries of mind are or we consider the whole issue of boundaries irrelevant, or as of limited value and applicability in archaeology. For in what sense could archaeology ever solve this metaphysical puzzle?

I want to argue that the question of boundaries is crucial and that little progress can be made in the study of tools before we come up with some not necessarily definitive but at least explicit and critical understanding of the epistemological use or abuse of those boundaries in archaeology.

To that end, it pays to look at some of the implications that follow naturally from the anachronistic ontological barrier we have placed between minds and tools. Take, for instance, the example of the Acheulean biface. One obvious implication of the current metaphysical predicament in archaeology is that the handaxe, a thing made of stone, cannot participate in the knapper's cognitive realm *per se*. It can only be the *index* of a mental process, as a footprint is the index of walking. In other words, the handaxe is simply the product, or external representation, of an "internal" pre-formed idea, or cognitive process, which was subsequently realized in the external physical world. Fixing "the marks of the cognitive" in this traditional dualistic sense, the handaxe, like any other tool, can only be seen as a kind of epiphenomenal cognitive residue left in the archaeological record by the operational sequence of the knapping gesture. Thus, the archaeology of mind is left with no other option but to use whatever "external" and "indirect" residual cognitive traces the handaxe has to offer for producing inferences about past ways of thinking. The handaxe, then, becomes our means of *entering into* the human cognitive realm, *"which is where we need to be* to answer questions about the mental abilities of early hominids" (McPherron 2000, 655, emphasis added).

But is this "internal" cognitive realm where we really need to be? Are there sufficient grounds, beyond mere habit or convenience, for archaeologists to uncritically accept the above popular "internalist" scenario? I think not. If one tries to look more closely at the ontological commitments underlying the ways most archaeologists think about and describe those early lithic assemblages, one will easily discover all the major components of the dualistic representational logic that I have been criticizing in this book. Three of those theoretical commitments are particularly relevant here. The first, which we might call "ontological" commitment, can be expressed as follows: Intentionality is a necessary condition of artifactuality. The second commitment, "agentive" commitment, usually takes the following form: The human agent (i.e., the knapper) "imposes" the intended "form" on the object. The third commitment, "temporal" commitment, can be expressed as follows: The form of the object exists before its objectification in stone.

Taken together, the above postulates mislead us into thinking of tools as secondary or derived entities. Their enactive dimension as "ready-to-hand" (Heidegger 1977) is reduced to the Cartesian metaphysics of mental representations. This denies the centrality of the lived experience of knapping as a form of embodying and of tools as enactive cognitive prostheses. As a result, we have a huge explanatory gap, the resolution of which is hindered by an implicit commitment to dualism that, unfortunately, implicitly affects how available data from actualistic and comparative studies are being interpreted. In the present context, this huge explanatory gap, as I hope I made clear in the preceding chapters, takes the following form: We can never understand and infer the nature of the "cognitive function" responsible for the creation and use of a tool without first recognizing that the various processes responsible for the transformation of raw material to tool, as well as the tool itself, actively and reciprocally participate in the co-construction of what counts as "cognitive function."

I am not denying that the complex combinatory character of human tool use and especially of later stone industries speaks of an emerging distinctive human mental architecture. Lyn Wadley's (2010; also see Wadley et al. 2009) experimental analysis of composite tools—that is, tools that require the use of compound adhesives to attach stone segments to hafts—clearly illustrates the increased demands for enhanced working memory and may provide evidence of forethought in humans 70,000 years ago and earlier.[1] My claim is, instead, that the practice and the skill of making and using tools is part of, rather than a product of, this emerging architecture.

I want to argue, following Material Engagement Theory, that the material physical qualities of artifacts do not depend on mental states but rather constitute those states.

Tools for a plastic mind

So far in this chapter, I have argued that the study of tools should be placed on an altogether different ontological foundation. The material-engagement approach enables us to abandon our common representational assumptions and to recognize knapping as an *act of thought*—that is, a cognitive act. But how does the proposal that we see early stone tools as enactive cognitive prostheses capable of transforming and extending the cognitive architecture of our hominin ancestors hold up against empirical evidence from neuroscience and comparative primatology?

From the perspective of neuroscience, understanding the precise effects of the making and the using of tools on the functional anatomy of the brain is not an easy task, and evidence that bears on this question is hard to come by, especially in humans. Until recently, our understanding of the brain mechanisms and of the functional architecture of tool use in humans came primarily from studies of apraxia or of similar behavioral deficits resulting from brain damage. For example, patients with ideomotor and ideational apraxia are able to name and describe a tool but are not able to grasp the tool and use it. (Deficits in which the opposite occurs can also be observed.) Moreover, some patients may show inability to use a tool unless the target of the tool's action is present (Holmes and Spence 2006; Johnson-Frey 2004). However, with developments in functional neuroimaging, the situation has been changing rapidly (Frey 2008; Johnson-Frey and Grafton 2003; Schaefer et al. 2004). From the perspective of archaeology, imaging studies of the making of stone tools (Stout et al. 2008; Stout and Chaminade 2007, 2009) offer good examples, providing the first concrete evidence of possible neural correlates of the changing lithic technologies in the human brain. But before I turn to those studies, I want to take a small detour to the world of our closest living relatives and offer a brief review of some interesting recent findings.

As was mentioned briefly at the beginning of this chapter, interpreting the tool use and the tool-making capacities of non-human primates remains highly controversial. For instance, monkeys rarely use tools in the wild (Tomasello and Call 1997). Monkeys have, nonetheless, been taught some basic skills in the use of tools, such as how to wield hand-held rakes to retrieve distant food rewards. More impressive are the observed effects of this novel behavior in the monkey's brain.

For present purposes, I want to explore what studies of the effects of tool use on the functional anatomy of the monkey's brain have contributed to our understanding of human embodiment. To that end, I will focus on three major experiments conducted and discussed by Atsushi Iriki and Osamu Sakura (2008).

In the first experiment, monkeys, after training, used a rake to retrieve distant food. When the monkeys were using the rake, their visual somatosensory receptive field extended along its axis; when they were not using the rake, it did not. According to Iriki and Sakura (2008, 2232), "it appeared that either the rake was being assimilated into the image of the hand or, alternatively, the image of the hand was extending to incorporate the tool."

In the second experiment, the monkeys again had to collect food with a rake. The only difference was that the experimental set-up blocked the monkey's view of the table and of its own arms. The only cue available for guiding the monkey's reaching was a video feed from a camera mounted under the barrier, which was projected onto a TV monitor in front of the monkey. Once the monkeys (after some training) seemed to have grasped the "abstraction" involved and become able to use the monitor view to guide their reaching, similar receptive field properties of their parietal bimodal neurons were observed. Could it be, then, that rake-trained monkeys might "be able to use their introspective body image to plan and sequentially combine the usages of their body parts in their minds before actually acting"? This was the question that Iriki and his colleagues set about to explore in the third experiment.

In the third experiment, the monkeys were again exposed to a food-retrieval challenge. This time, however, meeting the challenge required a "pre-planned" sequential combination of tools. In particular, the food was placed at a distance from the monkey and could be reached only with a long rake that lay beyond the reach of the monkey's arms but within the range of a shorter rake. To accomplish the task, the monkey had to use the short rake to pull in the long rake, then switch rakes in order to retrieve the food. Surprisingly, and in contrast to the initial tool-use training, which required approximately two weeks of intensive daily practice, monkeys quickly solved their new problem within a few trials.

What should we make of all this in the context of our question of human embodiment? There are two important points to emphasize. The first relates to the neural mechanisms behind the ability of the human body to flexibly assimilate and incorporate tools as if they were parts of the body. That long-recognized property of human embodiment, which dates back at least to the time of Head and Holmes (1911), has now placed on a more concrete and evolutionary plausible foundation by the findings by Iriki and colleagues (1996) about the receptive field properties of the intraparietal neurons and their abilities to flexibly code a modifiable body schema upon tool use. As a neuroanatomical study by Sayaka Hihara and colleagues clearly showed, even two weeks of tool-use training can forge a novel cortico-cortical connection linking the intraparietal area and the temporoparietal junction. This is the first evidence of induction of novel connections in the adult monkey cerebral cortex by a demand for behavioral learning (Hihara et al. 2006; see also Iriki 2005, 2006; Iriki and Sakura 2008). The second issue concerns the gradual emergence of a novel research paradigm that explicitly recognizes the efficacy of material culture in the development of higher cognition and self-awareness in primate and hominid evolution:

If external objects can be reconceived as belonging to the body, it may be inevitable that the converse reconceptualization, i.e. the subject can now objectify its body parts as equivalent to external tools, becomes likewise apparent. Thus, tool use may lead to the ability to *disembody* the sense of self from the literal flesh-and-blood boundaries of one's skin. As such, it might be precursorial to the capacity to objectify the self. In other words, tool use might prepare the mind for the emergence of the concept of the meta-self. (Iriki and Sakura 2008, 2232)

The experiments discussed above provide clear evidence of training-induced morphological modification of the intraparietal neural circuitry. (The intraparietal sulcus is where the bimodal neurons described above reside.) But how do we explain why tool-use learning might drive those links between temporoparietal junction and intraparietal cortex? One possibility that has been proposed is that rake training may have forced the monkey into "explicit awareness of its own body and intentions" (Iriki and Sakura 2008). I doubt that "explicit awareness" or "intentions" can be easily extrapolated in the case of monkeys. Nonetheless, I think Iriki and

Sakura make a valid point when they say that if improving a monkey's ability to focus its own awareness on the task helps the monkey to incorporate the external object into its body schema and thus to obtain more food, then the Hebbian mechanisms will reinforce, amplify, and even create the additional neurobiological connections that are needed (Hihara et al. 2006; Iriki 2006; Iriki and Sakura 2008).

With the last remark in mind, let us now consider humans' tool use more specifically. A fluorodeoxyglucose positron emission tomography (FDG-PET) study of Oldowan tool making by Stout and Chaminade (2007) provides an excellent starting point for looking at the intra-cranial side of tool making in humans. The study of six inexperienced modern subjects learning to make stone tools of the early Oldowan or Mode 1 type indicated reliance on a parietofrontal perceptual-motor and grasp system, as well as bilateral activations in the dorsal intraparietal sulcus related to human visual specializations (Orban et al. 2006). What does this tell us? The absence of recruitment of prefrontal cortex activations associated with strategic action planning is certainly interesting. It suggests the possibility that evolved parietofrontal circuits, enhancing sensorimotor adaptation and affordance perception rather than higher abstract level prefrontal action planning systems and conceptualizations, were central to Early Stone Age technological evolution. This provide yet another clue against the predominant prefrontal or "executive" bias that characterizes most research in human cognitive evolution.

But what about skilled rather than novice knappers? Would expert flaking performance involve strategic elements and neural substrates not implicated in novice tool making? To address this question, a follow-up study involving skilled flaking (expert Oldowan and complex Acheulean tool making) was conducted (Stout et al. 2008).[2] Comparisons of imaging data and activation patterns between Oldowan and Late Acheuelan knapping methods reveal a transition to more complex action organization in the latter, accompanied by increased anterior frontal and right-hemisphere contributions. Of particular interest is the right-hemisphere ventrolateral prefrontal cortex activation, seen only in Late Acheuelan knapping, which may indicate the emergence of higher levels of intentional organization in flake removal. These higher levels of intentional organization and technical competences in stone knapping can emerge only through deliberate practice and skill acquisition, which would have been greatly enhanced and facilitated by joint action and communication; this adds support to the view that human technological, social, and linguistic capacities evolved together in a mutually reinforcing way (Gibson 1993).[3]

What can these imaging studies tell us? Obviously, experimental studies with modern humans and other animals present a number of problems, not least because of the constraints imposed by using functional imaging. For what is it that a brain activation map actually represents, and how does it relate with broader archaeological issues and questions? Establishing testable, empirical, and at the same time philosophically and anthropologically sound conceptual links between brain structure, cognitive function, and archaeologically observable behaviors is a challenging task. Naturally, there are important restrictions to the inferences that can be drawn about past cognitive operations from imaging data based on experiments with modern subjects. However, although imaging data from modern humans cannot directly reveal the neural organization of extinct hominin species, they could, if carefully combined with available archaeological, comparative, and fossil data, help to clarify the relative demands of specific evolutionarily significant behaviors and thus constrain hypotheses about human cognitive evolution (Stout et al. 2008, 1944). It should be emphasized that the cognitive processes and associated neural systems engaged in a complex natural situation may differ substantially from those observed in the purified environment of the lab (cf. Kingstone et al. 2008), which also means that there might well be "external" components, with a constitutive role for the enactment of a given cognitive operation, that do not correlate to any observed brain activation pattern, or to any evoked blood-oxygenation-level-dependent response, simply because they do not participate in the brain's space or time.

A final potential pitfall should be pointed out. The epistemic power of the neuroimage, as an enchanting device able to translate and visualize some of the most complicated aspects of human mental life by way of a "snapshot" view of brain activity, may mislead us to adopt an unwarranted "neurocentric" view of human intelligence. We should resist this by adopting a critical neuroscience perspective (Choudhury et al. 2009) and by explicitly grounding neuroarchaeology in the principles of Material Engagement Theory and the idea of metaplasticity. As Dietrich Stout reminds us, "PET images do not explain *how* neuronal activity contributes to mental behavior" (2005, 280); they indicate *where* this activity takes place. From the perspective of MET, I doubt that simply knowing which area of the brain lights up during some task performance—knapping, for example—is the sort of information that will, in itself, make a big difference in the study of human cognition. Moreover, neuroimaging techniques often fail to capture the dynamical aspects of thought and behavior that consist of "softly assembled" patterns of activity that arise as a function of time (van Gelder 1995; Van Gelder and Port 1995a,b; Thelen and Smith 1994). (For a good review of the problems and the prospects of neuroimaging technologies, see Miller 2008.) Real progress can be made only through a systematic attempt to contextualize the available knowledge about "locality" within the temporal and socio-cultural frame of some working hypothesis.

Most archaeologists would agree that the first intentionally modified stone tools appear in the archaeological record of Africa at least 2.6 million years ago (Holloway 1999), before any fossil evidence of significant hominin brain expansion. Stone tools are not an *accomplishment* of the hominin brain; they are instead an *opportunity* for the hominin brain—that is, an opportunity for active material engagement. Stone tools have given hominins a window onto a whole new set of skills and ways of thinking that allow for great variation and flexibility. Only some of those potential skills and ways of thinking may have actually been realized, and even fewer may have survived in the visible archaeological record. The material-engagement approach that focuses on explaining the mutual constitution of brain, body, and culture across the scales of time may have much to offer to this end, protecting us from a sterile neurocentrism that has no place in the archaeology of mind.

In the next section, focusing on the example of the handaxe, I will show that tool use offers us a unique and archaeologically visible example of an integrative cognitive system whose constitutive parts, states, and components are spread beyond skin and skull. Yet it has rarely ever been seen as such.

The "handaxe enigma" revisited

In the remainder of this chapter, I will return to the "Acheulean handaxe" and use the "handaxe enigma" to explore the postponed yet crucial issue of intentionality. First, let us consider the shape and the technical properties of this tool. (See figure 7.3.) As I have said, technically this object is a "biface" first constructed and evolved in Africa by *Homo erectus* and subsequently dispersed with hominin populations migrating into northern and western Eurasia (Lycett and von Cramon-Taubadel 2008). In its long cultural biography, this kind of object encompasses a great variety of forms and technical qualities. Proposed accounts of the main influences on the handaxe morphology differ a great deal. Some interpretations see the symmetry of the biface as an adaptive means of increasing its efficiency as a butchery tool (Mitchell 1996; Simao 2002; Machin et al. 2007; McBrearty 2003), others as a form of sexual display (Kohn and Mithen 1999). Some even take symmetry as evidence of early symbolic capacities (Le Tensorer 2006), or as an indication of an aesthetic sense in Early and Middle Pleistocene hominins (Pelegrin 1993; Schick and Toth 1993). However, underlying the above differences concerning the precise selective factors there seems to be a common agreement (whether implicit or explicit) on a single important fact: Whatever the precise adaptive reason (e.g., functional, social, sexual, aesthetic, or symbolic) behind the symmetry of the handaxe, it is a product of "conscious deliberate intention."

Take, for instance, the classical exposition of the "handaxe enigma" by Thomas Wynn (1995, 2002). Wynn's analysis explicitly identifies in the symmetry of these objects the intentional execution of a preconceived mental plan. Without the operation of such an "internal" image manipulation, the various kinds of three-dimensional symmetries that we perceive as almost inscribed on the surface of these objects could have never been produced. On this construal, the mind of the Paleolithic knapper did not simply *recognize* the shape of a handaxe as a perceptually familiar construct, but was also able to *identify* the handaxe as a category—that is, an independent concept (Wynn 2002, 395–397). Simple, familiar, and convincing as this type of argument may be, it is far from the last word on the matter. Some archaeologists would object to the above line of thinking, arguing instead that the perceived symmetry in the Acheulean stone tools is simply a consequence of the manufacture technique rather than the product of explicit human intention or design (Noble and Davidson 1996; McPherron 2000). Their claim, in other words, is that the handaxe's elaborate form might have been produced without the intervention of conscious intentional deliberation about the final shape of the product. (For examples see

Lycett 2008.) Davidson and Noble went so far as to suggest that the "belief that the final form of flaked stone artefacts as found by archaeologists was the intended shape of a 'tool'" is simply a fallacy; they call it the "finished artefact fallacy" (1993, 365). In their view, the handaxe was not an idea imposed on the natural world, as archaeologists following Wynn (1995, 12) are proposing, for the simple reason that the symmetrical object we call a handaxe was actually the unintended residual core left after successive removal of flakes.

Are we justified in attributing some kind of concept of symmetry to the knapper, or is the property of symmetry simply a part of our modern perceptual apparatus that was in no way intended by the Pleistocene knapper? Was the handaxe a shared idea, or a representation imposed on the natural world, or was it simply the unintended product of a new way of striking one stone with another? Was it a symmetrical core or a sharp blade that constituted the aim of the knapper?

I think the main obstacle to our facing the challenge of the Acheulean biface is nothing more than the way the question of the Acheulean biface has been traditionally framed and understood. In particular, I want to argue that the "handaxe enigma" embodies much more than a simple question about what precise goal the knapper pursues. The Acheulean biface comes in different shapes and sizes (Lycett 2008; Lycett and Gowlett 2008), and, as Tim Ingold suggests, it has probably, "in the course of time, been many things to many people" (1993, 341). Instead, I propose that the root of the Acheulean problem turns on a far more significant issue: the very nature of human action and *intentionality*. In other words, it is not simply a problem about the precise content of the knapper's "intentional states" (e.g., a cutting instrument rather than a symmetric cutting instrument). It is, instead, a problem about the actual nature, location, and constitution of these intentional states in human cognitive evolution. The handaxe can certainly be seen as a sign of that special something we call human intentionality, i.e., the property of *aboutness*. But the main issue underlying the handaxe enigma is not whether humans in the Stone Age were producing intentional states of one sort rather than another. The issue does not lie in deciding between a core and a blade. Rather, the challenge that the "handaxe enigma" poses to the archaeology and philosophy of mind comprises two questions: How did humans, but not other animals, come to possess the special property that we call "intentionality"? How and when did humans become aware of the intentional character of their actions and of the actions of others? At this point it might be useful to separate two components of our problem that can easily be conflated. One component refers to the intentional character of the handaxe. The other concerns the internal constitution and implementation of the intention that brings forth the handaxe.

Reassembling the mind of the toolmaker

As we work to meet the challenge set forth above, we cannot take the knapper's "intentionality" for granted. Doing so might lead us to misconceive the way the knapper relates as a cognitive agent to its surrounding environment and the role the handaxe itself might have played in the constitution of human intentionality and sense of agency. This is precisely the main shortcoming underlying all major accounts of the Acheulean problem: Despite their differences, they all implicitly identify knapping with some sort of unidirectional causal and intentional transaction between the active mind and the passive stone. Following the traditional formulation, the knapping process can be described as a sequential process in which an intentional state in the mind of the knapper causes an external movement into the outside world. In other words, the knapper's intentional states are perceived as internal representational states, or "prior intentions," which are presumably formed inside the knapper's head in advance of the action itself. Thus, the intention, an internal representational state, temporally and ontologically precedes and causes the agent's movement, which then, as an external physical act, produces the handaxe. Knapping, then, is erroneously construed as the intermediate behavioral state between the intention and the tool—in other words, as the process that translates or transforms human "intention" into an "artifact" (the handaxe). The ontological commitments here are that knapping is essentially a form of "intentional" behavior and that tools are the products of the intentional mental states that produce such behavior. This also means that the ontology of tools is derivative of human intentionality, which explains the derivative and rather ephemeral metaphysical status of tools and material culture in the archaeology of mind.

Given this widely held implicit assumption about human intentionality, we archaeologists are left with no other option but to choose between two predetermined available possibilities: either to argue, following Wynn, that in the case of knapping the goal of this intentional transaction, or else the content of the intentional state, is the symmetry of the handaxe, or to propose, along the lines of Davidson and Noble (1993), that the goal of the knapper is to produce blades, and that to produce a blade one doesn't need a plan or a symmetry concept, one simply needs the ability to use one stone to strike another in a skillful way. Although in the latter case the relationship between the goal of the action (blades) and the action itself (knapping) is more intimate and direct, it is the knapper who remains the agent. The knapper might not be the one to decide or "aim for" the symmetry of the core, but he or she remains the one who supposedly makes all the important decisions about the sequence, the force, the direction, and the angle of the blows. In short, it is the knapper who possesses the "intentional states." It is this strongly internalist, broadly Cartesian, and, in my opinion, grossly misleading commitment to the representational character of these intentional states that we need to overcome. Here, then, lies the crux of our "troubles with handaxes": Intentional states are *of* or *about* things, whereas things in themselves may not be *of* or *about* anything. In other words, as far as intentionality is concerned, the boundary between the mind and the tool remains intact. Thus, the process of knapping as an intentional physical act is expressive of a neurally or otherwise mentally realized process of thought that causes the body to move and produce the handaxe. But is this really the case? Why I believe this view to be fundamentally mistaken should be clear from the preceding chapters.

Enactive intentionalities: The merging of flesh with stone

My suggestion is that the stone held in the knapper's hand did much more than simply and passively offer the necessary "conditions of satisfaction" to the knapper's intention. In line with the enactive dimension of Material Engagement Theory, I believe that the directed action of stone knapping does not simply execute but rather *brings forth* the knapper's intention. The decisions about where to place the next blow and how much force to use are not taken by the knapper in isolation; they are not even processed internally. The flaking intention is constituted, at least partially, by the stone itself. Information about the stone is not internally represented and processed by the brain to form the representational content of the knapper's intentional stance. Instead, the stone, like the knapper's body, is an integral and complementary part of the intention to knap. In the case of knapping, intentionality is not a property that stops at the boundary of the biological organism. The best angles for flake removal are neither identified nor imagined in the knapper's head before the act. The topography of the knapping activity and the accurate aiming of a powerful blow are neither pre-planned nor recollected; they are embodied, and therefore they must be *discovered* in action. Every stroke prepares and carves the platform for the next. Every stroke can also reveal something new about the stone's characteristics. One of the first things the knapper must learn comes from the senses and relates to the skill of understanding the qualities of stone as formless material—what we might call the "feeling" or "tactility" of stone. This sort of tacit thinking and this sort of engaging with the material constitute a cognitive skill that is of primary importance for at least two reasons: First, it influences the design of the tool. Contrary to what most archaeologists tend to think, I argue that material qualities of the tool, such as the feeling of weight, the sense of sharpness at the edge, or the smoothness of its surface, must have been of at least as much concern as the symmetry of the tool's shape. Second, it influences the sensory hierarchy of the process of manufacturing and using tools. In the Pleistocene, the caring, the carrying, and the owning of tools were based on a different "logic" than that prevalent in the analytical and cognitive schemata that define archaeological interpretation.

This is not to deny that knapping as a form of embodied manual skill is intrinsically associated with, follows from, and leads to specific patterns of neural activation. (See Stout et al. 2008.) It is simply a way to avoid the wrong image of a central neural engine that merely uses the stone and the human body to materialize, and thus externalize, pre-formed ideas and plans. In an important sense, one could argue, then, that the central executive for early humans is not to be found at pre-frontal areas of the hominin brain, but at the power grip and morphology of the hominin hand. In the absence of syntactic language and recursiveness (Corballis 2011), the locus of early human thought stays *with* the body rather than *within* the body; it is *handmade*. The tool guides the grip, the grip shapes the hand,[4] the hand makes the tool, and engaging the tool shapes the mind. When it comes to tool making and tool using, it is not appropriate to see the brain

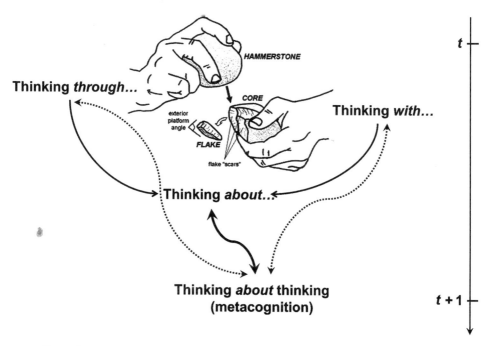

Figure 7.4
Knapping as enactive cognitive prosthesis. The knapper first thinks through, with, and about the stone (as in the case of Oldowan tool making) before developing a meta-perspective that enables thinking about thinking (as evidenced in the case of elaborate late Acheulean technologies and the manufacture of composite tools). Image of Oldowan knapping redrawn and modified from figure 1 of Stout and Chaminade 2007.

as the executive controller for embodied activity; rather, it is the other way around: Now embodied activity controls the brain. What we call "knapping" (and it remains for us to define the precise ontological and epistemic contours of that term) is the chief element or the gravitational center of the complex sequence of causes and events that unfold. In a way, then, knapping is what causes the movement of the hand, the changing of the stone, and the neural activation pattern in the parietal cortex of the knapper. Knapping, then, is the true agent and controller—if these concepts make any sense in the context of mediated action. The action of knapping binds time as it binds intention. Causality and human agency are simply the products—very often illusory—of such an experience. The stone, in the hand of the knapper, is not simply a blank surface upon which the knapper's pre-existing mental plan will be realized; it is a tightly coupled, transparent, and intrinsic part of knapper's cognition. The force and the angle of knapping are parts of a continuous and thoroughly temporal web of interactions that "involve complex feedback between limbs, objects, the visual sub-system, and the acoustic sub-system (because there are distinctive sounds associated with the successful removal of a flake)" (Davidson and McGrew 2005, 812). If any mental template is active during the knapping process, it is to be found in the interactive space between the affordances (Gibson 1977, 1979) of the raw material and the sensorimotor properties of the hominin hand, not in some sort of fixed "idea" stored in the knapper's head.

This minor shift in perspective has some important implications for our discussion of the handaxe problem, because in this case intention no longer comes before action but is *in the action*; the activity and the intentional state are now inseparable. Thus, the boundary between the mental and the physical collapses. The line between intention and material affordance (Gibson 1979; Knappett 2004) becomes all the more difficult to draw. In the dynamic tension that characterizes the process of knapping, sometimes the stone becomes the "extension" of the knapper. At other times, however, the knapper becomes the "extension" of the stone. There are no fixed agentive roles in this process; instead there is a constant struggle toward a "maximum grip" (Merleau-Ponty 1958). The stone projects toward the knapper as much as the knapper projects toward the stone, and together they delineate the cognitive map of what we may call an *extended intentional state*. The knapper first thinks *through* and *with* the stone before being able to think *about* the stone and hence about himself as a conscious and reflectively aware agent. (See figure 7.4.) In tool making, all formative thinking activity happens where the hand meets the stone. There is little deliberate planning involved (not, at least, in the sense implied in most archaeological interpretations), but there is a great deal of approximation, anticipation, guessing, and thus ambiguity about how the material will behave. Sometime the material collaborates; sometime it resists. In time, out of this evolving tension comes precision and thus skillfulness. Knapping, then, is not about externalizing pre-formed ideas or imposing form on matter. It is, instead, about learning how to make and sustain an idea and developing an explicit "sense of agency." The knapper's sense of agency emerges out of his artificial alliance with the material at hand. It is this hybrid coalition that enabled the directedness of knapping. If the knapper's predictions and aims come true, it is because his action was structured in the right way.

Tools are us: A "cyborg" species

I have proposed in this chapter that the problem of human intentionality that the handaxe "enigma" primarily embodies is grounded on the false assumption that intentional states are "in the head" whereas in fact they can, in many cases, be seen to spread out into the world. I have attempted instead to describe knapping as an embodied cognitive process that criss-crosses the boundaries of skin and skull, since its effective implementation involves elements that extend beyond the purely mental or neural realm. I have argued that the material qualities of the stone make a causal contribution to the spontaneous implementation and realization of the plan that brings forth the tool as an artifact. Thus, form is not *imposed* from the outside; it is, rather, brought forth or revealed from the inside. What we call "form" exists as a surface property rather than a static mental event. It exists where the projective mind meets the material at hand (stone, clay, or metal). More important, "form" is always "informed" by the properties of the material to which it gives shape. In the words of André Leroi-Gourhan (1993 [1964], 306), "the making of anything is a dialogue between the maker and the material employed."

Perhaps, as Thomas Wynn observed, the handaxe tell us, if nothing else, that it does not easily fit into our understanding of what tools are and do, and "its makers do not fit easily into our understanding of what humans are" (1995, 21). Naturally, in itself the Acheulean handaxe cannot give us the answer to the question of how we came to be human. But it certainly gives us a good indication about where we should be looking for it. The mark left on the core after each directed blow marks the spot for the next one. It is upon these marks that "the biological rubber meets the purpose-built road" (Clark 2001b, 142). In later periods these marks would take many different shapes and forms. Produced by different techniques, at different times, and in different cultural settings, they would become memory, symbol, and number—they would become us. I suggest that we should be looking to these marks for an answer to the question of what it means to be human.

8   Thoughtful Marks, Lines, and Signs

For people inhabit a world that consists, in the first place, not of things but of lines
—Tim Ingold (2007, 4)

Mark-making humans

Much of the discussion in the earlier chapters boils down to the ways we are accustomed to drawing lines of an ontological and epistemological sort—that is, lines between the "inside" and the "outside." I have argued that these lines often are misdrawn or misidentified to create rigid artificial boundaries where there should be permeable soft interfaces and semi-permeable membranes. Thus, from the perspective of Material Engagement Theory, I questioned the ecological validity of this sort of delimiting lines and argued for the need of adopting new ways for marking the mental or for identifying the marks of the mental. Sometimes the discourse surrounding the metaphysics of marks, signs, and lines may seem too abstract to be of any obvious empirical service to archaeology. Yet, as I hope I have made clear, the ontology of mark making relates directly to the archaeological record and the material practices associated with both the construction and the interpretation of this record. In any case, this chapter makes mark making the object of its study in a literary sense. Indeed, much present-day discussion and debate in the archaeology of mind revolves around the making, the dating, and the marking of various edges, surfaces, and materials. (See also Davidson forthcoming.) Our understanding of what it means to be human seems to be inextricably intertwined with our ability to create and make sense of marks of various sorts—particularly, as was shown in chapter 5, of the sort we call symbolic or representational.

In chapter 7, the discussion of tool making, from the Oldowan chopper to the Late Stone Age (LSA) microlithic technologies, presented an opportunity to follow the effects of precursion on the marking and making of surfaces and, through that, on the shaping of hominin minds. The scars of flaking on the surface of the stone offer the first archaeologically visible trace of human mark making. In this chapter I will continue to explore different forms of mark making. In particular, I will focus on what makes these markings so special, how they differ, and what they have in common. I will also address the relations and transformations of those marks: How did the human activity of mark making move from one material medium to the other? How are all these different kinds of marks related? Is mark making a necessary condition for symboling? Finally, I will look at the phenomenology or experience of mark making.

For most researchers, the understanding of mark making appears to be grounded upon conventional ideas of symbolism and representation. I am interested, instead, in exploring mark making as an evolving enactive cognitive system of material engagement. What does this mean? Two things are important to note. First, I will be studying what connects or separates different assemblies of mark making (e.g., abstract geometric patterns, iconic depictions, or symbolic representations) in order to understand what, if anything, they tell us about the changing relationship between cognition and material culture. Second, I will be using Material Engagement Theory to account for the role of mark making in the long-term development of human signification rather than treating markings as passive markers of cognitive symbolic modernity. This dissociation of mark making, symbolic communication, and behavioral modernity is the key to my argument in this chapter. I aim to show that early markings and lines *do not externalize anything but the very process of externalization.* I will approach mark making not as a passive representational object but as an active prosthetic perceptual means of making sense. That is, marks will be treated as enactive projections.

The anthropologist Tim Ingold suggests in his comparative anthropology of lines that focusing only on the lines themselves, or on the hands that produced them, is not enough. Rather, it is in the changing relations between lines, hands, and surfaces that the crucial differences are to be found (Ingold 2007, 39). In this chapter, inspired by Ingold's proposal, I will attempt a comparative prehistory of mark making, seeking to understand the cognitive life and ecology of different kinds of marks and surfaces, from the Blombos cave engravings to the markings of the La Marche antler.

The prehistory of mark making

Figure 8.1 presents a sample of some of the oldest widely known and well-studied Paleolithic markings. They differ in type, in material, and in period, ranging from Middle Stone Age (MSA) incised ochre and ostrich egg shells to the "notational" objects and images of the Upper Paleolithic.

The object illustrated in figure 8.1a, known as KRM 13, is the oldest piece, dating from between 100,000 and 85,000 years ago. It is nothing more than a fragment of "ochre" (red pigmentatious material) bearing a sequence of sub-parallel linear incisions made by single and multiple strokes produced by a lithic point (d'Errico et al. 2012; Henshilwood et al. 2009). KRM 13 is the only engraved piece, among thirteen ochre pieces, recovered from Middle Stone Age II levels of Klasies River Cave 1 in South Africa.

The objects shown in figures 8.1b and 8.1c are from Blombos Cave and from the Diepkloof Rock Shelter in the Western Cape Province of South Africa. The M1–6 piece (figure 8.1b) is one of fifteen incised ochre pieces recovered from the Blombos Cave (Henshilwood et al. 2009, 31–34). The fragment of engraved ostrich eggshell shown in figure 8.1c is one of some 270 ostrich eggshell fragments that have been found in the Howiesons Poort of Diepkloof Rock Shelter (Western Cape, South Africa) (Texier et al. 2010). The engraved pattern of the M1–6 piece consists of two sets of superimposed oblique lines crossed and framed by three horizontal lines on the long edge of this relatively large (166.6 grams) reddish-brown rectangular piece. Similarly, the ostrich eggshell fragment recovered from Howiesons Poort is showing evidence of three separate hatched bands motifs. Morphometric analysis has shown that the hatched lines always post-date the band (horizontal lines) (Texier et al. 2010).

In figure 8.1d we see five sets of marks from the well-known La Marche antler. Found in a cave in Lussac-les-Chateaux in western France, the antler came from an Upper Magdalenian layer. The figure shows only a small sample of the various sets of marks engraved on the two faces of this unique object, which was interpreted by Alexander Marshack (1972, 1996)

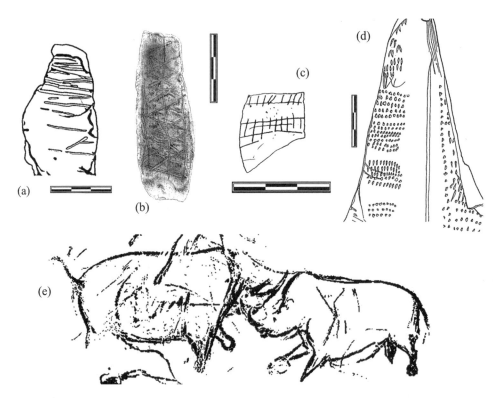

Figure 8.1
(a) Engraved lines on KRM 13 ochre fragment from Klasies River Cave 1, South Africa (between 100,000 and 85,000 years ago) (redrawn after d'Errico et al. 2012). (b) The M1–6 engraved ochre from the Blombos Cave MSA layers (redrawn after Henshilwood et al. 2009). (c) Fragment of engraved ostrich eggshells found in the Howiesons Poort of Diepkloof Rock Shelter (Western Cape, South Africa) showing evidence of three separate hatched bands motifs (redrawn after Texier et al. 2010). (d) Part of the La Marche antler found at a cave in Lussac-les-Chateaux in western France (redrawn after d'Errico 1995). (e) Detail from the "panel of the Horses" of Chauvet Cave (Vallon-Pont-d'Arc, France) (redrawn and modified from Fritz and Tosello 2007).

as a lunar calendar. Marshack's interpretation was based on the counting of the incisions and the assumption that the various sets of marks were engraved by different tools at different times. The archaeologist Francesco d'Errico (1995, 1998) challenged Marshack's interpretation. His analysis showed that the large majority of morphological changes thought to be due to changes of tool instead correspond to the antler's being turned over.

In figure 8.1e we see a small but, I believe, representative detail of the phenomenon we call "cave art." This example comes from the "panel of the Horses" (Clottes 1996, 2001) in the cave of Chauvet (Vallon-Pont-d'Arc, France). Here mark making takes on new significance: It makes the emergence of depiction possible. We no longer see simple patterns of lines; we now see "something": two rhinoceroses confronting each other. I am intentionally not using the word 'representation' here. Although representation might offer the modern observer a familiar way to approach and understand the coming into being of an image as an intricate form of mark making, it is also misleading. The reasons for that will become more obvious later in this chapter when we examine the role of the image in human cognitive evolution. I will argue that although our familiarity with pictures is what enables us to identify, experience, and talk about the image as a representational entity, it also constrains how an image should be understood. Representation may offer an easy way to answer the question of what does a picture do, but it is certainly not the only way either of making sense of pictures or of participating in the process of picture formation.

What is so special about these marks? The tyranny of modernity

There are a number of ways to answer the question posed in this section's heading. Let us look at one way that has been very popular among archaeologists and which is also important for our purposes in this chapter: Markings are special because they potentially allow the archaeologist to infer explicit symbolic intent. Technically simple and aesthetically unimpressive as they may seem to the untrained eye, markings matter because, for reasons yet to be properly established and explicated in the literature of archaeology, they constitute putative evidence for the presence, or the origin, of symbolically mediated behavior. Why is that important? It is important because symbolism, in the "representational" sense of the word, is generally considered to be one of the few universal markers of cognitive modernity and a proxy for language (Davidson and Noble 1989; d'Errico et al. 2003; d'Errico and Nowell 2000; d'Errico and Henshilwood 2007, 2011; Henshilwood and d'Errico 2011; Henshilwood and Dubreuil 2009, 2011; Henshilwood et al. 2001, 2002, 2004, 2011). It appears as if we have come full circle: Markings are special because they mark the symbolic, which marks the mental, which marks modernity, which marks what it is to be human. Put simply, early human mark making is important because behind the coming into being of a simple pattern of intersecting or parallel lines and grooves may lie part of the answer as to when and how we came to be human.

It is fair to say that it has been on the basis of those broad assumptions that the mental and symbolic properties of mark making has been used, but also abused, in the archaeological quest for the origin of the so-called modern symbolically competent human. Archaeology, of course, has yet to reach a consensus on how to approach and answer that question, but most archaeologists would agree that markings like those described above may be our best evidence of the existence of such a well-formed symbolic representational mechanism. Naturally, not every marking can be a symbol. Thus, from the moment when early markings began to attract archaeological attention there was a need for some normative hierarchical scheme that could provide some basic means of evaluating the ontology of the different kind of markings recovered in the early archaeological record. Such a scheme never became explicit and systematic, but it can be presented by way of four general conditions or criteria: antiquity, artificiality, intentionality/deliberateness, and symbolism. Let us take a closer look at these criteria in order to better understand their underlying logic and explanatory validity.

The first criterion, antiquity, is quite straightforward. Archaeology is concerned with time and with positioning things in their temporal frameworks. In the case of the marks and lines under discussion, time is of the essence. Take, for instance, the KRM 13 piece from Klasies River Cave 1 (d'Errico et al. 2012). The linear incisions on its surface may look unimpressive, yet, as has already been mentioned, this fragmented piece of ochre furnish us with the oldest occurrence of mark making, dated to between 100,000 and 85,000 years ago. The incised ochre pieces from Blombos Cave date from approximately 75,000–100,000 years ago (Henshilwood et al.

2009) and the ostrich eggshell fragments recovered from Howiesons Poort levels from about 60,000 years ago (Texier et al. 2010). The La Marche antler and the depiction of rhinoceroses from Chauvet date from the European Upper Paleolithic—much later. Clearly, the earlier the strata from which the markings derive, the more important the message they may carry about human cognitive evolution. That also explains why a Late Bronze Age engraved ochre recovered in the Aegean normally would pass unnoticed. Even if the incised mark takes the form of a Linear B sign, it has very little to tell us. However, an object found in the MSA layers of the Blombos cave in Africa is immediately transformed into something entirely different. Why? I will return to that question after discussing the other criteria.

I said that providing a secure stratigraphic and chronological context for the incised pieces in question is a major concern for archaeology. Still, all our efforts to ascertain their antiquity would count for nothing if those marks were to be results of a natural process. Marks are important only if they can be shown to be anthropogenic—that is, made by humans. For markings to have value, they must be artificial. The footprints of an animal or the scratch marks made by bears in the Chauvet cave (Clottes 2009) have no such value, though they could have been treated as indexical signs by humans.

Still, artificiality in itself is not enough. Any such engraving might be a product of accident or might be a non-deliberate by-product or consequence of human action. As a result, an additional quality is needed if these marks are to gain more epistemic value. The name of this quality is *deliberateness*. Marks are important when they seem to exhibit intentionality. Accidental marks or markings produced in the processing of carcasses (d'Errico and Villa 1997; Mania and Mania 1988), or absent-mindedly, as would be the case for a doodle (Wynn 2000; Balter 2002a), are of lesser epistemic status. This raises an important methodological question: How do we evaluate the degree of deliberateness behind some engraved parallel or converging lines we find on the surface of an MSA ochre?

From "deliberateness" to "symbolic or representational intent"

The KRM 13 from Klasies River Cave 1 (figure 8.1a) is currently considered to be one of the earliest examples of deliberate engravings. Why is that?

Recent detailed microscopic, x-ray fluorescence, and colorimetric analyses of this object (d'Errico et al. 2012) revealed three interesting clues about the manufacturing process. The first clue comes from the fact that the object's surface was ground until smooth before the act of engraving, which provides an indication of deliberate preparation of the blank on which the engraving was made. The second clue comes from the comparative analysis of the motion of the scraping process, the depth of the grooves, and their degree of intersection. This indicates that the grooves of KRM 13 were not consequences of an action intended to extract pigment powder, but rather were deliberate marking of the surface (d'Errico et al. 2012, 949). The third clue concerns the distinct darker brown color and heavier manganese-rich composition of the raw material. This contrasts with the composition of the other twelve pigment pieces recovered from the same level, and may suggest that the specific geochemical type of material may have been selected specifically for engraving purposes. Relatively dark and hard pieces of ochre are also used in most of the unambiguous examples of abstract engraved ochre from Blombos Cave (ibid., 949).

As Henshilwood et al. point out (2009, 41–42), most of the incisions on the Blombos ochre can be attributed to deliberate motions. Incising lines on ochre requires focused attention, with both hands working together in order to stabilize the piece, apply the right pressure, and keep the depth of the incision constant. In addition, as we saw in the case of the KRM 13 piece, incisions were often made after the initial grinding of the facet. This was certainly the case for the M1–6 piece (figure 8.2), which was flattened by grinding and scraping before a cross-hatched pattern was incised. Examining of the motion and the morphology of the oblique and horizontal lines in the engraved pattern revealed that the oblique lines were incised in three sets. The first set of incised lines were cut in sequence from top right to bottom left, the second set were cut from top left to bottom right, and the horizontal lines crossing and framing the sets of oblique lines were incised from left to right (ibid., 31–34).

To recap: Microscopic and other analyses can confirm the anthropogenic and deliberate nature of the MSA markings. Moreover, in some cases they provide valuable information about sequence of actions and choices made by the engraver. But if it is granted that the way in which the lines that we see juxtaposed and superimposed on the MSA pieces of ochre was indeed deliberately selected, what does this really tells us about the epis-

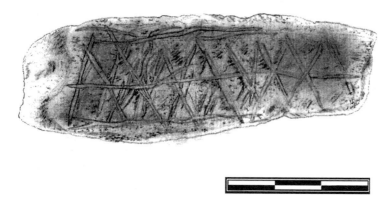

Figure 8.2
The M1–6 engraved ochre from the Blombos Cave MSA layers. Drawing by Odysseus
Malafouris.

temic significance of these incised lines and their patterns? I suggest that
it doesn't tell us much. More than simply being deliberately made or
selected, it is a special kind of "intent," namely "symbolic or representational intent," that makes marks stand out in the early archaeological
record and transforms their epistemic status.

Were they symbols?

Marks of any sort are truly special only when they are shown to embody
symbolic properties and qualities. But how can we establish that? We have
now come to the last and most difficult question: How do we measure for
symbolic intent behind the engraved patterns of MSA ochre?

In the case of KRM 13, d'Errico and his colleagues suggest that, although
the sub-parallel engravings were made deliberately, they "may not in fact
have been produced to create and convey a distinct design or 'message' to
an audience that could visually distinguish it" (2012, 949). But can the
more elaborate cross-hatched pieces from Blombos have been made with
explicit representational intent? According to the Peircean model of semiotics, a symbol can be defined, broadly speaking, as a sign that has only a
conventional rather than a causal or resembling connection with its referent. Can the Blombos markings have had such conventionalized meanings?

Clearly, for Henshilwood et al. (2009) the Blombos markings are not
"doodles." But they are not "notations," like the markings on the La

Marche antler. According to d'Errico (1995, 1998, 2001), the word 'nota-tion' refers to a system of sequential markings (usually produced by differ-ent tools) specifically conceived to store information outside the physical body. In the case of the Blombos engravings, however, individual marks cannot be visually identified as discrete signs used for the accumulation of information over time (Henshilwood et al. 2009, 41). Were the marks symbols, then?

Henshilwood et al. rightly suggest that the engraved patterns from Blombos "certainly do not display the high degree of standardization that we generally associate with structured symbolic systems" (2009, 43). None-theless, they also propose that four basic categories of patterns—cross-hatched designs, dendritic shapes, parallel lines, and right-angled juxtapositions—can be distinguished, and that "a sufficient case can been made that some of the engraved pieces were perceived as symbolic" (ibid., 43). On the basis of that assumption, Henshilwood et al. then ask whether there is also evidence to establish that these ochre markings represent a tradition in the sense of continuity in technique, style, or symbolic practice. How can that be ascertained? Henshilwood et al. consider mor-phology, surface preparation, engraving techniques, expertise, locations of engravings, types of patterns, evidence for additional modification, and how the piece may have been curated or disposed (ibid., 43). The main findings of their analysis can be summarized as follows:

Ochre is the only raw material on which engravings were made across all three phases at Blombos.

Grinding before engraving of the same facet is present on eight pieces recovered, which can be seen as evidence for prior selection and prepara-tion of the surfaces.

Single stroke lines occur in all phases, but multiple stroke lines in only one phase.

A high degree of engraving expertise can be seen in two phases.

Although there is some variation in the design of the motifs across the different phases, almost all of the designs are made up of straight or slightly curved lines.

If the changes in the engraving techniques and the type of design found in different phases are put aside, all the other features considered here strongly suggest, according to Henshilwood et al., "a continuity in engraving practices over a period of at least [25,000 years]" that represents "the longest span yet recorded at any one site" (ibid., 43).

What conclusion can we draw? Somehow paradoxically, Henshilwood et al. (ibid., 45) claim to have demonstrated in the case of the Blombos engravings the presence of a tradition in the production of a number of different patterns of geometric engraved representations in the MSA that goes back to at least 100,000 years ago: "The fact that they were created, that most of them are deliberate and were made with representational intent, strongly suggests they functioned as artefacts within a society where behaviour was mediated by symbols." (ibid., 45) I do not wish to deny that those marks are special in that they can provide some insight into the nature and emergence of early human signification activity. But I believe that the efforts to interpret MSA markings symbolically or semantically have been unconvincing if not altogether misleading. To my mind, there is little doubt that there is nothing symbolic—in the arbitrary representational Peircean sense of the word—in the Blombos engravings.

However, the example of the MSA engraved ochre pieces is of particular interest to us for two reasons. First, the sense in which those engravings have been interpreted conforms quite precisely to the Cartesian conception (explored and critiqued in earlier chapters) according to which the various sorts of incisions were produced to create a deliberate design and to convey a "message" to an audience. I suggest that to understand what is special about those early marks we need a different conceptual lens—one that breaks away from the representational information-processing models of mind. Regarding early human markings and depictions, the main problem of representational theory is the assumption that they are constituted primarily as a symbolic externalization on matter of a preconceived mental image. Against this mentalist claim, I maintain, from an enactivist point of view, that markings and later pictures are emergent products of perceptual semiotic dynamics of a non-representational sort that might have played an active role in the subsequent development of symbolic dynamics of the representational sort.

The second reason I find the example of MSA engraved ochre particularly interesting is that it nicely reveals the inherent ambiguity in the archaeological use of the notions of symbolism and modernity and the inconsistent and vague ways in which early engravings appear to be linked to these notions. For instance, I think that the prevalent archaeological tendency to treat as symbolic any aspect of the archaeological record that has no obvious pragmatic or utilitarian function is obviously wrong and should be abandoned. A more productive and constructive way to look at these early engravings as cognitive scaffolds and tools for thinking is needed. In this connection, the interesting question to ask first might not be "What do the Blombos cave incisions *mean* as carriers of some symbolic message from the past?" but instead "What did the activity of mark making *do* for the ancient mind?" Before turning to that question, however, it is important to clarify that I do not dispute in any way the usefulness of microscopic analysis as means of gaining valuable information on the act of engraving and the thinking of the engraver. The enactive logic of Material Engagement Theory does not, in any way, undermine the validity of empirical analysis. On the contrary, it enables us to make sense of the information microscopic analysis provides about lines, surfaces, grooves, patterns, tools, gestures, and their intersections from a new perspective. For Material Engagement Theory, to look at the terminations of an incised line, at the observed changes in its shape, depth, and direction, and at the morphology and chronology of motions is to look at one aspect of the *chronostratigraphy* of the cognitive act. By the same token, information gained from actualistic comparative studies provides additional insights into the phenomenology of the cognitive act. The material-engagement approach departs from most empirical methods for studying engravings, however, in how it perceives the epistemic and ontological status of those engravings. For the established conception, those lines represent the physical end product of the engraver's mental template (d'Errico et al. 2012, 943). For Material Engagement Theory, if such a mental template exists, it is those lines that constitute its shape and morphology. Put simply, *mark-making action and thinking are the same.*

What kind of line? Getting outside the engraver's mind

How should those early markings be understood, and on what aspects or properties of the process of making marks should we focus? As I said, the dominant way to look at those markings is to see them as the material residues of symbolic or representational intent. That, I contend, is the wrong way to make sense of early markings, as it deprives them of any real significance. Engravings, on that construal, do nothing; they are epiphenomenal. Products of a symbolic act that takes place in a different mental realm, they just happen to manifest on the ochre's surface. Not only does that view undermine the agency of those markings; it offers no explanation for the emergence of symbolism. As I noted in chapter 5, talk of early symbolic material culture (in any form) makes little sense, and is of limited use from a long-term evolutionary or developmental perspective, in the absence of an account of how this symbolic representational ability might have emerged. This is why I suggested that the conventional focus on identifying and reading static symbolic objects and structures should be replaced with a concern to understand material signification as a process of enactive projection and sense making. Such processes, even when they incorporate what we may call external representations (e.g., notational objects, Linear B tablets, or clay tokens), have their basis in dynamic coalitions of networks of material, bodily, and metaphorical signification that operate on the basis of a non-representational logic. Indeed, seen from the perspective of Material Engagement Theory, markings gain some additional phenomenal qualities: More than representational residues of human intentionality, they now become thoughts or actions of a sort, or what in chapter 6 I called *intentions in action*. That is, they are not so much the trace (and thus the end mark) of a human gesture as they are an actual part and thus a continuation of such a gesture in time and space. Thus, it can be useful to approach and describe those markings through the notion of enactive signification that was discussed in chapter 5.

An example having to do with the ontology of lines may be of use here. Imagine that you take a pen and draw a rough circle on a sheet of paper (Ingold 2008, 1796). What do you see when you look at this shape (figure 8.3)? How can you interpret and perceive the line you have just produced? Ingold suggests that there are two ways. The first is to see the line as the end product, of human intention and design abilities. The line then becomes a static geometric perimeter that delineates the form of a circle— that is, a fixed totality. The second way of seeing the line is as the dynamic trace of a human gesture rather than as a fixed totality. The line then becomes the index of an open process. It resembles a vector more than a static shape, and the trajectory of a movement more than the perimeter of a figure. Ingold's argument is that each of these two ways of seeing emanates from, reiterates, and signifies the operation of a specific logic that determines our ways of thinking about human perception and design.

In particular, the logic operating behind the seeing of a circle refers to a tendency, deeply entrenched in the structure of modern thinking, to "turn the pathways along which life is lived into boundaries within which life is contained." Ingold calls that tendency the "logic of inversion" and suggests that it is responsible for transforming our perception of the line from that of an active trajectory of movement into a dividing line between "what is on the 'inside' and what is on the 'outside'" (2008, 1796). Now put this "logic of inversion" into reverse and you get the second kind of logic, one that sees lines and force trajectories instead of boundaries and closed circles. This is the "logic of inhabitation," and it characterizes an "open" world—that is, a world that is inhabited rather than occupied.

I think this Heideggerian[1] methodological shift from "occupation" to "inhabitation" provides a useful and applicable metaphor for the comparative analysis of mark making as a form of enactive signification. It reminds us that what might seem to our well-trained eye to be deliberately imposed form can be seen from a different angle as an "open" and "formless" dynamic assemblage of lines. However, marks and lines of the latter sort no longer constitute boundaries of "closed" patterns but now construct indexical "surrogate structures" (Clark 2010) that open new possibilities for material engagement and signification. If the Blombos engravings, as I

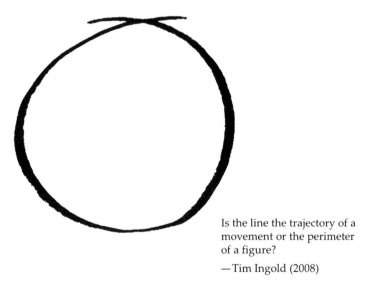

Is the line the trajectory of a movement or the perimeter of a figure?

—Tim Ingold (2008)

Figure 8.3
What kind of line? Redrawn after Ingold 2008.

suggest, are "formless," that is not necessarily because they lack intent; it may be because their "intent" is not about form but rather is about the forming process itself. More simply, I argue that MSA marks and lines *externalize nothing but the very process of externalization.* That is, they are enactive projections. It is important that this kind of enactive projection not be confused with conventional representational ideas about the "externalization" of human thought. There are no pre-formed ideas here, only potentialities or possibilities which are being loosely and flexibly objectified as part of an unfolding creative process. The role of this partial objectification is to enhance and make visible the situational affordances (Gibson 1977, 1979), freeing up but also restructuring the available cognitive resources (e.g., working memory). This constant transformation of what is out there to be perceived facilitates further projections. Over time, these projections may construct a creative ecology of recursiveness and metacognition. If the markings and engravings of the Middle Stone Age represent anything, it is the crafting and exploration of human perception within the changing limits and affordances of the new creative ecology. In contrast with other prosthetic gestures (e.g., tool use), the activity of mark making leaves a permanent perceivable dynamic trace that can be interpreted as an index of the crafting gesture. Crafting gestures will build the necessary scaffold for making a proper representational sign out of a mark. It is only then that the question of what this mark *stands for* arises. Further evidence on that can be found by looking at recent psychological studies exploring the effect of "scribbling" actions in the development of children's symbolic abilities. Such studies suggest that scribbling leaves perceivable consequences that act to stimulate further actions, which often result in self-organized changes in the scribbling action and recursion (Stamatopoulou 2011, 166). This point has received little attention from archaeologists who are inclined to dissociate early engravings from seemingly trivial non-representational activities such as doodling and scribbling. Yet I suggest that by looking at the impact of the constructive structure of scribbling in children we might gain some useful insights into how early mark making contributes to symbolic functioning. From an ontogenetic developmental perspective, young children's scribbling, as an embodied kinesthetic action, can also be seen as a "self-responding interactive system to one's own actions, subsequently imbuing scribbles to contain/express meaning" (ibid., 163).

Although MSA markings can certainly be seen as having an epistemic dimension and potentially also a semiotic one, I do not think they bear the right recursive semantic relation to social convention or activity to qualify as arbitrary symbols. Markings and mark-making activities are not reflective of pre-established traditions and symbolic schemes. Instead, they provide a possible and indeed a strong basis for enactive construction and establishment of such schemes. Whether, where, and when that happens depend on a variety of other reasons that, although associated with the mark-making process, are largely external to it. And it is my contention that it will take millennia of repeated experimentation and accumulated perceptual learning before humans will be able to develop conscious use of symbols—that is, meta-representation. This explains, to some extent, the far greater antiquity of mark making in comparison to image making or the appearance of the first notational marks. Nonetheless, even image making is essentially a complex form of mark making and participates in the same enactive logic of signification. This also means that the difference between the early-MSA markings and the magnificent depictions of the Upper Paleolithic is not one of representational ability and symbolic capacity but one of "pictorial skill" and "tectonoetic awareness" (Malafouris 2008a), which require explicit event-related timing control of the technical gesture in ways that we don't see in the case of the Blombos markings. In the case of "notation," mark making undergoes a further important transformation. Once the trace of a continuous gesture, it has now been fragmented into a succession of independent points or dots that constitute analogous inscriptive traces. Mark-making activities can now be described as what Kirsh and Maglio (1994) call "epistemic actions"—that is, as actions whose purpose is not simply to alter the world so as to advance physically toward some goal, but rather to alter the world so as to help make available a new way of thinking about it.

Learning to see: On being conscious of marks and pictures

I would like to point out three distinctive features that I found particularly striking about the image shown in figure 8.1e and again in figure 8.4. I will use the term *re-presentational economy* to refer to the efficiency with which this complex binding or combination of lines is presented to us as a piece of meaningful information—that is, as a picture. The second feature

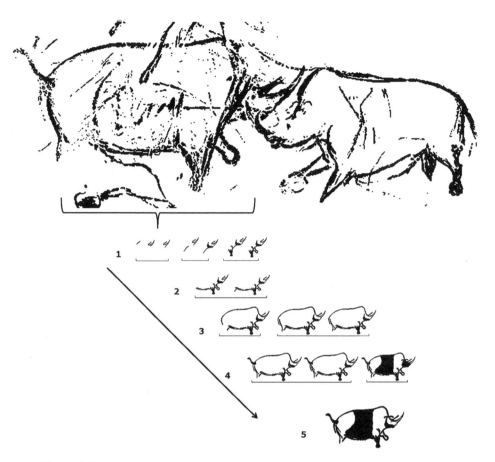

Figure 8.4
The making of a rhino. Redrawn and modified after Fritz and Tosello 2007.

might be called *re-presentational mobility*. I know that it may sound strange
to talk about mobility in reference to "parietal" art, but one of the defining
characteristics of the sort of things we call pictures is that they are primarily about movement and motion. Pictures are a very efficient way to trans-
fer information from one time to another. Take, for instance, our rhinos
from Chauvet. They were created more than 30,000 years ago in a very
specific and isolated locale, yet, thanks to modern representational technologies, they are with us today in a thousand different locales and forms
(e.g., printed on paper, stored in jpeg files, and projected on the walls of
classrooms and museums around the world). And I call the third and final
feature of picturing that I want to point out *re-presentational illusion*. Thanks

to the picture's cognitive economy, it takes us only a single look to identify, without any particular conscious effort, the rhinos. But there is more to this than a simple perceptual identification. Not only can we easily identify what this is a picture of; more important, we seem to possess some kind of intuitive grasp or feeling about the *what it is* that makes the image an image. We seem to have an immediate and genuine perceptual intuition that tells us that what we see depicted is not a real living animal, but rather a drawing of it—a representation of the animal as depicted on the walls of the cave by our Paleolithic ancestors. This may seem to be a trivial observation ("Of course this is not a real animal"), but only because we live in a particular historical situation in which images play a big part in our daily activities. The familiarity that enables us to identify, experience, and talk about an image as a representational entity also blinds us to the non-representational aspects of the image's cognitive life. The ease with which we "modern" humans process such identifications belies the complexity of the cognitive operations behind them and renders some especially interesting phenomena invisible. How can we draw out those hidden phenomena and processes?

A good way to begin would be to try go deeper into the phenomenology of human perception by asking some more basic and perhaps slightly more difficult questions. For instance, exactly how do we see, and exactly what do we see when we look at the picture of the rhinos? What does our experience of seeing really consist of? For one thing, we can easily identify the content of this picture: two rhinos confronting each other. For another, we can immediately recognize that these are not real rhinos but simply depictions of rhinos originally painted on the walls of the Chauvet cave. Is this printed depiction what we really see when we look at the drawing of our two rhinos? The answer is probably both Yes and No—Yes because, whatever the origin of this drawing, it is certainly a printed version of it on a page that we are looking at right now; No because if we turn to neuroscience for expert advice on the precise whereabouts and contents of our present visual exploration we are probably going to get an answer that goes something like this: What you really see when you look at this picture—what your experience of seeing really consists of—is essentially an internal representation of the retinal image of this picture that is automatically constructed and processed in the so-called V1 area in the occipital lobe at the back of your head. In other words, according to the neurocentric view of reality what you really see is not the picture before your eyes; it is instead an internal representation of this picture behind your eyes, in the visual center inside your brain, which is made of neural tissue and electrical impulses. It seems, then, that if we were to construct a simple diagram of the main representational stages responsible for our current visual experience we would end up with a scheme that can be described as, more or less, a representation (R6 in figure 8.5) of a representation (R5) of a representation (R4, R3, R2, R1). This chain of representational events is not without problems. It might well be, for example, that the so-called V1 area at the back of the head plays a crucial role in our visual experience, but I think we can all agree that our personal experience of seeing tells us a different story. Looking at the drawing of the rhinos, we do not feel that we

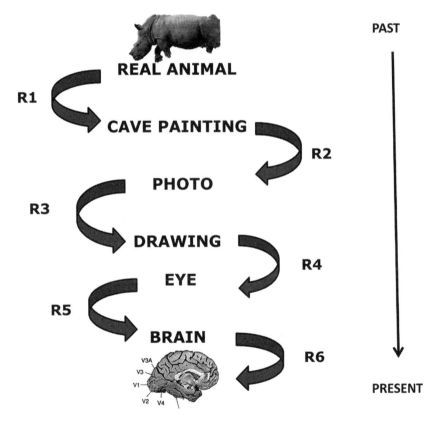

Figure 8.5
What makes a picture?

are seeing them inside our heads; we see them right where they are, printed on the page in front of us.

I believe that every image one encounters in the world embodies an analogous perceptual puzzle. The cognitive efficacy and the affective power of this perceptual trick emanate primarily from the creative conflation of appearance with reality that every picture is capable of bringing forth. However, we are rarely aware of this fact. This crucial property of every picture usually escapes our conscious attention. The reason is not difficult to imagine. We are immersed in a predominantly visual epistemic environment, and we are well trained from early childhood to create and make sense of visual phenomena of this "pictorial" sort. They often appear so familiar to us as "sense data" that we rarely find it necessary to stop and think about images as entities. We don't ask "What is this thing?" or "What does this thing do?" Rather, we immediately assume that we are dealing with some sort of visual representation and move on to more important questions about pictorial content, style, aesthetics, or possible symbolic meaning and intent.

This is the problem that I want to tackle in this section. The moment we look at the drawing of the rhinoceroses from Chauvet we have already identified it as an image. It is already a *picture of* something—that is, a *representation of* something. Of course, I do not deny the representational character of pictures altogether. Representation is part of what a picture does. However, I wish to object to the idea that representation is the only way, or the best way, to understand what images do. From a Peircian (1955, 1991) semiotic perspective, the representational character of the picture can be understood either in the sense of an *icon* (that is, a "motivated" sign that operates through some sort of visual resemblance) or in the "arbitrary" sense of a symbol (that is, a signifier that operates via convention). It is not the *iconicity* of those images that I am disputing here. No doubt the rhinos from Chauvet "look like" the real animals. But does this also imply symbolic intent or what Lewis-Williams refers to as an "already-existing mental symbology" (2002, 2003)? Contrary to what many researchers think, I believe that the answer to this question should be No. I think that to say that a painting from Chauvet "resembles" or "looks like" a rhinoceros does not necessarily imply that the painting also represents a rhinoceros in a concept-mediated manner. Iconicity does not, in itself, imply the existence of consciously manipulable content-bearing tokens, though it certainly sets up a visually stimulating channel of influence for their creation. It is one thing to ask what it means to see a rhino on the wall of Chauvet; it is another thing to ask what it means to see a rhino as a *representation* of a rhino. In other words, I am not questioning that the picture can be taken as evidence of *seeing* a rhino; I am, rather, questioning that it can be taken as evidence of a consciousness that represents or *stands for* something to be found beyond the depicted thing itself. The experience of pictures and the awareness of pictures *as representations* are not the same, and it would be a mistake to confuse them.

Upon that point, I suggest, instructive lessons can be derived from developmental studies of how young children of various ages interact with pictures. Such studies also suggest that having identified the pictorial content of an image does not necessary mean that one has also identified the relation of this image with the world (Costall 1997, 56; DeLoache 2004; DeLoache et al. 2003, 1998). It is interesting to note in this connection that even in a pictorially rich society such as ours the manual investigation of pictures (e.g., grasping) is routinely displayed by the majority of young infants, although it becomes increasingly less common as they grow older. According to DeLoache et al. (2003, 1998), manual exploration of pictures should be interpreted to reflect a conceptual deficit, not a perceptual deficit. For one thing, their research has ruled out the possibility that infants cannot distinguish depictions from real objects:

[I]nfants do not know *what kind of thing* a picture is. Not understanding the significance of two-dimensionality, they respond to realistic pictures as if they were three-dimensional objects. (2003, 117)

It takes several months of pictorial experience to appreciate the fact that a picture shares only a few of the qualities of its referent. By the time children are 19 months of age, they understand the difference between real objects and depicted objects and have fully adopted the convention that a picture is to be looked at in a particular orientation. Thus, instead of trying to interact directly with depicted objects, they seem to have a substantial amount of pragmatic knowledge about how pictures are used to recognize the pictures as means "of contemplation and communication" (ibid., 117). From an anthropological perspective, it is important to note that, as one would expect, this developmental pattern will be different in societies in which children receive substantially less exposure to pictures. We should also recall that even in today's educational environment it takes a child nearly a year to "realize that the word 'three' is a number without knowing the precise value it refers to" (Dehaene 1997, 107).

Though with present-day habits of seeing and perceiving it probably makes good sense to interpret the Paleolithic image as a representation *of* something, to assume uncritically that this was also how the image was experienced in its original context—which was to a large extent uniniti-ated, untrained, and naive about the psychological power of the image—is to take as our starting point what should have been the end of our analysis. I am not saying that the light projected from such an image in the past would have followed a different path than the physiology of our present visual system would allow. What I am saying is that if we could compare our *perceptual experience* of this image *in the present* with that of our Paleo-lithic ancestors *in the past*, I doubt that we would find much in common.

If the chief property that defines the picture as an object, and "picturing" as a process, is not that of representation, what else can it be? Again an interesting suggestion comes from Tim Ingold (1998, 183): In a non-modern context, activities whose products a modern observer might unproblemati-cally identify as representational art might well be "understood as ways not of representing the world of immediate experience on a higher, more 'sym-bolic' plane, but of probing more deeply into it and of discovering the sig-nificance that lies therein." But to exactly what would this "probing" or "discovering" amount in the case of early Paleolithic pictures?

The liberation of sight

From the perspective of Material Engagement Theory, I have already gone some way toward showing how to answer that question: Instead of think-ing in terms of static and closed pre-designed representational "objects," we should be thinking in terms of open enactive "processes." What does this mean, more specifically? Let us focus on the depiction of rhinos from Chauvet. What do we see when we look at that drawing? Recall also the reference to Ingold's example of the circular line in the preceding section, where it was suggested that, instead of the "closed," "delimiting" lines of modern "occupational" design, we need to discover something alive and "inhabitable" in the act of mark making (depictional or not). How can that be done? What could be our escape route from the representational predicament?

A good empirical starting point can be found in the recent work of Carole Fritz and Gilles Tosello, from which I borrowed the picture of the rhinos. Earlier in this chapter, discussing the M1–6 engraved ochre piece from the Blombos Cave, I said that microscopic analysis of the incised lines and their motion made it possible to discern the sequence of their manufacture (Henshilwood et al. 2009, 31–34). I argued that by focusing on the temporal unfolding of action we can transform what initially appears to be a static pattern (designed or not) into a dynamic process. What Fritz and Tosello (2007, 61–64) tried to do is very similar but on a different scale. In particular, they attempted to decipher the engraved or painted walls of Chauvet by focusing on the most basic visual element: the individual stroke. The forms and contours of the depicted animals are made of lines—a combination of charcoal drawing (modified using the fingers to blur or smudge the lines) and fine engraving—and the lines, in turn, are made of successive strokes. Taking the stroke as the guiding principle, Fritz and Tosello undertook a precise examination of each line by locating where the mark of a tool (e.g., flint, pigment, brush, or finger) begins and ends on the surface of the cave wall. This procedure, combined with overlays of a *relève* of the images and careful examination of the final movements of the tool on the basis of technical marks, enabled Fritz and Tosello to identify the direction of the execution of the layout and to reconstruct the actual sequences of the hand's movements and gestures. Since the order of execution of the various graphic elements (head, antlers, limbs, chest, and so on) necessary to make up the contour of an animal figure is usually not random, reconstructing the chronological sequences by examining the superpositions of tool marks reveals the temporality of gestures, which suggests, as I will explain below, the inseparability of hand and mind in the construction and perception of form. Tosello and Fritz's gestural reconstruction of forms and contours can be used to illustrate the proposed shift from "occupation" to "inhabitation." By identifying the whole sequence of movements or gestures, we can see what was initially a "closed" and "delimited" contour of two rhinos facing each other as an "open" process. On the basis of such a reconstruction, it becomes easier to adopt the perspective of the material-engagement approach and to follow the enactive thread it embodies. Seen from this angle, lines are no longer solid boundaries that separate domains of experience; instead they are *enactive signs* that can help us visualize the constitutive intertwining of cognition with material culture.

In this regard, it can be argued that in constructing images the Paleolithic person was not simply externalizing the contents of his or her mind but was exercising what Paleolithic people could do better than any other species: construct external patterns for sensorimotor engagement and let the resulting dense and reciprocal mind/world interaction construct their perceptual and experiential content. Early depictions are not material residues of human consciousness; instead they are open interactive possibilities or techniques through which a new consciousness of the physical world was attained.

Recall that in chapter 5, in discussing the emergence of symbolism in the context of numerical thinking, I argued for a similar enactive developmental process. I suggested that counting with the fingers or with clay tokens was an integrative projection between a mental domain of experience—the basic biological approximate "number sense" (Dehaene 1997)—and physical domains—e.g., fingers or clay tokens. Moreover, I suggested that it was the resulting structural coupling or blend that brought about the possibility of the meaningful cognitive operation we know as counting, and not some innate biological capacity of the human brain. At these early developmental stages (and this applies both from an ontogenetic and phylogenetic perspective), the use of body parts (e.g. fingers) or other available forms of external scaffolding had a dynamic and constitutive role for the emergence of arithmetic competence. The fingers did not stand for numbers, as it may seem; the fingers brought forth the numbers and made the manipulation of their properties visible and tangible. To illustrate this point from an archaeological perspective, I have used the case of the small clay tokens found all over the Near East from about 8000 B.C. According to Denise Schmandt-Besserat (1992, 161), these can be linked according to their shapes (cylinders, cones, spheres, etc.) with specific quantities of particular agricultural commodities—for example, the ovoid stood for a jar of oil. I argued that the partial counterpart projection that links (for example) an assemblage of five ovoids with five jars of oil did not necessary imply or presuppose the abstract notion of fiveness. At this early stage in the development of mathematical thinking, the concept of fiveness had not yet been separated from what was actually being counted. In fact, I proposed, the concept of fiveness could not have arisen as a meaningful notion if not preceded by such concrete integrative projections between experiential domains, such as that of an oil jar and that of an ovoid clay token.

I suggest that it is precisely such an enactive logic that characterizes, above anything else, the cognitive life of the Paleolithic image. In other words, those early pictures *bring forth* a new process of acting within this world and, at the same time, thinking about it. This thinking, however, should not be understood as thinking of the "higher-level" abstract or symbolic type. Rather, it should be understood in the more basic "lower-level" sense: as a new form of what Kevin O'Regan and Alva Noë call "active sensorimotor engagement" (O'Regan 1992; O'Regan and Noë 2001; Noë 2004). This enactive sensorimotor account has two major implications. The first is that it enables us to understand seeing and perceiving as a form of "skillful interactive engagement"—as a form of acting in the world rather than as a form of representing the world:

> [U]nder the present theory, visual experience does not arise because an internal representation of the world is activated in some brain area. On the contrary, visual experience is a mode of activity involving practical knowledge about currently possible behaviors and associated sensory consequences. Visual experience rests on know-how, the possessions of skills. Indeed, there is no "re"-presentation of the world inside the brain: the only pictorial or 3D version required is the real outside version. What *is* required, however, are methods for probing the outside world—and visual perception constitutes one mode via which it can be probed. (O'Regan and Noë 2001, 946)

The second implication, correlated with the first, is that once we recognize visual perception as a mode of probing the outside world rather than representing it, we may well also conceive the role of the Paleolithic image as a continuous prosthetic part of this probing mechanism, and thus a cultural extension of the visual brain. Although no symbolic cognitive requirement is needed, the emergence of the image made possible a new special kind of perception of the world that was not previously available. To understand the meaning of this statement, we have to understand the Paleolithic image as a perceptual device. This means that we have to account for how lines of pigment depict anything, rather than taking for granted that they do so.

To this end, an analogy may be useful: Whereas the toolmaker brings forth the possibility of a new form of tactile thinking, the image maker brings forth the possibility of a new form of visual thinking. As the liberation of the prehensile hand from the requirements of locomotion allowed it to become a privileged interface between the organism and its physical environment, so, it seems to me, the liberation of sight from its ordinary experiential requirements, in the case of the Paleolithic image, allowed the eye to gradually become the privileged interface of human perceiving. To appreciate this point better, one should bear in mind that our visual system has arms and legs, and that it has evolved so as to visually engage the world, not pictures (a remark originally made by the father of ecological psychology, James Gibson) (Costall 1997, 50). In other words, the effected "liberation of sight" emanates from the unique ability of the image to disrupt or question how the world is experienced under normal conditions. By that I do not mean that the image impinges upon the retina of the visual system differently than the rest of the world does. What I mean is that the image makes it possible for the visual apparatus to interrogate itself and thus acquire a previously unavailable sense of perceptual aware-ness. More simply, the image provides a scaffolding device that enables

human perception to become aware of itself. The materialization of such basic perceptual gestalten as those manifested in the use of occluding contours, in the use of canonical perspectives, or in the changes of component scale that characterize the Paleolithic image (Clottes 1996; Deregowski 1989, 1995; Halverson 1992a,b) testifies to this process of cre-ative engagement and of sensory learning. Those features offer us some of the earliest examples of moments in the engagement of mind with the world in which structures of mind meet and identify with structures imposed on materiality. Through the process of "picturing," the underlying mechanisms of human perception were transformed into an object *for* perception and contemplation. Those invisible mechanisms became per-ceivable visual patterns arrayed and combined in real time and space. In this sense, the image offered a new mode of epistemic access to the world of visual experience. The Paleolithic image maker constructed an external scaffold that made it possible to see and experience the world in ways that the physiology of the naked eye by itself did not allow. This scaffolding also made possible a new direct understanding of the human perceptual system and thus offered the Paleolithic person the opportunity to become, in some sense, maybe for the first time, the engineer of his or her own perception. The image, as is also the case with language, enabled humans *to think about thinking.*

Becoming symbol-minded

My aim in this chapter was to attempt a comparative prehistory of mark making, starting with the first engravings from the Blombos Cave and ending with the magnificent cave paintings of Chauvet. The discussion focused primarily on questions that so far have received little if any attention in the archaeological literature. The first question concerns how we understand the intentional link between the self and the engraving. The second concerns our understanding of the putative referential link between the engravings and their referents. The analysis revealed that a common feature of mark making is that it is able to transform humans' direct and immediate perceptual relation to the world. Such a shift in perception affords and stimulates new opportunities for enactive thinking. An interesting feature of this cognitive ecology of mark making is that it can leave persistent and visible material traces that alter the epistemic landscape of activity and thinking. Mark making can transform a thing into an object of one's attention. It can also turn such an object or surface into a sign. It is through the transformation of objects into signs, I argue, that symbols are brought into being. Whether the people who made and perceived prehistoric marks possessed a modern symbolic mind seems of less significance in this particular connection than the fact that they came to possess such a freeing device.

In this ~~page~~ chapter. Malafouris is buried in jargon. Could we understand him better if we expressed his ideas in ordinary language?

9 Becoming One with the Clay

Thrown on the wheel

Two questions that emerged repeatedly in different forms in the earlier chapters were a question about the intentional link between the self and material culture and a question about the nature of creative material engagement between persons and things. Underlying those questions is the theme or problem of agency, which I addressed in chapter 6 when presenting the hypothesis of material agency. For the purposes of this chapter, I find it useful to revisit agency in order to explore in depth the kinds of projections, relations, and bodily skills that are needed for transforming a collection of things and materials into something new. Of course, to explore those issues fully will require a different method and a different level of description than are afforded by long-term archaeological analysis. Thus, in this chapter I will be drawing primarily on ethnographic material I have been collecting while conducting fieldwork in pottery workshops in Greece in the last three years.

I have two aims in this chapter: to present a cognitive ecology of pottery making and to situate and explore the issues of self, agency, intentionality, and creativity I have identified above in an ethnographic setting in which the process of material engagement can be observed directly and thus can be used to illustrate the phenomenological requirements of some of the principal assertions I have made.

The phenomenological and ecological traditions in philosophy (e.g., Merleau-Ponty 1958; Polanyi 1958) and anthropology (e.g., Bateson 1973; Ingold 2000, 2007, 2008, 2010; Hutchins 1995, 2008, 2010a,c) have offered rich descriptive characterizations of embodied and situated action that provide a good starting point for approaching some of those issues. (See also Mauss [1934] 1973; Rogoff 1990; Rogoff and Lave 1984; Lave 1988; Lave and Wenger 1991.) However, phenomenology in itself generally lacks the contextual and historical specificity needed for a rigorous comparative anthropological approach to decomposing the unfolding of human creativity in action. Current theoretical and experimental paradigms in the cognitive sciences have approached and explored the experience and meaning of agency either at the level of the isolated individual or at the level of joint attention and cooperation between individuals. (See, e.g., Knoblich and Sebanz 2008.) No doubt this methodological decision is to a certain extent both sensible and productive, in view of its great potential for experimental implementation. Nonetheless, this decision also has limitations that threaten to obscure many important aspects of embodied experience and material engagement. Besides the usual problems of "ecological" and "cross-cultural" validity, the failure of most experimental designs to capture the relational character of creative agency threatens any conceptual, functional, or phenomenological account of expressive bodily action that fails to consider the analytical implications of context and interaction. The body, as Andy Clark's notion of "profound embodiment" nicely expresses, is "just one element in a kind of equal-partners dance between brain, body, and world, with the nature of the mind fixed by the overall balance achieved" (2008b, 56–57). Consequently, my approach to creative agency as a property of material engagement and mediated action avoids mistaking the properties of the system for the properties of the isolated body. Recall also that cognitive science, as Edwin Hutchins pointed out in *Cognition in the Wild* and as I have discussed extensively using different examples in the earlier chapters, has made a similar "fundamental category error." We are condemned to repeat this old "category mistake" each time we think that minds, bodies, and things can be understood in isolation or confuse their artificial analytic distinction for ontological reality. We also risk losing sight of some aspects of mind, agency, and action that archaeology and anthropology were meant to explain. The categorical separations mentioned above are popular and are somewhat useful for heuristic purposes. They become, nonetheless, badly misleading each time they become the natural measure of what counts as cognitive and blind us to the complex dynamic interactions between humans and things.

In this chapter, I attempt to marry cognitive ethnography and ecology with neurophenomenology in order to provide an integrative account of human creative agency. In particular, I seek to identify some of the empirical and conceptual challenges associated with the study of agency and to see how they can be understood if placed against the background of real-world practice and situated action, or if thrown on the wheel.

At the potter's wheel: Agency in action

Imagine a potter throwing a vessel on a wheel. (See also Malafouris 2008c.) Try to follow the complex orchestration of action throughout the stages of the creative process. Consider, for instance, the moment the potter's intention to act is formed. The potter's hands are skillfully sensing and grasping the wet clay so that the potter can decide precisely how much forward or downward pressure is needed to center the lump of clay on the wheel. What is it that guides the dexterous positioning of the potter's body? How do the potter's fingers come to know and control the precise force and position of the appropriate grip for the shaping of the vessel? The ease with which the potter seems to accomplish the task makes these questions even more fascinating. An experienced potter does not have to attend to the movements of his or her hands. Most embodied motor control is non-conscious and automatic. Moreover, the potter seems to possess the tacit knowledge needed to do what is necessary to construct a vessel without necessarily being able to communicate or explicitly reflect upon what this know-how consists of. In the case of embodied skill, explicit representational thinking and verbal description are not needed and can hardly capture the phenomenological perturbations of real activity or the reciprocality between the crafted and the crafter. This observation becomes particularly visible in the context of learning and skill acquisition, where the affordances of the technique of throwing a lump of clay on a wheel must be discovered each time, in real time and space, through extensive apprenticeship. Someone may object here that all these questions have little to do with agency, action, and creativity as such, and that instead they relate primarily to embodied sensorimotor control, tacit knowledge, and practical skill. But this is precisely the assumption that I want to question in this book by collapsing the divisions between perception, cognition, and action and rejecting the methodological separation between individual creative experience and the material mediational means and collective structures through which it becomes realized. I will

Figure 9.1
A potter's wheel. Photo by author.

Figure 9.2
An expert potter at work. Photo by author.

Figure 9.3
Stages of creative material engagement. Photo by author.

show that underlying the effortless manner in which the potter's hand reaches for and gradually shapes the wet clay is a set of conceptual challenges to the embodied nature of action and the meaning of agency that go well beyond mere motor control processes.

But let us return to the question that was raised at the beginning of this chapter: What kinds of projections, relations, mental, or physical representations are needed for the enaction of the creative performance by which an amorphous mass of clay is being transformed into a new object? Traditionally there are two major ways of answering questions of this sort. According to the first approach, which might be called "externalist," the focus of analysis would be the final end of the creative process—that is, the products of creativity. According to the second approach, which might be called "internalist," we should be looking at the beginning of the

This is what we are encouraged to avoid.

creative process. To put it more simply, we should be searching for the origins of creativity inside the mind/brain. Creative experience is now a quality of mind rather than a perceivable property of things, materials, and techniques. Similarly to my discussions of tool making and mark making in chapters 7 and 8, the "internalist" approach sees the creative process as something that exists entirely inside the potter's head. Whether one speaks of "combinational," "exploratory," or "transformational" creativity (Boden 2010), understanding the nature of the creative processes is based on information processing and computation.

On the analytical level, each of the two approaches has its merits. The "externalist" approach has the advantage of bypassing the uncertainty and the fluidity of the creative process The products of creativity stand still long enough to be treated as "objects," and objects can be perceived with sufficient clarity to be named, classified, compared, and interpreted. However, simply looking at the products of human creativity as static entities not only fails to accommodate the temporal dynamics and the embodied aspects of the creative process; it also fails to accommodate the cognitive, social, and cultural effects of the products themselves. Similar problems appear in the case of the "internalist" perspective. From the perspective of neuroscience, the only way to deal with the inextricable intertwining of the fingers, the body, and the task environment is to erroneously assume that the potter's fingers do nothing but to execute the orders of the potter's brain. (For a more detailed argument see Malafouris 2008c.) It is within the brain that the ultimate source of the creative agency that guides the effortless movement of the potter's hand as it reaches for and gradually shapes the wet clay is to be found.

In contrast to the above "internalist" or "externalist" ways of looking at human creativity, I want to explore a number of different conjectures about the emergence and locus of creative agency. I start with a very simple observation that comes naturally from the perspective of Material Engagement Theory but which most studies of human creativity fail to consider, or are unable to consider: The problem of creative agency in mediated action is that the purity of action and causality is lost. The potter's thinking, enmeshed in the mediated practice that we call pottery making, cannot be as rigidly defined and circumscribed as traditional cognitive theories of creativity might prefer. The being of the potter is co-dependent and interweaved with the becoming of the pot. This also means that the constituents of the creative process are not to be found before or outside the throwing or the shaping of the pot. The constituents of creativity are *in the throwing, in the shaping*. The creative process becomes, then, a binding of materials—a dynamic flow of the organic into the inorganic that can be understood as a new or "surprising" blend of ingredients that can act or be acted upon.

How should we proceed, then? First, I propose, we should get rid of any *a priori* assumption about causal or agentive hierarchy of potter's brain/ body/wheel/clay. Similarly, in terms of cognitive topology—that is, the question of where those cognitive processes reside—we should begin from a locationally uncommitted position. We should assume, instead, that every mental recourse needed to grow a vessel out of clay may well be extended and distributed across the neurons of the potter's brain, the muscles of the potter's body, the motions of the potter's sense organs, the affordances of the wheel, the material properties of the clay, the morpho- logical and typological prototypes of existing vessels, and the general social context in which the activity occurs. The components mentioned above can be broken down further, but none of them should be allowed to deter- mine the contours of activity in isolation.

Based on that foundation, we can then attempt to build a *chrono- architecture* of creative action. In particular, I suggest that in order to under- stand creative agency we have to understand the temporality of creative action, and in order to do that we have to understand its constitutive web of causal antecedents. This temporal stratigraphy of creative action will enable us to understand what causes the potter's intention to grow a vessel out of clay. It will also give us an opportunity to test our suspicion that this growing may involve or demand a number of "neural activations" or "presentations" but few if any "internal representations" in the computa- tional sense of the word. Our working hypothesis would be that first the hand grasps the clay in the way the clay affords to be grasped, then the action becomes skill, skill selects and effects results, and creative agency emerges from the results that matter.

But first some further clarifications about the concept of agency are in order.

Agency and "sense" of agency

To start with it, would be useful to differentiate from the outset between agency and "sense" of agency (Tsakiris et al. 2007a,b; Tsakiris and Haggard

2005a,b; Gallagher 2005). Agency, or the agentive capacity, is something
we share with other animals. In contrast, "sense" of agency—that is, conscious agency—is distinctively human. Although a nut-eating chimpanzee,
for example, can certainly cause the nut-cracking act, like any other tool-
using animal it lacks a sense of agency or authorship, and it may lack any
true understanding of causality. (For good discussions of causal cognition
in non-human animals, see Visalberghi and Tomasello 1998 and Penn and
Povinelli 2007.) To the extent that the sense of agency involves not only
generation and awareness of voluntary behaviors but also conscious perception of the effects of such behaviors and a sense of responsibility, I
consider such a sense of agency to be uniquely human. Similarly simple
inanimate material things and artifacts can be argued to have agency
although they certainly lack any "sense" of it. As was discussed in chapter
6, the notion of material agency is somewhat artificial, or even a misnomer,
but it helps us to get on with our question and to avoid the well-entrenched
anthropocentric biases.

This distinction between agency and "sense" of agency may seem trivial
from the perspective of psychology and neuroscience, which are preoccupied with dissociating the bodily and intentional aspects of agency and
discerning their neural correlates. In fact, many cognitive neuroscientists
and psychologists think of agency more as an illusion or a confabulation
than as a *bona fide* mental state (see Wegner 2002, 2003, 2004), and therefore much of the empirical research has focused on the unconscious initiation of voluntary behavior rather than on the subjective experience of
agency. But differentiating between agency and "sense" of agency may
make a huge difference in the context of real-world experience and situated
action, where "much of what matters about human intelligence is hidden
not in the brain, nor in the technology, but in the complex and iterated
interactions and collaborations between the two" (Clark 2001a, 154). It is
one thing to say that only humans have a sense of agency (that is, an
ability to refer to oneself as the author of one's own actions); it is another
to say that only humans are agents or have agency in the sense of being
able to initiate causal events with intentional character. In the context of
material engagement and situated action, to ask whether we can account
for the sense of agency either by looking at the realm of voluntary body
movement and motor control or at the realm of intentionality is to ask
the wrong question. The above distinctions are important for the brain's

time, not for an activity's time, and thus can be misleading when applied in the natural setting of mediated and situated human activity.

Thus, what differentiates the agency of the potter from the agency of the clay or the wheel through which agency is enacted is not the fact that it is the potter, rather than the clay or the wheel, that is actually the cause of the sequence of actions that produces the vessel—in fact, many resources (physical, mental, or biological) are needed for the enaction of this creative process. What makes the potter an experiencing enactive agent is the fact that, in contrast to the clay and the wheel, the potter possesses a "sense" or an "experience" of agency. In other words, it is not causality but consciousness that differentiates the human sense of agency from agency proper.

A further distinction is that between the feeling of agency in the sense of being conscious of causing something to happen and the feeling of agency as being conscious of being in control of one's own actions. Being in control does not necessarily makes you the cause of a happening. Thus, we may also differentiate between the feeling of agency (the experience of being in control) and judgment of agency (the explicit conceptual attributions of whether one produced an action or caused an effect) (Synofzik et al. 2008a,b).

These are important distinctions not only from a philosophical and phenomenal perspective but also from an evolutionary and developmental perspective. If we accept that agency is a basic and evolutionary primitive capacity that we share with other species, and we acknowledge the inextricable linking of agency, action, and embodiment, then understanding how human conscious agency emerges may be the key to understanding the origins of human consciousness and self-awareness. To this end, our starting point cannot be that of conscious agency as an innate property of humans. The feeling of agency should be seen as an emergent property of action rather than as an *a priori* possession of the embodied biological organism. From this perspective, achieving agency is a process inseparable from becoming human.

"I did it": The problem of agency

If we accept the unity of agency, embodiment, and mediated action, we can reduce the problem of agency to two major questions. The first *ambiguous use of this word,*

concerns the authorship and causality of the doing. It is the question about who or what is causing the act (in this case, the making of the pot). That is different from asking who or what feels as, or believes to be, the cause, or author, of the doing. For example, a potter might well think of himself as the author of and the main cause behind the production of a pot, but a careful analysis of the operational sequence might reveal a far more complicated picture of the causal chain and of the nature of causes and agents involved in the act. The second question concerns causality, time, and sense of agency. It is a question about how we go about delineating the appropriate time scale and thus the portion of phenomenal time against which the causal contributions (human or non-human) will be evaluated. Depending on the scale of analysis, there are two major ways to approach these questions.

modular and hierarchical again

From a macro-level perspective (characteristic of anthropology, archaeology, social sciences, and other disciplines that seek to define agency at the point of intersection between individual and society), one could focus on describing the activity chain in material procurement and manufacture, identify the technical choices responsible for the making of the pot, then ask who or what is responsible for those choices. The archaeologist Sander van der Leeuw writes:

Suppose the potter has in mind to make a jar to pour water from. That imposes certain minimal constraints both on the shape of the vessel (a high centre of gravity, a handle, a spout) and on the characteristics of the vessel wall (it has to be waterproof). The tools he or she uses impose other constraints: on a potter's wheel, ceteris paribus, there is more potential variation in shape than when the potter is using a mould, for example. Other constraints derive from the nature of the kiln and fuel: if the kiln can be fired above 1050°C, the potter can usually ensure impermeability of the vessel wall by vitrification, but if that is not the case, the vessel either has to be glazed or impregnated with another substance to make it impermeable. Yet other constraints derive from the availability of raw materials: if the clay is fine and plastic, and the potter is working on a wheel, the clay may be used as is, but if it is found with larger non-plastic admixtures, it will have to be purified. On the other hand, if the potter is working in a mould, the "rougher" paste may be used, and a fine clay will have to be mixed with some form of temper, etc. (2008, 237)

At first sight, according to the above observations, it may appear that it must be the potter to whom we should attribute responsibility for the activity, but a closer look in the sequence of events will reveal that discerning the causal links and determining the direction of causality is not as

Both levels of causes are equally acceptable but in different contexts and for different purposes.

direct and straightforward as we might initially think. The wheel may seem to serve as a passive means or instrument for the potter's manufacturing purposes, but in any stage of the dynamic operational sequence it can also subsume the plans of the potter and itself define the contours of activity.

From a micro-level perspective (characteristic of psychology, neuroscience, philosophy, and other disciplines that seek to define agency as the universal and strictly mental property of human action), one could instead attempt to break down the activity of manufacturing pottery into the greatest possible number of component voluntary acts (e.g., squeezing, supporting, and controlling the shape of the vessel while it is plastic, turning the pot in the hands, cutting, scraping, smoothing, and so on) and look inside the potter's brain for the "internal" mental mechanism and/or neural network responsible for "executive processing," planning, ordering, and behavioral execution.

Despite differences in the temporal and the spatial scale of the activities the micro-level approach and the macro-level approach attempt to describe, they seem to share a commitment to the potter's potentiality of being a causal agent. Let us call this deeply rooted agency judgment the "I did it" stance. It is important to note, as I mentioned in the preceding section, that this agency judgment should not be confused with the feeling or sense of agency, and that the potter seems to be committed to this "agency judgment" early in the sequence of events, long before the vessel is actually produced. By that I mean, on the one hand, that the potter knows that he possesses the requisite knowledge, skills, and technical means before the action itself, and, on the other hand, that the potter is ready to project or otherwise use this self-as-agent knowledge or component of his acquired personal identity to fill in or interpret the gray zones in the phenomenal experience of action. An example from Gregory Bateson (1973, 318) should serve to bring all this into better view:

Consider a man felling a tree with an axe. Each stroke of the axe is modified or corrected, according to the shape of the cut face of the tree left by the previous stroke. This self-corrective (i.e., mental) process is brought about by a total system, trees-eyes-brain-muscles-axe-stroke-tree; and it is this total system that has the characteristics of immanent mind. . . . But this is *not* how the average Occidental sees the event sequence of tree felling. He says, "*I* cut down the tree" and he even believes that there is a delimited agent, the "self," which performed a delimited "purposive" action upon a delimited object.

By the same token, although the potter may again be entirely unaware of how or when his brain and body are making all these fine small decisions, when confronted with his final product he is, in most cases, going to answer the agency question, with ease and certainty, as follows: "I did it." In fact, this tendency or "proclivity for constructing self-referential narratives" (Graham and Stephens 1994, 101) is a common feature not only of our experience of action (allowing us to explain our behavior retrospectively) but also of our agency judgments in contexts in which we are "participant observers" rather than the subjects of the action.

However, the fact that common sense rarely demands that we question our sense of agency does not mean or warrant that it should be treated as an innate and homogeneous universal human attribute. Clearly the idea of the isolated human agent that acts upon the inert world can hardly be accommodated, or even make any sense, in a number of ethnographic contexts in which the categories of persons and things are inseparably interlinked (Gell 1998; Bird-David 1999) and in which notions of "agency" and "causality" lose their traditional meanings. The case of Melanesia offers an excellent example of how action and doing, although associated with a basic sense of body ownership, may not necessarily be associated with a sense of authorship. In Melanesia, as the anthropologist Marilyn Strathern observes in her ethnography of the "Melanesian person" (1988, 273), "agents do not cause their own actions; they are not the authors of their own acts. They simply do them. Agency and cause are split." (See also Busby 1997; Ramsey 2000.)

These considerations can become clearer if we attempt to look more closely at what lies behind the agency judgment and, more precisely, where the macro-level and micro-level approaches differ in respect to this judgment.

At the macro level, the agency judgment seems to be a product of many cultural and social factors that involve a great deal of higher-level cognition. For instance, elaborate capacities for planning, decision making, behavioral control, and memory are activated and contribute to the experience of agency. All these capacities become realized in specific cultural and social contexts and thus are situated and mediated processes. Although a macro-level approach is much better equipped to capture the totality of practice and thus the possible respective contributions of these various elements to the experience and constitution of agency, the complexity of the event so revealed presents serious analytic obstacles.

Too simple, and too confident.

At the micro level, the agency judgment is sensed like a feeling, or rather the aggregate of feelings, experienced during the long sequence of activity. The question is no longer about who made the pot; now it breaks down to a series of micro events (voluntary or non-voluntary, self-generated or externally generated, and so on) that constitute the operational sequence of the pot's production. Though we are now dealing with scales of time and activity that are more easily controllable and that may be experimentally replicable, we still cannot escape the complexities of action. Methodologically, the only way to deal with the inextricable dynamic coupling between the potter's fingers and body and the task environment is to assume, wrongly in this case, that the potter's fingers and body do nothing but execute the orders of the potter's brain—more simply, to assume that it is inside the head that we should be looking for the true source of agency. The above inevitably shifts the locus of agency from the realm of embodied action to the realm of motor control and/or intentionality. That is a shift from the *performative* realm of situated action to the *representational* realm of brain processes and mental action. Thus the question of agency ceases to be a question about the phenomenology of action and becomes a question about the neural correlates of action. Agency is no longer an "enactive" problem; it is transformed into a "computational" or "representational" problem. I do not mean to deny that an intricate computational problem may well arise for the brain the moment the potter touches or is touched by the clay; I simply mean to emphasize that part of the problem's solution is offered by the clay itself, without any need for mental representation (Brooks 1991). As the enactive perspective on mind and action reminds us, "cognition is not the representation of a pregiven world by a pregiven mind but is rather the enactment of a world and a mind on the basis of a history of the variety of actions that a being in the world performs" (Varela et al. 1991, 9). Unfortunately, this part of the cognitive equation is left out each time we decide to reduce the coexistence of the active and receptive elements of practice to a mental process inside the head.

How do we account for this agency-attribution problem in the context of situated action? One way to answer this question is by following Daniel Wegner's formulation about "apparent mental causation" (2004, 654) and seeing the problem of agency as an "illusion" whereby people tend to experience conscious will, and thus agency, quite independent of any actual causal connection between their thoughts and actions. This is not, however, because, as one would have expected from an embodied perspective, the potter's hand often has reasons of which the potter's mind is not aware and which the clay may resist or accommodate. According to Wegner, it is instead the potter's brain that has the reasons, in the form of a "readiness potential" (RP), at least 350 milliseconds before the potter's conscious awareness of the wish to act. (See Libet 1985, 1999.) There is much we do not yet know about the nature of agency, but I doubt that the way to tackle the question of agency is simply by looking deeper inside the brain.

Another way to answer the question about "agency attribution" is to adopt a phenomenological enactive approach. This may allow us to understand the dynamic coupling between the potter and the task environment as a dance between equal partners, the potter leading the dance at some times and the potter's "situation" leading it at other times (Malafouris 2008c; Pickering 1995). Unfortunately, although a good phenomenological description can pull us inside this seamless flow of activity and agency, when we cut the flow and press the question of agency our inner Cartesian self or "interpreter" wakes up to take control of the situation. To be sure, many external factors (from the texture of the clay and its physical properties to the material affordances of the tools available to the potter) may be allowed to influence or determine some parts of the action. But final responsibility rests with the potter. It is the potter who "really" decides what sort of vessel to produce, and thus it is the potter who is to blame if the vessel produced is of low quality or if it explodes during firing—a price that not only potters but people in general are willing to pay for the sake of free will or the "illusion" thereof (Wegner 2002, 2004).

The question of agency may seem innocent enough in the context of pottery making, but it carries some major ethical and social implications of which we should be constantly aware. Consider, for instance, the question whether people or guns kill, as expressed by Bruno Latour (1999, 177):

What does the gun add to the shooting? In the materialist account, *everything*: an innocent citizen becomes a criminal by virtue of the gun in her hand. The gun enables, of course, but also instructs, directs, even pulls the trigger. . . . Each artifact has its script, its potential to take hold of passerby and force them to play a role in its story. By contrast, the sociological version . . . renders the gun a neutral carrier of will that adds nothing to the action, playing the role of a passive conductor, through which good and evil are equally able to flow.

Both the materialist account and the sociological account fail to recognize that agency "resides in the blind spot in which society and matter exchange properties" (ibid., 190). It was precisely that conviction that led Latour to rediscover the notion of "mediation" originally developed by Lev Vygotsky (1978, 1986) and the Russian activity-theory school. Neither the isolated gun nor the isolated individual can bear the responsibility for the act of killing. The responsibility lies, on the one hand, in the way those two agents come together to construct a new hybrid agent—the gunman—and, on the other, in the socio-technical network that supports and makes possible such a meeting. Action involves a coalescence of human and non-human elements, and thus the responsibility for action must be shared among those elements (ibid., 180–182). No distinctions between human and nonhuman entities can be sustained in terms of agency.

In the remainder of this chapter I will argue that neither the micro-level approach nor the macro-level approach is sufficient to capture the phenomenon of agency in its totality and thus to answer our question of agency attribution. To understand agency we need to understand the meaning of mediation and recognize the priority of action and material engagement.

Agency in pottery making

As the sociologists John Law and Annemarie Mol (2008, 57) are careful to observe, questions about agency "are usually asked as part of a search for explanation. What is the origin of an event?" The problem with agency in mediated action is that the purity of action has been lost. The potter, by being a potter, possesses a different body. The common distinction between an internally driven biologically constituted physical body and an externally imposed technologically enhanced enculturated body collapses. The potter's body, being messy and leaky (Clark 1997), cannot be as rigidly circumscribed as a body observed in a controlled experimental setting would have been. Entering into the cultural realm of skill and practice that we call pottery making, the potter's body becomes more than a body; it becomes a *situated* body.

However, "being situated" does not simply mean that the potter is located somewhere, for the same reason that "being embodied" does not simply mean that the potter has a body. Instead, "being situated" means that "situatedness" *matters*. It means, in other words, that the situation (environmental, technological, cultural, or social) can shape and/or become part of the embodied thinking process. By the same token, "being embodied" means that "embodiment" *matters*. It means, in other words, that the body shapes and/or becomes part of the process (Gallagher 2005; Chemero 2009). Two major premises follow the claims made about the meaning of "situatedness" and "embodiment": that different bodies think differently and that situatedness presupposes embodiment. In other words, the way our brains and bodies are put together and are situated in different activity contexts is not irrelevant either to how the mind works or to how agency is experienced and constituted. There are significant physiological and experiential differences involved in being a potter, and those differences differentiate the experience and thus the agency of the potter. More simply, the phenomenology of a simple bodily movement in the context of pottery making may differ a great deal from an identical bodily movement that happens in a different context. There are very few points of resemblance—although kinematically they may seem identical—between the potter's hand touching the clay and the experimenter's hand engaged in an voluntary or involuntary key press in the context of a neuroimaging study. What in the latter case seems to be a controlled hierarchical sequence of causal events is in the former case more a motivated sequencing of relational events that often take on a life of their own. By the same token, the meaning of situated agency is that of an agency extended, mediated, and thus shaped by the instruments, tools, media, and technologies that characterize a particular situation. This also means that a great deal of ordinary experiences and thoughts—thoughts about who is the cause of what, who is controlling what, and who owns what—become seriously enmeshed. Indeed, "trying to *separate cause from effect inside the loop of pottery making is like trying to construct a pot keeping your hands clean from the mud*" (Malafouris 2008c, 25). Is there any way out of this?

Time, agency, and material engagement

One way to proceed is to take time as our starting point and, by cutting across the scales of time, try to develop a detailed temporal anatomy or chrono-architecture of the act. Constructing such a chrono-architecture would be essential for understanding how the sense of agency is generated.

A precondition of that is that we carefully define the portion of time encapsulating the event we want to describe and then decide whether this portion of time constitutes a meaningful event in the larger enchainment of events constituting the activity we seek to explain. This is necessary if we want our account of the causal hierarchy of events not to trivialize the complexities of their cognitive ecology.

Now not only does time become important but the experience of time has changed. As the "intentional binding effect" (Haggard et al. 2002a,b) suggests, the experience of agency links actions and effects across time, producing a temporal attraction between them. In other words, time is shorter—or at least is experienced as such—during the enaction of the operational sequence that will bring about the pot. Simple judgments of whether or not an action caused a specific sensory effect are now distributed among a number of participating elements and resources that extend and mediate the prosthetic body. Higher-order thinking and memory must now come into play in order to disambiguate the situation.

To see that better, let us focus on the basic distinction between the sense of agency and the sense of ownership (Gallagher 2005; Tsakiris and Haggard 2005a,b). "Sense of agency" refers to the potter's feeling that it is he who is moving his hands and spreading, pounding, and shaping the clay. "Sense of ownership" refers to the potter's feeling that it is his hand that is moving. Many recent studies have shown that the sense of agency ("I am the author of the act") and the sense of ownership ("This is my body") dissociate. For instance, experiments by Tsakiris, Prabhu, and Haggard (2006) and by Tsakiris and Haggard (2005a,b) provided empirical evidence that our sense of ownership might be generated by afferent sensory feedback (as in involuntary acts, passive movements, or sensory stimulation) and that the sense of agency might be generated by efferent signals (as in voluntary acts). Comparisons of active and passive movement define agency as an additional component over and above the normal experience of one's own body. Recent evidence suggests that agency transforms the experience of the body. A number of studies have compared the effects of voluntary action and passive movement on proprioceptive awareness of one's body. Agency generally enhances both spatial and temporal processing of proprioceptive information (Tsakiris et al. 2005) and modulates time perception (Haggard et al. 2002), and voluntary action appears to integrate distinct body parts into a unified awareness of the body (Tsakiris, Prabhu, and Haggard 2006). While this approach treats the sense of agency as an addition to the sense of body ownership, it also predicts a two-way interaction between the two, such that the addition agency will change the experience of ownership and, at the same time, this altered sense of ownership can change the very experience of agency.

? sensation
may not
does not imply cause

But how do these experimental observations figure in the real-world setting of mediated action and pottery making? On the one hand, pottery making, when seen from what previously was called a macro-level perspective, can certainly be classified as a voluntary rather than a passive act—the potter certainly intends to perform a sequence of goal-directed bodily movements aimed at producing a pot. On the other hand, when seen from a micro-level perspective, pottery making, as a demanding skilled action, can be described as a dynamic chain of voluntary, passive, and reflexive action elements. One implication of that for the above-mentioned distinction between agency and ownership is that, in the case of mediated action, the way our sense of agency and the way our sense of ownership correlate or dissociate during the course of action are not fixed and stable but vary depending on different temporal scales and stages of action (before action, during action, after action, and on the degree of expertise in performing that action, novice or skilled). For example, although an experienced potter immersed in the shaping of a vessel will often report that the sense of ownership (that is, the sense that it is his hands that touch and move the clay) is experienced throughout the activity, the sense of agency (that is, the feeling that it is he that is causing the movement) is often disrupted. In other words, it is one thing for the potter to feel that it is his body that moves and thus to have a sense of ownership for it; it is indeed another thing to say that the potter is always conscious that it is he that moves his hand, as in the case of skilled action.

Meanwhile, the acquisition of a new skill is generally associated with a decrease in the need for attention leading to the development of automaticity. However, automaticity in the sense of effortless performance of a task is usually associated with a sense of loss of agency or loss of self—a feeling of being immersed in, rather than causing, the act. The opposite phenomenon can be observed in novices at the early stages of skill acquisition. Practice effects (reorganization, redistribution, scaffolding—see Kelly and Garavan 2005) can affect or contribute to the sense and feeling of agency. A similar observation about the effects of practice and time can be made for the distinction between the feeling of agency (the experience of being in control) and judgment of agency (the explicit conceptual attributions of whether one did produce an action or cause an effect) (Synofzik et al. 2008a,b). The sense of agency (feeling and judgment) will differ between, say, time t_a and time t_b, where t_a refers to the first minutes of action, when the potter attempts to center the lump of clay on the wheel, and t_b to the final minutes, when the pot has almost been shaped and the potter adds the final touches. The above observations suggest that the potential contributions of the different stages of the action sequence to our sense of agency would be different.

In the time and space of pottery making, afferent sensory feedback (visual and proprioceptive/kinesthetic information that tells that potter that he is moving) and efferent motor commands conflate and operate synergistically. The potter's sense of agency may be generated by efferent signals that send motor commands to the muscle system, but we should keep in mind that these efferent signals derive from the potter's sense of the clay (Malafouris 2008c).

Situated bodies and the feeling of clay

The ongoing controversies about agency in psychology, anthropology, and social science derive in part from the fact that agency has many different manifestations and that those manifestations cannot be captured in their totality at any single analytic level or in any single experimental setting. It is customary that an attempt to explore the nature of human bodily experiences will use the Western skin-bounded individual as the principal analytic unit. In other words, the basic assumption is that any bodily dimension on which one may choose to focus can and should be accounted for entirely by physiological processes occurring within the organismic skin bag. As a consequence, on the one hand, some of the most interesting aspects of our bodily physical, social, and technological constitution remain neglected; on the other hand, important new findings about the neural correlates of human embodiment and the nature of agency as a bodily experience fail to influence and engage with the anthropological perspective. No doubt the fluid nature of these extra-organismic factors and forces means that they cannot be easily accommodated by conventional experimental protocols (imaging, clinical, or behavioral). By the same token, localizing the experience of agency in the brain fails to account for real-world action. However, I have argued in this chapter that some of the most interesting questions about agency in the context of embodied mediated action (Wertsch 1998) can be found only "in the wild." Using the example of the potter's wheel as an illustration of such a bio-interface, I have reviewed some important findings about the different facets of agency, placing them against a natural and ecologically valid context of mediated action. My aim has been to contribute toward the grounding in action and the cultural embedding and possible cross-cultural evaluation of current findings on agency. I have argued that the important question is not how to separate the pre-reflective aspect of bodily experience from the reflective aspect (Legrand 2006), or how to separate the active element of action from the passive element, but how to put them back together and account for their ongoing and irreducible causal coupling. It remains to be seen whether agency can offer a way to bridge the neural and cultural correlates of our bodily selves.

What is the difference between "caused by" and "constituted by"? Is the first one way, and the second two way?

10 Epilogue: How Do Things Shape the Mind?

and how does the mind shape things?

In this book I have sought to expose some of the prejudices, and have questioned some of the preconceptions, that are prevalent in our ways of thinking and in our ways of doing cognitive archaeology. In a radical and perhaps for some a puzzling manner, I have tried to reformulate the question of human cognition in a manner that will challenge us to reassess our intuitions about what counts as a cognitive process. Drawing on the general hypothesis of the extended mind, I have depicted human cognitive processing as a *hylonoetic field*—a mindscape quite literally extending into the extra-organismic environment and material culture. This is not simply the view—much more compatible with common sense—of a cognitive agent that depends heavily on external props and tools, as when we use pencil and paper to do a large multiplication. Such a view would simply recognize the importance of mediation in human thinking—a proposal already put forward, most famously by the psychologist Lev Vygotsky, in so-called cultural-historical activity theory, decades before the cognitive revolution of the 1960s began.[1] Nor was it simply my intention to rehearse the well-known criticisms of the computational ideal of mind as an algorithmic, rule-governed, and sequential representational engine (an ideal that is characteristic of "good old-fashioned artificial intelligence"). Instead, the chief innovation of this book lies in the more radical idea that human cognitive and emotional states or processes literally comprise elements in their surrounding material environment. According to the hypothesis of the constitutive intertwining of mind with the material world that I set out in chapter 4, our ways of thinking are not merely causally dependent upon but *constituted by* extracranial bodily processes and material artifacts. Some people may find this stronger version of extended-mind theory hard to defend and difficult to embrace fully. Such a reaction is, of course, to be anticipated, because once the conventional demarcations of skin and skull are removed it appears that conventional cognitive science loses the analytical purity of its object of study. More important, as the philosopher Alva Noë points out (2009, 185), in view of the influential if not foundational role that the classical "internalist" plays in cognitive sciences, "whole research programs have to be set aside." But what may appear to be a loss from one point of view may be an important gain from another. In any case, it is important to remember that, radical as it may be, the approach to the study of mind that I have set forth in this book emerges as a legitimate and natural ontological possibility once we "rid ourselves of the idea that our brains are somehow touched with the magic dust that makes them suitable to act as the physical machinery of mind and self, while the non-biological stuff must forever remain mere slave and tool" (Clark 2007b, 118).

But why does it matter, for archaeology, where the boundaries of mind are drawn? Why should we abandon the well-entrenched view of human cognition as a strictly or primarily intracranial affair? How far are we willing to go with the idea of extended cognition? Precisely how does extended-mind theory relate to the study of material culture? In this epilogue, I will offer a few summary remarks on some obvious and some less obvious ramifications that Material Engagement Theory has for the archaeology of mind and for the study of material culture.

Methodological ramifications

What do cognitive archaeology and anthropology gain by adopting the perspective of Material Engagement Theory? Starting at the level of method, one immediately obvious consequence, and one potential payoff, is nothing less than a reconfiguration of the intellectual landscape inhabited by the archaeology of mind. (See also Wheeler 2010b; Knappett 2005.) The spreading of mind transforms material culture into an important cognitive extension, not in some symbolic or secondary representational sense, but in a more immediate and direct way. As a result of this shift, we need no longer divorce thought from embodied activity, as we need no longer adopt the stance of methodological individualism and thus reduce the complexity of an extended and distributed cognitive system to the isolated brain of a delimited human agent. Embracing the relational ontology of Material

Engagement Theory means that archaeology no longer condemns material culture to a life outside of cognition proper. Past ways of thought are not just expressed in material culture; now they can also be seen as partly *constituted by* material culture. Ben Jeffares makes a similar argument about the role of early stone tools in shaping human thinking. Turning around the traditional view of archaeological evidence as the secondary visible product of some pre-existing invisible cognitive skill, Jeffares (2010, 504) proposes that we view this evidence as "one half of a feedback loop" between cognition and material culture, so that the archaeological record no longer looks like a black box but "rather like a clock with some of the mechanisms available for inspection, even while some elements remain hidden" (ibid., 505). The archaeologist, thus, is freed from the "unhappy state of being a frustrated mentalist condemned to materialism" (Knappett 2005, 169). Mind and matter are one and can be approached and studied as such. This puts material engagement at center stage in the study of mind and cognitive evolution.

At the same time, a cognitive archaeology that is no longer committed to an "in-the-head" representational ontology of mind is better protected from the Darwinian-inspired intellectual syndromes of "Darwinitis" and "neuromania," or from "Darwinized neuromania." The latter terms have been recently employed by Raymond Tallis (2011; for a full review of the argument see Malafouris 2012) to criticize the currently dominant tendency to explain everything about human life in terms of biological evolution and the brain. Taking proper measures to avoid the trap of neurocentrism is particularly important in the developing field of neuroarchaeology, in which there is a strong temptation to locate all that really matters in human cognitive evolution inside the head. (See Malafouris and Renfrew 2008; Malafouris 2008, 2009; Renfrew et al. 2008.) Material Engagement Theory and the Extended Mind Hypothesis remind us that brain imaging, no matter how convincing and enchanting a statement about the inner workings of the human brain it might be, should under no circumstances be confused with a technology able to delimit the realm of the "truly cognitive." The notion that we are (rather than simply have) a brain is mistaken and should be abandoned. We are more than a brain. *The mind is more than a brain.*

One could even argue that the excavation trench objectifies and brings to light—at a different temporal and spatial scale—what functional

Agreed, but again so what?

magnetic-resonance imaging (fMRI) fails to capture and visualize about human cognition.

How?

Focusing on the cognitive life of things also fosters a new concern with the way boundaries (ontological and epistemological) are drawn within archaeology and beyond. Boundaries have a great effect on our understanding of who we (as cognizers) are, and thus on our conceptions of agency and persons. Collapsing the boundaries between the "inner" and the "outer" offers archaeology and anthropology a new window onto the human mind, but it also leave us with the important epistemological challenge of taking material culture seriously and developing common relational ways of thinking about the complex interactions among brain, body, and world. Of course, this challenge extends beyond the field of cognitive archaeology and qualifies material culture as an analytic object for the sciences of mind: The study of things matters not simply because things can spread the properties of mind to the external world (and possibly vice versa), but also because things are capable of changing the established ways in which these cognitive properties are approached and defined. This implies that traditional ways of doing cognitive science must change.

Like This vvv

vvv

Obviously, rethinking the boundaries of the mind has major implications for our understanding of the role of things far beyond the context of cognitive archaeology and human evolution—in technology, in design, in critical theory, even in ethics. (See, e.g., Verbeek 2011; Bennet 2010, 2004; Brown 2001, 2003.) As minds and persons spread, so does freedom and moral agency. As the philosopher of technology Peter-Paul Verbeek points out in his book *Moralizing Technology*,

Things

Just as intentionality appeared to be distributed among the human and nonhuman elements in human-technology associations, so is freedom. Technologies "in themselves" cannot be free, but neither can human beings. (2011, 60)

What are we, then? Exactly how might Material Engagement Theory help us to rethink the traits that mark the origin of our species? Exactly how might it advance the ongoing debate over the making of modern humans?

What is it to be human?

Think of Darwinian evolution. So far as its basic biological endowment is concerned, *Homo sapiens*, like any other species, came into being over time

[handwritten marginalia: "confuses With What we are Not we do -"]

through a process of adaptation and natural selection. Yet, in contrast with all other species, *Homo sapiens* did not stop there. It became the only species to transform its biology by manufacturing a distinctive, collective, self-aware cognitive realm of social interaction and material engagement. Does this mean that some of Darwin's insights into the cognitive continuity between humans and animals, and their modern re-instantiations in neo-evolutionary theories, might be wrong? So far as the hybrid bio-cultural realm of human mind and consciousness is concerned, the answer is probably Yes. Darwinian accounts are far from being the last word on what we are. In many important ways, as Tallis rightly points out, "we are as remote from animals when we queue for tickets for a pop concert as when we write a sublime symphony" (2011, 151). The question, however, remains: How did *Homo sapiens* get to be so different from other species? Above all, what is the difference that makes the difference?

The image of human intelligence that emerges from the discussion in this book is clear enough: The human mind is a product of biological evolution as much as it is an artifact of our own making. Humans, Jonathan Kingdom has argued, became different by becoming "artefacts of their own artefacts" (1993, 3). Nicole Boivin (2008, 192–193), discussing Kingdom's hypothesis, agrees that "human technological achievements have not only defined but also shaped our species." More recently, John Hoffecker has set out to explore how humans' effective use of ever more refined forms of artifacts and technologies provided a medium for externalizing their minds and redesigning themselves. Although his approach is firmly grounded on the "internalist" computational ideal of cognition that I have criticized heavily in this book, Hoffecker explicitly acknowledges the conflicting character of human lives in that they are rooted in the natural world and yet quite different from it (2011, 171). In particular, he proposes that humans have "redesigned the environment, both abiotic and biotic, in ways that have completely altered their relationship to it as organic beings" (ibid., 7). For Hoffecker, the distinctive feature of human cognitive evolution is the unprecedented complexity of the human "super-brain," which he sees as a product of the gradual externalization of thought and symbolic expression and as exhibiting "properties that are unknown or had not been evident in organic evolution" (ibid., 77). Clearly, then, the idea of becoming human by way of self-engineering and transformation is not something new or strange. (See also Gamble 2007.) Nor, as has been

[handwritten marginalia in right margin: "? intellectual evolution"; "? + culture"]

[handwritten marginalia at bottom: "Human identity in prehistory."]

nich constructi

noted many times in this book, is this idea peculiar or restricted to the fields of archaeology and anthropology.[2]

Not only, then, does the idea of humans as a "cyborg" and "self-made" species come very naturally from the perspective of Material Engagement Theory; in addition, it must be rather important. Yet the same idea can be extremely puzzling if seen against the background of many taken-for-granted evolutionary ideas in archaeology. Why is that? One part of the answer comes from Tallis' criticism of Darwinitis: "We are held captive by a picture of ourselves from which we cannot escape because it is written into the very language in which we think about our nature." (2011, 184) The other part of the answer can be found in my discussion in earlier chapters of how prevalent conceptions about mind's location, together with a flawed ontology of material culture, have largely undermined archaeology's contribution to the debate over the causes of human unique-ness. As I have described, if one accepts the current orthodoxy about the epistemological status of the archaeological record, especially insofar as it is relevant to questions of human cognition, there is little direct material evidence that an archaeologist could use to substantiate any suspicion or intuition he or she might have against the dominant "computational" and "neo-Darwinian" trends and ideas, which, as Tallis points out (2011, 182), "are now woven into the very language in which we are invited to think about ourselves."

How can human nature best be understood, then? What might be a good archaeological example to focus upon in order to better illustrate "our fundamental cyborg humanity" (Clark 2003)? Two notions with long tradi-tions in archaeology and human evolution can be used to that end: *Homo faber* and *Homo symbolicus*.

Homo faber

As I discussed briefly in chapter 7, neo-evolutionary accounts in compara-tive cognition tend to discard tool use as a hallmark of human cognition. On that construal, any argument for cognitive discontinuity that contra-dicts the long-held evolutionary ideal according to which the cognitive abilities of human and nonhuman animals exist along a "continuum" is ill-conceived and anti-Darwinian. But I hope I have made it clear that if the notion of *Homo faber* became obsolete in archaeology and comparative cognition it was because of three common erroneous prejudices: that mind and body are fundamentally separable, that the mind has executive control over the body, and that our interactions with the world don't affect or transform the presumed ontological separation and asymmetry of mind over matter in any significant sense. Given these deficiencies, and the way they seem to encapsulate both Descartes' dualism and "Darwin's mistake" (Penn et al. 2008), one can explain the recent neo-evolutionary trends.

To remedy these deficiencies, I suggest, we should look at the making and the using of tools as means of understanding the nature and the scope of embodiment in our species' development. Tool use offers new possibilities for cognitive extension. It affords new forms of embodied praxis, and thus opportunities for the development of the experience of agency and self-awareness.

I am not saying that only humans make and use tools. Other animals seem capable of doing so to some degree. What I am saying is that there is more to the notion of *Homo faber* than the sheer variety and sophistication of human technologies. What truly stands out is the profound complexity of our engagement with tools and technologies. There simply is no ontological offense or epistemological mistake involved in saying that we humans "alone" define and shape ourselves by the tools we make and use. In the words of Andy Clark (2003, 136–137), we are just "shifting coalitions of tools." But why is that? What does that co-dependency imply for our species? Should we perceive early stone tools as capable of transforming and extending the cognitive architecture of our hominin ancestors? Would it be safer, instead, to continue looking at them as merely passive "external" mechanical aids for cutting meat, with no real cognitive bearing on the developmental trajectories of our species?

I hope to have demonstrated that the former view emerges as plausible. Even the skeptical reader, who may still find the pill of extended-mind theory too bitter to swallow, must admit that recent studies exploring the effects of the temporary or permanent incorporation of inanimate objects and tools into the "body schema" (Cardinali et al. 2009a,b; Farnè et al. 2007; Farnè and Làdavas 2000; Iriki et al. 1996; Berti and Frassinetti 2000; Maravita et al. 2001; Holmes and Spence 2006; Holmes et al. 2004; Maravita and Iriki 2004) offer plenty of evidence as to how even the simplest acts of material engagement can change the way the human brain perceives the size and the configuration of body parts. Also relevant here is a

comment by Carl Ratner (1991, 50) on the importance of material mediation in human action:

> [Tool use] fosters consciousness by imparting a sense of mastery of things. The tool
> user develops an attitude that he can use things to serve himself. To use objects is
> to impart a use to them, to make them do what they don't do naturally, to make
> them "for-oneself" rather than "in-themselves." This stimulates purposiveness and
> intentionality.

Comparative archaeological study of tool use can help us answer questions about the primacy of embodiment and about how basic capacities
for embodied action relate to our capacities for reflective reasoning and
abstraction. This brings us to symbolism.

Homo symbolicus: When is a symbol?

There seems to be little doubt that humans are the "symbolic species."
(See, e.g., Deacon 1997.) The human ability for signification and symbol-
ization expands and reshapes the "cognitive ecology" of thought and
communication, liberating them from the immediate experiential constraints of time and space. But *when* is a symbol? When does a simple mark
become an arbitrary sign for people to think with? I touched on these
questions in chapters 5 and 8, where I said that there are two principal
ways in which the above questions can be understood. According to the
first (common among archaeologists), 'when' refers to a point in time. That
is, it relates to the origin and development of human symbolic behavior,
which remains contentious. (For recent reviews see Henshilwood and
d'Errico 2011; Henshilwood and Dubreuil 2011; Wynn and Coolidge
2010.) The second way to understand our questions has a deeper ontological sense; 'when' now refers to what it is that transforms some-*thing* (for
example, an engraved mark or a shell bead) into a symbol. I have argued
that archaeology has made much progress with the first question. Yet it
still struggles with the second. Why is that? I have discussed several major
shortcomings. Here I will summarize those that truly stand out.

Intentionality

One particular weakness, stemming from the Cartesian way of thinking
about how minds relate to things and bearing directly on the issue of
symbolism, concerns "intentionality," "causality," and "action." The main

assumption behind this drawback amounts to the following: Intentional states are *of* or *about* things, whereas things in themselves may not be *of* or *about* anything. Things, on this view, may constrain or become the objects of human thought and action, but they do not actively participate or shape it in any real sense. Things, in other words, are simply "products" or "passive recipients" of human intention and creativity. They may "stand for" something, but in themselves they can "do" nothing; they have no life of their own.

For Material Engagement Theory this is the wrong way to approach the question of artifact metaphysics. It implies what Tim Ingold (2010, 97) calls the "hylomorphic ontology" of mind over matter, which mislead us to read creativity "backward." What this backward reading means, to use the example of tool making, is that we start with tools in the material world and then trace their origin in the knapper's intracranial mental world. A characteristic example of this tendency can be seen in the way many archaeologists continue to interpret the form of bifacial tools as exhibiting "a mental template imposed on rock." (For a recent example see Hoffecker 2011, 4.) On that view, tools reflect arbitrary preconceived designs that were imposed on materials to produce standardized forms (e.g., a handaxe). Ingold (2010, 92), drawing upon the work of the philosophers Gilles Deleuze and Félix Guattari, rightly suggests that we replace this hylomorphic ontology with "an ontology that assigns primacy to the processes of formation as against their final products, and to the flows and transformations of materials as against states of matter." But how can that be done in practice? How can we best approach intentionality, and infer the direction of motion and causality among the various ingredients of action (brains, bodies, materials, tools, surfaces, markings)? Ingold proposed two simple rules of thumb that might offer a useful starting point: to follow the materials (2010, 94) and to look between lines and the surfaces on which they are drawn (2007, 2). More remains to be done, however. Trying to sketch Material Engagement Theory's conception of "action as thinking" and "thinking as action," I argued that in order to break away from this dominant "hylomorphic" trend we need to replace it with an "enactive" one. I proposed enactive signification as a model akin to the underlying principles of Material Engagement Theory and able to highlight the relational properties of human creativity. Thus, instead of seeing in the shaping of the handaxe the execution of a preconceived "internal" mental plan, we should see an "act of embodying." In tool making, most of the thinking happens where the hand meets the stone. There is little deliberate planning, but there is a great deal of approximation, anticipation, and guessing about how the material will behave. Sometimes the material collaborates; sometimes it resists. In time, out of this evolving tension comes precision and thus skillfulness. Knapping, then, should be seen more as an active "exploration" than as a passive "externalization" or "imposition of form." The knapping intention is essentially constituted through an act of collaboration between human and material agency, one of the earliest manifestations of human "tectonoetic awareness" (Malafouris 2008a,b). This argues against the "hylomorphic" ontology of "imposing form" *on* matter and supports a "hylonoetic" (from the Greek *hyle* for matter and *nous* for mind) ontology of thinking *through* and *with* matter.

Choosing the right boundaries for our unit of analysis is important. As Edwin Hutchins (inspired by Gregory Bateson) points out, "every boundary placement makes some things easy to see, and others impossible to see" (2010b, 706). Then what constitutes a meaningful boundary in the prehistory of human signification? One way to tackle questions of this relational sort—a way I have employed repeatedly in this book—is to extend and expand the conventional demarcation lines of skin and skull into the world. A more radical way, also employed often in this book, is to abandon the logic of "boundaries" and "delimiting lines." Things may not think and feel, but neither do brains. Instead, it is humans that do the thinking, and humans, we should not forget, are the product of "worlds ambiguously natural and crafted" (Haraway 1991, 149). The latter also means that the human brain, with its properties, is an artifact of culture as much as it is a product of human biology. The "inner" mental domain, far from neutral and pure, is already shaped by and inseparably linked with the "external" domain. As the philosopher Anthony Chemero suggests from the standpoint of a radical embodied cognitive science, "It is only for convenience (and from habit) that we think of the organism and environment as separate; in fact, they are best thought of as forming just one nondecomposable system." (2009, 36) One major postulate that Material Engagement Theory shares with the view of "enactivism," besides that of "sense making," relates precisely to a point made by Evan Thompson and Mog Stapleton (2008, 26):

The spatial containment language of internal/external or inside/outside (which frames the internalist/externalist debate) is inappropriate and misleading for understanding the peculiar sort of relationality belonging to intentionality, the lived body, or being-in-the world.

Human beings, as living organisms, constantly enact the world they live in. Thompson and Stapleton, citing Martin Heidegger, also remind us that "a living being is 'in' its world in a completely different sense from that of water being in a glass" (ibid., 26). Nonetheless, it is also the case that often the problem we face in archaeology is not about if or where we should draw a line but instead about how to make sense of the different kinds of lines that people have drawn. This brings us to the second major shortcoming of the archaeology of material signification: the fallacy of representation.

The representational fallacy

A common fallacy in the way archaeology usually makes sense of signification and symbolism is what I have called the representational fallacy. It can take different forms, and can operate at different levels, but essentially it involves an attempt to account for the relationship between cognition and material culture by way of some representational mechanism. I have argued that the representational approach to mind-world interaction simply leaves out many phenomena that are of great value to the study of cognition and material culture.

There is, however, an alternative. Instead of approaching material culture as a mere vessel or "external storage medium," we should look at things as a fundamental cognitive resource in their own right. Although we may well be able to construct a mental representation of anything in the world, the efficacy of material culture in the cognitive system lies primarily in the fact that it makes it possible for the mind to operate without having to construct a mental representation—that is, *to think through things, in action, without the need of mental representation.* For Material Engagement Theory the world of material things can be seen as its own best representation (Brooks 1991). The brain need not waste its time producing internal replications of what is directly available in the world. The artist's sketchpad isn't just a storage vehicle for externalizing pre-existing visual images; it is a tightly coupled and intrinsic part of artistic cognition itself (Clark 2001a, 147–150).

In this book I have set forth a vision of the cognitive life of things that encompasses much more than a simple reconfiguration or spreading of our modes of mental encodings (from in the head to in the world). It is a vision inspired more by the distributed and compositionally plastic image of the potter skillfully engaging the clay to produce a pot than by the linear architecture of a Turing machine. In the former case, "it may make little sense to speak of one system's *representing* the other" (Clark 1997, 98). Although the function of extra-neural recourses may well be a representational one, such recourses can also take on a radically enactive, and thus non-representational, cognitive function. We have seen some good examples of this in technologies and artifacts—for example, a Linear B tablet—that seem to fall under the category of "external symbolic storage" and therefore can be approached from a representational stance. Even in those cases, an important type of cognitive event should not be neglected: A cognitive system does not make use of external representations only for what they *stand for*, but also for what they *are*. I demonstrated in chapter 4, using the case of the Linear B tablets, that thinking is not simply a matter of reading a series of meaningful linguistic signs inscribed on the surface of a tablet, but also a matter of meaningfully engaging with the tablet itself as a material sign. As Hutchins remarks, many people wrongly assume that "the status of external representations qua representations" is unproblematic. "But what makes a material pattern into a representation," Hutchins asks, "and further, what makes it into the particular representation it is? The answer in both cases is enactment. To apprehend a material pattern as a representation of something is to engage in specific culturally shaped perceptual processes." (2010c, 429–430) As I said in my discussion of the origin of symbolic numerical thinking in chapter 5, the concept of number does not have initially to be stored in a verbal format, or to activate the brain regions we traditionally associate with language; it can be grasped directly by engaging the material world. This is possible because of the basic property that constitutes above anything else the cognitive efficacy of material culture: A thing can act as its own best representation. Even if we agree that the understanding of "external representations" and the origins of symbolism are what really matters in the archaeology of mind (something I seriously doubt), the question we should ask is not about *when* humans begun to represent one thing with another but rather about *when* and *how* they *became fully aware* of their doing so. In other words, we should be focusing on meta-representation or on meta-cognition (that is, thinking about thinking).

A particularly telling example was considered in chapter 8: How do ochre engravings or lines of pigment come to depict anything? Answering a question of this sort did not help to advance our knowledge about what those engravings or cave images might have meant, but it certainly helped us to understand *how* they meant. The attempted comparative prehistory of mark making proposed a shift in perspective from the usual question ("What kind of mind was needed to made those marks?") to "What kinds of minds are constructed by making and perceiving those marks?" The crucial question, I suggested, was "To what extent could the human ability for external representation and meta-representation have emerged or developed in the absence of those marks?" I proposed that the principal role of early mark making, and later of imagery, was to provide a scaffolding device that enabled human perception gradually to become aware of itself. That is, it enabled humans to *think about thinking*.

Unlearning modernity

How is all this relevant to the question of the origin of so-called modern human cognition?[3] Despite many archaeologists' confidence in the notion of a "modern mind," one could question the existence of such an identifiable human core that is sufficiently stable and enduring to be used as a single universal designation for the cognitive status of our species. In particular, I think the concept of "modernity" is too vague, underdetermining, and potentially question-begging to serve as a justification for such a transition in the mental profile of our species. I do not wish to question or deny the existence of a distinctly human mind; I only deny that such a mind exists as an essence—that is, as a set of fixed and biologically determined capacities whose origins can be explained by appeal to some fortuitous genetic mutation and whose products can be seen reflected in the archaeological record in a series of preconceived fixed behavioral traits, as the notions of cognitive or behavioral modernity seem to imply. Against that view, I hope, I have demonstrated in this book that the human mind exists as a historically situated actuality—that is, an emergent product of complex ecological relationships and flexible incorporative forms of material engagement.

Whichever list of early modern human behavioral traits one chooses, Eurocentric or not (see Henshilwood and Marean 2003), and whichever precise model of change one subscribes to, gradualistic or sudden (see d'Errico and Stringer 2011), there are two major and deeply entrenched implicit assumptions behind the debate over the origin of modern human intelligence. The first is that the brain's anatomy and structure stayed the same after the main speciation event, whenever and wherever we decide to situate that. The second is that material culture, though it can be seen to express possible changes (genetic or other) in human cognition, has no causal efficacy with respect to these changes and no direct relationship with the mechanisms that underlie these changes, which should be sought in the domain of human biology. This means that the role of objects and things in the overall evolutionary scheme remains instrumental and their status remains epiphenomenal. Things are treated as a difference that doesn't make a difference. For instance, changes in technology and innovations in materials such as those discussed in chapters 7 and 8 may suggest cognitive changes, such as enhanced working memory, inventiveness, recursion, and creativity, but ultimately they depend on, and must have originated because of, some sudden genetic mutation, such as the FOXP2 gene associated with the development of human ability for speech and language (Enard et al. 2002). This attitude, as I have pointed out, is symptomatic of a more general tendency in the mainstream cognitive sciences to leave material culture outside the cognitive equation proper. I consider this epistemic neglect of the object one of the most pressing problems in the study of mind.

From the perspective of Material Engagement Theory, none of the assumptions mentioned above can be sustained. For one thing, what is it about the human brain that remains the same? Although recent DNA studies (Mellars 2006a,b) suggest that the human genetic structure doesn't seem to have changed much, the human brain almost certainly has. As was discussed extensively in chapter 3, cognitive development is no longer seen as the progressive unfolding of information laid out in the genome. The traditional view of a one-directional flow of cause and effect from genes (DNA) to RNA to the structure of proteins which they encode gives way to a subtler picture in which physical, social, and cultural aspects of environment and behavior can trigger the expression of genes (Westermann et al. 2007, 76; Quartz and Sejnowski 1997; Gottlieb 2003, 2007). If the intrinsically plastic human brain undergoes constant change subject to various developmental, environmental, and cultural factors, it cannot simply be assumed that "anatomically modern human intelligence" refers to a fixed and stable speciation event. As we saw in chapter 3, for Material Engagement Theory the hallmark of human cognitive evolution is metaplasticity—that is, ever-increasing extra-neural projective flexibility that allows for environmentally and culturally derived changes in the structure and functional architecture of our brain.

This brings us to the second of the previously stated assumptions concerning the epiphenomenal role of material culture in human cognition. As I said above, a major methodological implication of Material Engagement Theory is that the observed changes in the material record should also be seen as indicative of possible plastic transformations and reorganizations in the human cognitive architecture, rather than as simply expressing pre-existing cognitive changes or magical genetic mutations. The direction of inferred causation must change. I am not assuming that the possession (or lack thereof) of a certain technology or material innovation correlates directly or causally with the possession (or lack thereof) of a certain capacity or ability. The proposed inversion and complication in the direction of a causal arrow is not meant to imply a new form of simplistic determinism. Material culture is not a cause in the linear mechanistic sense; it is a cause in a dynamic ontological sense. It does not replace one efficient cause with another; rather, it redirects efficient causes relevant to one another. This redirection does not necessarily mean that any change in the material record coincided precisely with fundamental changes in human biology. On the contrary, it is meant to remind us that not only does it *require* intelligence to make and use a tool, but "a tool *confers* intelligence" on those (human or nonhuman) "lucky enough to be given one" (Dennett 1996, 99–100).

The real challenge for cognitive archaeology is not to establish the material correlates of human "modern" cognitive capacities by way of some pre-fixed behavioral trait list. The objective should be to discover the trajectories of co-constitution and explore the types of information flows that each coupling enables in any particular time and space. This also means that not just any "coupling" or "link" will do. Any instance of tool use and manufacture may share a number of elements in common, so far as this dense coupling is concerned, but it also has important differences.

One challenge for the archaeology of mind is to try to understand when the coupling takes just the right form. It is at this point that cognitive, social, demographic, and technological components become interlinked in such a way that one component defines and is defined by the others. I propose, then, that moving beyond grand narratives about the origin of human modernity should be the first step toward a convincing explanation of human cognitive becoming. This *unlearning* of human modernity will clear the field of study of many unnecessary assumptions and free us from many unproductive dichotomies and strong asymmetrical biases.

Although separating biology from culture sometimes makes good ana-lytic sense when one is approaching some archaeological problems, it should not be confused with an ontological statement about the way things are. Nor should this artificial separation be allowed to obscure the question of how cognition and material culture are combined and bring each other into being (Renfrew et al. 2008; Gibson 1996; Knappett 2005; Gamble 2007). Human cognitive lives are "bio-psycho-social totalities" (Knappett 2005, 169) rooted in the natural world and yet quite different from it, which is also why I think Tallis (2011) is right to insist that humans cannot be seen as parts of nature *in the same way* that other animals are parts of nature, and that Darwinian natural selection cannot explain how human consciousness could have come into being.

The need arises to come up with new explanations about the making of the human mind that are not based on clean delimiting lines and clear-cut evolutionary stages but instead are sensitive to the complexity and the emergent character of the phenomena they seek to account for. Clearly the notions of cognitive and behavioral modernity, which still dominate much of current archaeological thinking, are not able to serve the above purpose. Not only is the concept of cognitive modernity poorly equipped to capture the embodied, collective, and situated character of human cognition and consciousness; it often forms a pervasive epistemological barrier. As a result, I believe that the notion of "modernity" has long outlived its useful-ness and should be abandoned. (See also Shea 2011.)

In this book I have tried to show that new things, and new ways of making and relating to things, are not simply products of cognitive change but also constitutive aspects of the constantly changing and extended anatomy of human intelligence. (See also Jordan 2008.) In a way, then, one could argue that innovations in early material culture are important not as evidence of human modernity but as evidence *against* it. Material innovations—from the Oldowan chopper to the Acheulean handaxe to the Blombos engravings and shell beads to depictional cave art to the more recent symbolic or "exographic" (Donald 1991) technologies, such as calendars, writing, and numerals—are neither accomplishments of the hominin brain nor symbolic statements about the presence of a new human representational capacity and thus the origins of human modernity. Instead, they are *opportunities* for the hominin brain. New forms of material engagement have given us a window onto a whole new set of skills and ways of thinking that afford great variation and flexibility. Of course, only some of those potential skills and ways of thinking may have actually been realized, and even fewer may have survived in the visible archaeological record. The important challenges for cognitive archaeology and philosophical anthropology are to look at people and things as dynamical interfaces and to try to understand their cognitive life in terms of mutual permeability, binding, and structural coupling rather than separation.

At the tip of the blind man's stick: "We have never been modern"

To pave the way for the main thesis of this book, I used the classical phenomenological thought experiment of the blind man with a stick (Merleau-Ponty 1958; Polanyi 1958, 1962; Bateson 1973) to raise an old but fairly intractable and timely question: Where does the blind man's self end and the world begin? Where do we draw, and on what basis can we draw, a delimiting line across the extended system that determines the blind man's perception and locomotion?

I said that I had chosen the example of the blind man's stick as my point of entrance to the realm of material engagement mainly for two reasons. The first was that it provides a good analogy for the profound plasticity of the human mind. The example of the blind man's stick reminds us that it is in the nature of human intelligence to remain always amenable to drastic deep reorganization and thus, potentially, to a constant pre-modern or non-modern state of change and ongoing cognitive evolution. As I mentioned in the preceding section, it strikes me as plausible, if not likely, that to an important extent, if I may borrow the words of Bruno Latour (1993), "we have never been modern." The human mind remains an incomplete and unfinished project, in some sense blind and yet "profoundly embodied" (Clark 2007, 279–280)[4]—that is, capable of flexible deep incorporation of new sensory and cognitive structure.

At the same time, the ontological unity of the blind man and the stick offers a powerful metaphor that enables us to conceptualize minds and things as *synechēs* (continuous). It is especially in the latter sense that the example of the blind man's stick encapsulates the spirit of Material Engagement Theory and thus can be used to summarize my overarching thesis in this book. The summary goes as follows:

> The functional anatomy of the human mind (which includes the whole organism, that is, brain/CNS and body) is a dynamic bio-cultural construct subject to continuous ontogenetic and phylogenetic transformation by behaviorally important and socially embedded experiences. These experiences are mediated and sometimes constituted by the use of material objects and artifacts (e.g., the blind man's stick) which for that reason should be seen as continuous, integral, and active parts of the human cognitive architecture.[5]

To make better sense of this assertion, it is important to keep in mind that, whatever actual form the "stick" might have taken in the history of our species, its primary function was that of a *pathway* instead of a *boundary*, or else a *thing* instead of an *object*. Through the "stick," the person feels, discovers, and makes sense of the environment but also enacts the way forward. And it is in that capacity that it can be seen as an exemplar of what in this book I have called the process of material engagement.[6] Think of the way the stick shapes the mind of the blind man. It is not simply a matter of expanding the boundaries of his "peripersonal space" (that is, the space surrounding the body). Neither is it simply a matter of delimiting a new range of action possibilities, dependencies, or sensory hierarchies (for example, substituting vision for touch). The stick does more than that. It becomes an interface of a peculiar transformative sort—what might be called a brain-artifact interface.

Generally, the word 'interface' is used to denote any mediation (natural or artificial) that enables, constrains, and in general specifies communication, flow, and interaction between entities or processes. The human body (or parts of it), language, and gesture are some obvious examples of such an interface, but one could think also of more distinctive comparative examples—for example, a rake used by a monkey in captivity to retrieve distant food rewards, or a stick used by a chimpanzee to dig for food in the wild (chapter 7 above; Iriki 2005; Iriki and Sakura 2008). However, in the context of Material Engagement Theory the notion of the brain-artifact interface has a more specific meaning—a meaning closely associated with the concept of metaplasticity that was discussed in chapter 3. In particular, it is introduced to denote the kind of material assemblies or enactive cognitive prostheses that enable the configuration of a dynamic alignment or tuning among brain, body, and culture. This sort of bidirectional dynamic coalitions can take many different forms—e.g., hard-assembled (stable) or soft-assembled (reconfigurable), epistemic or pragmatic, invasive or non-invasive, representational or performative, transparent or non-transparent, constitutive or instrumental—and can be empirically observed through diverse examples, including early Paleolithic stone tools, the most recent brain-machine interfaces that enable a monkey or a human to operate remote devices directly via neural activity (Nicolelis 2001, 2003; Donoghue 2008), and the QWERTY keyboard of the laptop computer I used to write this book. Yet, despite the multiplicity and variation in form of those ontological coalitions of brains, bodies, and things, they delineate and occupy the hybrid "lived" space at the intersection of "personal," "peripersonal," and "extrapersonal" space. (See Cardinali et al. 2009a.) I propose that, when seen in this broader context of metaplasticity, where mediated action takes place and where neural and cultural plasticity meet and exchange properties, the main transformative effects of things in human cognitive life and evolution can be, very broadly, put in three major and closely interrelated categories: mediational, temporal, and plastic.

Mediational effects

I start with the most obvious way things shape our minds. Things, as dynamic perturbatory mediational means, drastically change and reconfigure the relationships between humans and those between humans and their environments. More simply, they reconfigure our cognitive ecologies or assemblies. As we know, an immediate implication of that is a change in evolutionary dynamics and selective pressures. The presence of things means that people no longer react or passively adapt to their environment;

instead they actively engage and interact with it. That is, things become agents of change and culturally orchestrated interventions, generating their own unusual evolutionary dynamics. This idea resonates with, and to a certain extent emanates from, the theory of niche construction (Laland et al. 2000; Day et al. 2003), but my emphasis on human environmental exploitation is not restricted to the sort of cumulative "epistemic engineering" (Sterelny 2004) that such a view might imply. (See also Wheeler and Clark 2008.) Things do much more than enable the mind to make maximal use of and/or transform the structure of information in the environment in ways that the naked organism wouldn't have been able to achieve. Things are more than simple adaptive moments within our cumulatively constructed cognitive niche serving to promote more efficient problem solving. Rather, they impose their own dynamics, consciousness, and temporality on our bio-cultural evolutionary continuum. Things affect the flow of time, our emotions, and the boundaries of our cognitive systems.

Temporal effects

It is apparent that time is of the essence for cognitive archaeology. A big part of archaeological practice is concerned with distinguishing what came "before" and "after" in the archaeological record, and with constructing a sequence of events over the long term. However, time is also one of the defining features of human phenomenal experience and thinking. This point is brought into high relief in the following quotation from Chris Gosden (1994, 17):

All action is timed action, which uses the imprint of the past to create an anticipation of the future. Together the body and material things form the flow of the past into the future. Human time flows on a number of levels. Each level represents a different aspect of the framework of reference.

But if, as Gosden implies, time flows on a number of different levels, how does the unity of human phenomenal consciousness emerge? I argue that things play an important part in the integration and coordination of processes that operate on radically different time scales (e.g., neural, bodily, cultural, and evolutionary).

Time, and thus consciousness, operates at different speeds, ranging from the millisecond of neural activity to the slower rates of muscular time to the millennia of human evolution. Things effect temporal anchoring and binding. They help us to move across the scales of time and to construct bridges between temporal phenomena that operate at different experiential levels. Through their physical persistence, they also help us to better understand the qualities of time and the complex ways in which these qualities become embodied in different cultural processes. They also work best over the long term, accumulating biographies and capturing time, through joint participation in cultural practices, in ways that often escape the temporal limits and rhythms of individual human life and experience. Of course the kind of duration encapsulated in things differs from the kind of duration encapsulated in human bodies and brains. Yet the phenomenal stability of the temporality of things relevant to the temporality of the human body is precisely what makes possible their ontological union in action. However, this temporal stability of things need not be interpreted as a "slowing down time" argument of the sort that is prevalent in many archaeological theories. (See, e.g., Hodder 2011a; Olsen 2010.) What may appear to be a slowing down of time is more of a fine tuning. Things act as dynamic attractors, operating in feedback circles that bind the different scales of time together.

Plastic effects

Finally, things change the brain. They effect extensive structural rewiring by fine tuning existing brain pathways, by generating new connections within brain regions, or by transforming what was a useful brain function in one context into another function that is more useful in another context.[7] More than that, things extend the functional architecture of the human cognitive system, either by adding new processing nodes to the system or by changing the connections among existing nodes. More important, they are capable of transforming and rearranging the structure of a cognitive task, either by reordering the steps of a task or by delegating part of a cognitive process to another agent (human or artifact).[8] This process of extended reorganization does not simply refer to an activity-dependent change in the neural architecture (either the addition of new processing nodes or the changing of connections among existing nodes). It refers to an outward expansion of the cognitive system in order to forge extra-neural connections objectified through material culture, bodily action, and learning. (Recall the example of numerical thinking in chapter 5.)

The spike of culture

I end by briefly outlining some future challenges.

Explaining how things shape the mind entails close reexamination of the basic ontological ingredients of human thought and of the embodied cultural practices that turn those ingredients into cognitive processes across the scales of time. The challenge ahead demands reconnecting the brain with the body and beyond, breaking with reductionistic explanations and the cognitivist past. Exactly how this can be done remains an open empirical question for the sciences of mind.

I hope to have demonstrated in this book that archaeology might have a clear and distinctive contribution to make to the interdisciplinary study of mind. As a research field preoccupied with the study of change and able to compare and follow transformations of things and their assemblies over time and across geographical space, archaeology can give us a particular awareness of the effects of things on human cognitive life. Material Engagement Theory's focus on "vital materiality" enables us to ponder what makes us all human and at the same time so different.

However, what I am trying to emphasize here is not simply that it would be in the interest of cognitive archaeology to adopt Material Engagement Theory and "active externalism" for the purpose of mapping the prehistory of the human mindscape. It is more than that. I argue that cognitive archaeology has an *epistemological obligation* to investigate in depth the whereabouts of mind and to explore the cognitive terrain of material engagement. I believe that it is the burden of those who are dealing with material culture *per se* to investigate the kind of life it leads. For many years now, archaeologists have emphasized the active nature of material culture and have recognized that things, like persons, have social lives (Appadurai 1986). The Extended Mind Hypothesis, I want to suggest, opens the way to discovering the cognitive life of things. I believe that Material Engagement Theory, by focusing on the dense reciprocal causation and on the inseparable affective linkages that characterize the ontological compound of cognition and material culture, may offer the optimal point from which to perceive what for many years remained blurred or invisible: the image of a mind not limited by the skin (Bateson 1973).

Obviously, the major question no longer concerns only the hemodynamic couplings of blood flow, metabolism, and behavior; it also concerns the dynamic structural couplings of brains, bodies, and the material world. Admittedly, none of the usual radionuclide tracers used in brain imaging would be of any help here. The question is not about the changes in cerebral blood flow; it is about the "leaks" (Clark 1997) of this flow into the world. The challenge, in other words, lies in figuring out how our plastic brains can be understood within the wider networks of non-biological scaffolds and enculturated social practices that delineate the spatial and temporal boundaries of the human cognitive system as a cultural artifact. To visualize that, a different kind of tracer—an "epistemic" kind—is needed. Adopting a long-term and rather object-oriented archaeological perspective, I propose Material Engagement Theory as a useful method and conceptual apparatus for integrating the different temporalities of cultural, evolutionary, and neuronal time and for bridging the gap between neural and cultural plasticity.

I cannot claim that we have the answers. I hope I have demonstrated that we can at least begin to ask the questions.

Material engagement must be at any appropriate level. Ie it must not rule out immaterial things and causes. It is only useful to consider things if we also consider the interrelationships between them. Some of these relationships are also material eg a pot made out of clay. But others may not be material eg the relationships between the materials in a clock that enable it to tell the time - or the relationships between neurons which enable an animal to respond and learn.

Notes

Chapter 1

1. For a good review of available imaging methods and their problems, see Miller 2008.

2. Merlin Donald (1998, 186) was one of the first to point out that "we cannot have a science of mind that disregards material culture as we cannot have an adequate science of material culture that leaves out cognition."

Chapter 2

1. Throughout this book the terms 'cognitivism', 'computationalism', 'representationalism', and 'internalism' will be used interchangeably to refer to the same "all-in-the-head" view of human cognition.

Chapter 3

1. An alternate "selectional" interpretation could interpret the findings mentioned above as meaning that people with increased hippocampal gray-matter volume are innately better navigators and thus may be more likely to become taxi drivers. However, a follow-up study of navigation expertise among non-taxi-drivers found no differences in gray-matter volume (Maguire et al. 2003), indicating that plastic change was actually effected by experience and practice rather than by innate factors. Another study comparing taxi drivers with bus drivers (Maguire et al. 2006) lent further support to the aforementioned findings.

Chapter 4

1. Another concrete example of this process can be seen in the case of "the 'land-tenure' tablets from Pylos, where a large set of small, individual tablets (as the Eb series) have been recopied in groups on large tablets (Ep) to form a long continuous document" (Chadwick 1976, 26).

2. The numerous examples of words or even complete lines of writing subsequently added over the main text—an annotation or continuation of the text for which there was not enough space (Chadwick 1987, 16)—clearly indicate that in the case of Linear B, as with many other activity contexts, Suchman's law—i.e., that internal plans and models are always too vague to accommodate in advance the manifold contingencies of real-world activity (Suchman 1987)—is confirmed.

3. The concept of affordances was coined by the psychologist J. J. Gibson (1979) to denote "the action possibilities of a thing." The term underlines the dense interaction between the physical properties of things and the experiential properties of an observer. According to Gibson, affordances can be conceptualized in terms of two fundamental properties: that an affordance exists relative to the action capabilities of a particular agent (human or nonhuman) and that the existence of an affordance is independent of the agent's ability or capacity to recognize, perceive, or actualize it. In Gibson's words (1979, 137), "the observer may or may not perceive or attend to the affordance, according to his needs, but the affordance, being invariant, is always there to be perceived." In other words, the affordances of an artifact are objective (as they exist independent of any valuation or interpretation—being or not being perceived), but at the same time they are subjective (as they necessitate a point of reference). An affordance is always an affordance in relation to the action capabilities of something. It is simultaneously objective and relational. In that sense the concept of affordance cuts across traditional subject-object dualities and proves useful in our attempt to draw out the interactive properties of the extended mind—an endeavor that, as Daniel Miller has observed (1987, 109), requires "the transcendence of cultural relativism in order to discuss objects in terms of their general potential" but "demands the recognition that these potential attributes need not necessarily be realized or acknowledged in any particular context."

4. Evaluating the evidence on engrams from fruit flies, Bertram Gerber, Hiromu Tanimoto, and Martin Heisenberg (2004, 737) summarize an important point about biological memory that also applies to humans: "Unlike technical storage devices, biological memory does not seem primarily designed to replay the past, but to integrate selected aspects of it into present behavior."

5. Although his perspective was essentially a dialectical one, Miller (2008, 287) argued that "objects create subjects much more than the other way around."

Chapter 5

1. The choice of the term 'material semiosis' in this context stems from my concern to emphasize the important differences between the semiotics of matter and of language. By using the term 'material sign' instead of 'material symbol', I aim to avoid the Saussurian connotations of this term.

2. A similar proposal can be found in a series of articles in which Byers (1992, 1999a,b) discusses what he calls "the referential fallacy": the common tendency in

archaeology to reduce "the pragmatic force of things to social referential commu-nication" (1992, 414).

3. It can be objected here that the above considerations don't necessarily mean that we should abandon our linguistic analogies. After all, there are various linguistic theories emphasizing the performative action-speech capacities of language that could be used as a model for the communicative properties of material signs. This may be true; however, the issue is not whether "words 'do' as much as they 'say'" (Hodder 1993, 255), but whether material things do much more than what they say and whether their physical affordances and material consequences are an insepa-rable dimension and are in most cases the important parameter of their semiotic significance. That is why their doings usually surpass, in social effects and in semi-otic force, their ability to operate as the conduit of a message or a verbal substitute. Most important, when and if they speak, they do so in an enigmatic language of their own—a language substantially different from human language systems both in grammar and in syntax (if to speak about grammar and syntax in the case of material things makes any sense).

4. This differentiation should not be understood in a firm ontological sense, since a sign can be simultaneously an icon, an index, and a symbol. A characteristic example of the above can be found in central Australian art, in which people and animals are often visually depicted on the basis of the marks they leave in the sand (Munn 1973, 132–145).

Chapter 7

1. The production of adhesives, in particular, demands the irreversible combination of different ingredients, such as plant gum and ochre. It also demands practical knowledge of the physical and heating properties of the different ingredients which demonstrates the ability for recursive combinatory thought (Wadley 2010, 111).

2. Following the same methods, this second study of expert Early Stone Age tool making was based on a limited sample of three professional archaeologists, each with more than 10 years of tool-making experience. Despite the small size of the sample, the FDG-PET procedure yielded a high signal-to-noise ratio sufficient for statistical analysis. Brain-activation data from two tool-making tasks—Oldowan flake production and Acheulean handaxe making—were compared against data from a control task consisting of bimanual percussion without flake production and against the results of the previous study with inexperienced subjects (Stout et al. 2008, 1941).

3. For further evidence of this important link between complex tool use and lan-guage, see Frey 2008. Frey's research combining data from brain-injured patients and data from functional neuroimaging studies suggests the possibility that a brain network participates in the representation of both familiar tool-use skills and

communicative gestures. Although from an evolutionary perspective these correlations cannot demonstrate the direction of causality, they constitute a significant development in the long-standing issue of the possible relations between language and tool use in human evolution.

4. For detailed discussions of precision grips, hand morphology, and tools, see Marzke 1997 and Marzke 2002.

Chapter 8

1. As Ingold points out, this relates to what the philosopher Martin Heidegger (1971) identified as the foundational sense of dwelling: not the occupation of a world already built, but the very process of inhabiting the earth.

Chapter 10

1. See Vygotsky 1978, 1986. Indeed, Vygotsky was one of the first psychologists to study systematically the transformative effects of material mediational means and psychological tools on the way we think. Though principally concerned with the study of language, Vygotsky offered important insights into how various cognitive artifacts, including systems of counting, mnemonic devices, maps, works of art, diagrams, and material signs in general, affect the human cognitive system and its development.

2. For instance, niche-construction theory (Laland et al. 2000; Sterelny 2004; Stotz 2010), autopoietic theory, embodied cognitive science (Clark, 1997, 2003; van Gelder 1995; Chemero 2009; Menary 2007; Wheeler 2005; Wheeler and Clark 2008; Hutchins 2010), actor-network theory, artificial intelligence, and robotics.

3. For reviews of "modern human cognition," see Balter 2002b; Henshilwood and Marean 2003; d'Errico 2003; d'Errico and Stringer 2011; Nowell 2010; McBrearty and Brooks 2000; Shea 2011; Mellars 1989, 1991; Powell et al. 2009; Zilhão 2007; Conard 2010; Wadley 2001.

4. "Humans," Andy Clark points out, "are *profoundly embodied agents*: creatures for whom body, sensing, world, and technology are resources apt for recruitment in ways that yield a permeable and repeatedly reconfigurable agent/world boundary. . . . They are not helpless bystanders watching the passing show from behind a fixed veil of sensing, acting, and representing, but the active architects of their own bounds and capacities." (2007a, 279–280)

5. For a more detailed exposition of this hypothesis, see Malafouris 2008b.

6. "The blind man's stick," Merleau-Ponty writes, "has ceased to be an object for him and is no longer perceived for itself; its point has become an area of sensitivity, extending the scope and active radius of touch and providing a parallel to sight. In

the exploration of things, the length of the stick does not enter expressively as a middle term: the blind man is rather aware of it through the position of object than of the position of objects through it. The position of things is immediately given through the extent of the reach that carries him to it, which comprises, besides the arm's reach, the stick's range of action." (1962, 143)

7. The latter is also known as cultural reconversion or neuronal recycling (Dehaene 2005, 147).

8. Neurobiologically, this shift in the cognitive processes underlying the performance of a task can be seen as a change in the actual location of brain activations (Kelly and Garavan 2005).

Nich   construction Theory

References

Abraham, W. C. 2008. Metaplasticity: Tuning synapses and networks for plasticity. *Nature Reviews Neuroscience* 9 (5): 387.

Abraham, W. C., and Bear, M. F. 1996. Metaplasticity: The plasticity of synaptic plasticity. *Trends in Neurosciences* 19: 126–130.

Adams, F., and Aizawa, K. 2008. *The Bounds of Cognition*. Blackwell.

Adams, F., and Aizawa, K. 2010. Defending the bounds of cognition. In *The Extended Mind*, ed. R. Menary. MIT Press.

Aizawa, K. 2010. The coupling-constitution fallacy revisited. *Cognitive Systems Research* 11: 332–342.

Akrich, M., and Latour, B. 1992. A convenient vocabulary for the semiotics of human and nonhuman actors. In *Shaping Technology/Building Society: Studies in Sociotechnological Change*, ed. W. Bijker and J. Law. MIT Press.

Allen, S. J. 2009. *The Lives of the Brain: Human Evolution and the Organ of Mind*. Belknap.

Ambrose, S. H. 2001. Palaeolithic technology and human evolution. *Science* 291: 1748–1753.

Anderson, M. L. 2003. Embodied cognition: A field guide. *Artificial Intelligence* 149: 91–130.

Appadurai, A. 1986. Introduction: Commodities and the politics of value. In *The Social Life of Things*, ed. A. Appadurai. Cambridge University Press.

Arthur, B. 1989. Competing technologies, increasing returns, and lock-in by historical events. *Economic Journal* 99: 116–131.

Ashby, W. R. 1952. *Design for a Brain*. Wiley.

Austin, J. L. 1975. *How to Do Things with Words*. Harvard University Press.

Balter, M. 2002a. Oldest art: From a modern human's brow—or doodling? *Science* 295: 247–249.

Balter, M. 2002b. What made humans modern? *Science* 295: 1219–1225.

Bar-Yosef, O., and Van Peer, P. 2009. The châine opératoire approach in middle Palaeolithic archaeology. *Current Anthropology* 50 (1): 103–131.

Barkow, J. H., Cosmides, L., and Tooby, J., eds. 1992. *The Adapted Mind: Evolutionary Psychology and the Generation of Culture.* Oxford University Press.

Bateson, G. 1973. *Steps to an Ecology of Mind.* Granada.

Bavelier, D., and Neville, H. J. 2002. Cross-modal plasticity: Where and how? *Nature Reviews Neuroscience* 3: 443–452.

Beer, R. 2003. The dynamics of active categorical perception in an evolved model agent. *Adaptive Behavior* 11: 209–243.

Bell, J. 1992. On capturing agency in theories about prehistory. In *Representations in Archaeology*, ed. J. Gardin and C. Peedles. Indiana University Press.

Bendall, L. 2007. *Economics of Religion in the Mycenaean World.* Oxford University School of Archaeology.

Bengtsson, S. L., Nagy, Z., Skare, S., Forsman, L., Forssberg, H., and Ullen, F. 2005. Extensive piano practicing has regionally specific effects on white matter development. *Nature Neuroscience* 8: 1148–1150.

Bennett, J. 2004. The force of things: Steps toward an ecology of matter. *Political Theory* 32 (3): 347–372.

Bennett, J. 2010. *Vibrant Matter: A Political Ecology of Things.* Duke University Press.

Bergson, H.-L. [1911] 1998. *Creative Evolution.* Dover.

Berti, A., and Frassinetti, F. 2000. When far becomes near: Remapping of space by tool-use. *Journal of Cognitive Neuroscience* 12: 415–420.

Binford, L. R. 1965. Archaeological systematics and the study of cultural process. *American Antiquity* 31: 203–210.

Bird-David, N. 1999. "Animism" revisited: Personhood, environment, and relational epistemology. *Current Anthropology* 40: 67–91.

Biro, D., and Matsuzawa, T. 2001. Chimpanzee numerical competence: Cardinal and ordinal skills. In *Primate Origins of Human Cognition and Behavior*, ed. T. Matsuzawa. Springer.

Blakemore, S. J. 2008. The social brain in adolescence. *Nature Reviews Neuroscience* 9 (4): 267–277.

Blakemore, S. J., and Choudhury, S. 2006. Development of the adolescent brain: Implications for executive function and social cognition. *Journal of Child Psychology and Psychiatry, and Allied Disciplines* 47: 296–312.

Boden, M. 1990. *The Philosophy of Artificial Intelligence*. Oxford University Press.

Boden, M. 2010. *Creativity and Art: Three Roads to Surprise*. Oxford University Press.

Boesch, C., and Boesch, H. 1984. Mental map in wild chimpanzees: An analysis of hammer transports for nut cracking. *Primates* 25: 160–170.

Boesch, C., Marchesi, P., Marchesi, N., Fruth, B., and Joulian, F. 1994. Is nut cracking in wild chimpanzee a cultural behavior? *Journal of Human Evolution* 26: 325–338.

Bool, F. H., Kist, J. L., Locher, J., and Wierda, F. 1982. *M.C. Escher: His Life and Complete Graphic Work*. Abrams.

Boivin, N. 2008. *Material Cultures, Material Minds: The Impact of Things on Human Thought, Society and Evolution*. Cambridge University Press.

Bourdieu, P. 1977. *Outline of a Theory of Practice*. Cambridge University Press.

Boyd, R., and Richerson, P. J. 1985. *Culture and the Evolutionary Process*. University of Chicago Press.

Brentano, F. [1874] 1995. *Psychology from an Empirical Standpoint*. Routledge.

Brooks, R. A. 1991. Intelligence without representation. *Artificial Intelligence* 47: 139–159.

Brown, B. 2001. Thing theory. *Critical Inquiry* 28 (1): 1–22.

Brown, B. 2003. *A Sense of Things: The Object Matter of American Literature*. University of Chicago Press.

Bruner, E. 2003. Fossil traces of the human thought: Paleoneurology and the evolution of the genus *Homo*. *Rivista di Antropologia* 81: 29–56.

Bruner, E. 2004. Geometric morphometrics and paleoneurology: Brain shape evolution in the genus *Homo*. *Journal of Human Evolution* 47: 279–303.

Buchli, V. 2004. Material culture: Current problems. In *A Companion to Social Archaeology*, ed. L. Meskell and R. Preucel. Blackwell.

Burge, T. 1979. Individualism and the mental. In *Midwest Studies in Philosophy*, volume 4, ed. P. French, T. Uehling Jr., and H. Wettstein. University of Minnesota Press.

Burke, K. 1966. *Language as Symbolic Action: Essays on Life, Literature, and Method*. University California Press.

Busby, C. 1997. Permeable and partible persons: A comparative analysis of gender and body in South India and Melanesia. *Journal of the Royal Anthropological Institute* 3: 261–278.

Byers, M. A. 1992. The action-constitutive theory of monuments: A strong pragmatist version. *Journal for the Theory of Social Behaviour* 22 (4): 403–446.

Byers, M. A. 1999a. Intentionality, symbolic pragmatics, and material culture: Revisiting Binford's view of the old copper complex. *American Antiquity* 64 (2): 265–287.

Byers, M. A. 1999b. Communication and material culture. *Cambridge Archaeological Journal* 9 (1): 23–41.

Byrne, R. W. 2005. The maker not the tool: The cognitive significance of great ape manual skills. In *Stone Knapping: The Necessary Conditions for a Uniquely Hominin Behaviour*, ed. V. Roux and B. Bril. McDonald Institute for Archaeological Research.

Callon, M., and Latour, B. 1981. Unscrewing the Big Leviathan. In *Advances in Social Theory and Methodology: Towards an Integration of Micro- and Macro-Sociology*, ed. K. Knorr Cetina and A. Cicouvel. Routledge & Kegan Paul.

Cardinali, L., Brozzoli, C., and Farnè, A. 2009a. Peripersonal space and body schema: Two labels for the same concept? *Brain Topography* 21: 252–260.

Cardinali, L., Frassinetti, F., Brozzoli, C., Roy, A. C., Urquizar, C., and Farnè, A. 2009b. Tool-use induces morphological updating of the body schema. *Current Biology* 12: R478–R479.

Chadwick, J. 1976. *The Mycenaean World*. Cambridge University Press.

Chadwick, J. 1987. *Linear B and Related Scripts*. University of California Press.

Charney, E. Forthcoming. Behavior genetics and post genomics. *Behavioral and Brain Sciences*.

Chase, F. G., and Dibble, H. L. 1987. Middle Paleolithic symbolism: A review of current evidence and interpretations. *Journal of Anthropological Archaeology* 6: 263–296.

Chemero, A. 2009. *Radical Embodied Cognitive Science*. MIT Press.

Chiao, J. Y., and Ambady, N. 2007. Cultural neuroscience: Parsing universality and diversity across levels of analysis. In *Handbook of Cultural Psychology*, ed. S. Kitayama and D. Cohen. Guilford.

Chiel, H. J., and Beer, R. D. 1997. The brain has a body: Adaptive behavior emerges from interactions of nervous system, body and environment. *Trends in Neurosciences* 20: 553–557.

Choudhury, S., Nagel, S. K., and Slaby, J. 2009. Critical neuroscience: Linking neuroscience and society through critical practice. *Biosocieties* 4: 61–77.

Clancey, J. W. 1997. *Situated Cognition*. Cambridge University Press.

Clancey, J. W. 2009. Scientific antecedents of situated cognition. In *The Cambridge Handbook of Situated Cognition*, ed. P. Robbins and M. Aydede. Cambridge University Press.

Clark, A. 1997. *Being There: Putting Brain, Body, and World Together Again*. MIT Press.

Clark, A. 2001a. *Mindware*. Oxford University Press.

Clark, A. 2001b. Reasons, robots and the extended mind. *Mind & Language* 16 (2): 121–145.

Clark, A. 2003. *Natural Born Cyborgs: Minds, Technologies, and the Future of Human Intelligence*. Oxford University Press.

Clark, A. 2007a. Reinventing ourselves: The plasticity of embodiment, sensing, and mind. *Journal of Medicine and Philosophy* 32 (3): 263–282.

Clark, A. 2007b. Soft selves and ecological control. In *Distributed Cognition and the Will: Individual Volition and Social Context*, ed. D. Ross, D. Spurrett, H. Kinkaid, and G. L. Stephens. MIT Press.

Clark, A. 2008a. *Supersizing the Mind: Embodiment, Action, and Cognitive Extension*. Oxford University Press.

Clark, A. 2008b. Pressing the flesh: A tension in the study of the embodied, embedded mind? *Philosophy and Phenomenological Research* 76: 37–59.

Clark, A. 2010. Material surrogacy and the supernatural: Reflections on the role of artefacts in "off-line" cognition. In *The Cognitive Life of Things: Recasting the Boundaries of the Mind*, ed. L. Malafouris and C. Renfrew. McDonald Institute for Archeological Research.

Clark, A., and Chalmers, D. 1998. The extended mind. *Analysis* 58: 7–19.

Clark, G. 1969. *World Prehistory: A New Outline*. Cambridge University Press.

Clarke, D. L. 1973. Archaeology, the loss of innocence. *Antiquity* 47: 6–12.

Clottes, J. 1996. Thematic changes in Upper Palaeolithic art: A view from the Grotte Chauvet. *Antiquity* 70: 276–288.

Clottes, J., ed. 2001. *La Grotte Chauvet*. L'art Des Origines Editions du Seuil.

Clottes, J. 2009. Sticking bones into cracks in the Upper Palaeolithic. In *Becoming Human: Innovation in Prehistoric Material and Spiritual Culture*, ed. C. Renfrew and I. Morley. Cambridge University Press.

Cochran, G., and Harpending, H. 2010. *The 10,000 Year Explosion: How Civilization Accelerated Human Evolution*. Basic Books.

Cole, M. 1985. The zone of proximal development: Where culture and cognition create each other. In *Culture, Communication, and Cognition: Vygotskyan Perspectives*, ed. J. V. Wertsch. Cambridge University Press.

Cole, M. 1996. *Cultural Psychology*. Harvard University Press.

Conard, N. J. 2010. Cultural modernity: Consensus or conundrum? *Proceedings of the National Academy of Sciences* 107 (17): 7621–7622.

Connerton, P. 1989. *How Societies Remember*. Cambridge University Press.

Coolidge, F., and Wynn, T. 2004. A cognitive and neuropsychological perspective on the Châtelperronian. *Journal of Anthropological Research* 60: 55–73.

Coolidge, F., and Wynn, T. 2005. Working memory, its executive functions, and the emergence of modern thinking. *Cambridge Archaeological Journal* 15 (1): 5–26.

Coolidge, F., and Wynn, T. 2009. *The Rise of* Homo sapiens: *The Evolution of Modern Thinking*. Wiley-Blackwell.

Corballis, M. C. 2003. From mouth to hand: Gesture, speech, and the evolution of right handedness. *Behavioral and Brain Sciences* 26: 199–260.

Corballis, M. C. 2009. The evolution of language. *Annals of the New York Academy of Sciences* 1156: 19–43.

Corballis, M. C. 2011. *The Recursive Mind: The Origins of Human Language, Thought, and Civilization*. Princeton University Press.

Cosmides, L., and Toody, J. 1987. From evolution to behavior: Evolutionary psychology as the missing link. In*The Latest on the Best: Essays on Evolution and Optimality*, ed. J. Dupré. MIT Press.

Costall, A. 1997. Things and things like them. In *The Cultural Life of Images*, ed. B. L. Molyneaux. Routledge.

Costall, A., and Dreier, O., eds. 2006. *Doing Things with Things: The Design and Use of Objects*. Ashgate.

Cushing, F. H. 1892. Manual concepts: A study of the influence of hand-usage on culture-growth. *American Anthropologist* 4: 289–318.

Damerow, P. 1988. Individual development and cultural evolution of arithmetical thinking. In *Ontogeny, Phylogeny, and Historical Development*, ed. S. Strauss. Ablex.

Damerow, P. 1998. Prehistory and cognitive development. In *Piaget, Evolution, and Development*, ed. J. Langer and M. Killen. Erlbaum.

Darwin, C. 1871. *The Descent of Man, and Selection in Relation to Sex*. John Murray.

Davidson, I. 2009. Comment on Bar-Yosef and Van Peer. *Current Anthropology* 50 (1): 119–120.

Davidson, I. In press. Origins of pictures: An argument for transformation of signs. In *Origins of Pictures*, ed. K. Sachs-Hombach. Herbert von Halem Verlag.

Davidson, I., and McGrew, W. C. 2005. Stone tools and the uniqueness of human culture. *Journal of the Royal Anthropological Institute* 11 (4): 793–817.

Davidson, I., and Noble, W. 1989. The archaeology of perception. *Current Anthropology* 30 (2): 125–155.

Davidson, I., and Noble, W. 1993. Tools and language in human evolution. In *Tools, Language and Cognition in Human Evolution*, ed. K. Gibson and T. Ingold. Cambridge University Press.

Day, R. L., Laland, K. N., and Odling-Smee, J. 2003. Rethinking adaptation—the niche construction perspective. *Perspectives in Biology and Medicine* 46: 80–95.

Deacon, T. W. 1997. *The Symbolic Species: The Co-evolution of Language and the Brain.* Norton.

de Beaune, S., Coolidge, F., and Wynn, T., eds. 2009. *Cognitive Archaeology and Human Evolution*. Cambridge University Press.

Dehaene, S. 1997. *The Number Sense*. Oxford University Press.

Dehaene, S. 2005. Evolution of human cortical circuits for reading and arithmetic: the neuronal recycling hypothesis. In From Monkey Brain to Human Brain: A Fyssen Foundation Symposium, ed. S. Dehaene, J.-R. Duhamel, M. D. Hauser, and G. Rizzolatti. MIT Press.

Dehaene, S. 2009. Origins of mathematical intuitions. *Annals of the New York Academy of Sciences* 1156: 232–259.

Dehaene, S., Spelke, E. R., Stanescu, R., and Tsivkin, S. 1999. Sources of mathematical thinking: Behavioral and brain-imaging evidence. *Science* 284: 970–974.

Delagnes, A., and Roche, H. 2005. Late Pliocene hominid knapping skills: The case of Lokalalei 2C, West Turkana, Kenya. *Journal of Human Evolution* 48: 435–472.

DeLoache, J. 2004. Becoming symbol-minded. *Trends in Cognitive Sciences* 8 (2): 66–70.

DeLoache, J. S., Pierroutsakos, S. L., and Uttal, D. H. 2003. The origins of pictorial competence. *Current Directions in Psychological Science* 12: 114–118.

DeLoache, J. S., Pierroutsakos, S. L., Uttal, D. H., Rosengren, K. S., and Gottlieb, A. 1998. Grasping the nature of pictures. *Psychological Science* 9: 205–210.

Dennett, D. C. 1987. *The Intentional Stance*. MIT Press.

Dennett, D. C. 1996. *Kinds of Minds: Towards an Understanding of Consciousness*. Weidenfeld & Nicolson.

Deregowski, J. 1989. Real space and represented space: Cross-cultural perspectives. *Behavioral and Brain Sciences* 12: 51–119.

Deregowski, J. B. 1995. Perception-depiction-perception, and communication. *Rock Art Research* 12: 3–22.

d'Errico, F. 1995. A new model and its implications for the origin of writing: The La Marche antler revisited. *Cambridge Archaeological Journal* 5 (2): 163–206.

d'Errico, F. 1998. Paleolithic origins of artificial memory systems. In *Cognition and Material Culture: The Archaeology of Symbolic Storage*, ed. C. Renfrew and C. Scarre. McDonald Institute for Archaeological Research.

d'Errico, F. 2001. Memories out of mind: the archaeology of the oldest memory systems. In *In the Mind's Eye: Multidisciplinary Approaches to the Evolution of Human Cognition*, ed. A. Nowell. International Monographs in Prehistory.

d'Errico, F., Henshilwood, C. S., Lawson, G., Vanhaeren, M., Tillier, A., Soressi, M., et al. 2003. Archaeological evidence for the emergence of language, symbolism, and music: An alternative multidisciplinary perspective. *Journal of World Prehistory* 17 (1): 1–70.

d'Errico, F., and Henshilwood, C. S. 2007. Additional evidence for bone technology in the southern African Middle Stone Age. *Journal of Human Evolution* 52: 142–163.

d'Errico, F., and Henshilwood, C. 2011. Origin of symbolically mediated behavior: From antagonistic scenarios to a unified research strategy. In Homo Symbolicus*: The Dawn of Language, Imagination and Spirituality*, ed. C. Henshilwood and F. d'Errico. Benjamins.

d'Errico, F., Moreno, R. G., and Rifkin, R. F. 2012. Technological, elemental and colorimetric analysis of an engraved ochre fragment from the Middle Stone Age levels of Klasies River Cave 1, South Africa. *Journal of Archaeological Science* 39: 942–952.

d'Errico, F., and Nowell, A. 2000. A new look at the Berekhat Ram figurine: Implications for the origins of symbolism. *Cambridge Archaeological Journal* 10: 123–167.

d'Errico, F., and Stringer, C. 2011. Evolution, revolution or saltation scenario for the emergence of modern cultures? *Philosophical Transactions of the Royal Society of London. Series B, Biological Sciences* 366: 1060–1069.

d'Errico, F., and Villa, P. 1997. Holes and grooves: The contribution of microscopy and taphonomy to the problem of art origins. *Journal of Human Evolution* 33: 1–31.

Di Paolo, E. 2009. Extended life. *Topoi* 28 (1): 9–21.

Dobres, A., and Robb, E. J. 2000. Agency in archaeology: Paradigm or platitude? In *Agency in Archaeology*, ed. A. Dobres and E. J. Robb. Routledge.

Donald, M. 1991. *Origins of the Modern Mind*. Harvard University Press.

Donald, M. 1998. Material culture and cognition: Concluding thoughts. In *Cognition and Material Culture: The Archaeology of Symbolic Storage*, ed. C. Renfrew and C. Scarre. McDonald Institute for Archaeological Research.

Donald, M. 2001. *A Mind So Rare: The Evolution of Human Consciousness*. Norton.

Donald, M. 2010. The exographic revolution: Neuropsychological sequel. In *The Cognitive Life of Things*, ed. L. Malafouris and C. Renfrew. McDonald Institute for Archaeological Research.

Donoghue, J. P. 2008. Bridging the brain to the world: A perspective on neural interface systems. *Neuron* 60 (6): 511–521.

Dreyfus, H. 1979. *What Computers Can't Do: The Limits of Artificial Intelligence*. Harper Colophon.

Dreyfus, H. 1991. *Being-in-the-World: A Commentary on Division I of Heidegger's* Being and Time. MIT Press.

Dreyfus, H. 2002. Intelligence without representation: Merleau-Ponty's critique of mental representation. *Phenomenology and the Cognitive Sciences* 1 (4): 367–383.

Dupré, J. 2008. Against maladaptationism: or what's wrong with evolutionary psychology? In *Knowledge as Social Order: Rethinking the Sociology of Barry Barnes*, ed. M. Mazzotti. Ashgate.

Dupuy, J. P. 2000. *The Mechanization of the Mind: On the Origins of Cognitive Science*. Princeton University Press.

Durham, W. H. 1990. Advances in evolutionary culture theory. *Annual Review of Anthropology* 19: 187–210.

Elbert, T., Pantev, C., Wienbruch, C., Rockstroh, B., and Taub, E. 1995. Increased cortical representation of the fingers of the left hand in string players. *Science* 270: 305–307.

Ellen, R. 1988. Fetishism. *Man* (N.S.) 23: 213–235.

Enard, W., Przeworski, M., Fisher, S. E., Lai, C. S. L., Wiebe, V., Kitano, T., et al. 2002. Molecular evolution of *FOXP2*, a gene involved in speech and language. *Nature* 418: 869–872.

Evans, A. 1935. *The Palace of Minos*, volume 4. Macmillan.

Evans, P. D., Gilbert, S. L., Mekel-Bobrov, N., Vallender, E. J., Anderson, J. R., Vaez-Azizi, L. M., et al. 2005. Microephalin, a gene regulating brain size, continues to evolve adaptively in humans. *Science* 309: 1717–1720.

Everett, D. L. 2005. Cultural constraints on grammar and cognition in Pirahã: Another look at the design features of human language. *Current Anthropology* 46: 621–646.

Farnè, A., and Làdavas, E. 2000. Dynamic size-change of hand peripersonal space following tool use. *Neuroreport* 11: 1645–1649.

Farnè, A., Serino, A., and Làdavas, E. 2007. Dynamic size-change of peri-hand space following tool-use: determinants and spatial characteristics revealed through cross-modal extinction. *Cortex* 43: 436–443.

Fauconnier, G. 1997. *Mappings in Thought and Language*. Cambridge University Press.

Fauconnier, G., and Turner, M. 1998. Conceptual integration networks. *Cognitive Science* 22 (2): 133–187.

Fauconnier, G., and Turner, M. 2002. *The Way We Think: Conceptual Blending and the Mind's Hidden Complexities*. Basic Books.

Feigenson, L., Dehaene, S., and Spelke, E. 2004. Core systems of number. *Trends in Cognitive Sciences* 8: 307–314.

Fodor, J. 1981. *Representations: Philosophical Essays on the Foundations of Cognitive Science*. MIT Press.

Foley, R., and Lahr, M. M. 2003. On stony ground: Lithic technology, human evolution, and the emergence of culture. *Evolutionary Anthropology* 12: 109–122.

Forty, A., and Küchler, S., eds. 1999. *The Art of Forgetting*. Berg.

Frank, M. C., Everett, D. L., Fedorenko, E., and Gibson, E. 2008. Number as a cognitive technology: Evidence from Piraha language and cognition. *Cognition* 108 (3): 819–824.

Frey, S. H. 2008. Tool use, communicative gesture, and cerebral asymmetries in the modern human brain. *Philosophical Transactions of the Royal Society of London Series B* 363: 1951–1958.

Fritz, C., and Tosello, G. 2007. The hidden meaning of forms: Methods of recording paleolithic parietal art. *Journal of Archaeological Method and Theory* 14 (1): 48–80.

Gallagher, S. 2005. *How the Body Shapes the MIND*. Oxford University Press.

Gallese, V., and Lakoff, G. 2005. The brain's concepts: The role of the sensory-motor system in reason and language. *Cognitive Neuropsychology* 22: 455–479.

Gamble, C. 2007. *Origins and Revolutions: Human Identity in Earliest Prehistory*. Cambridge University Press.

Gardner, H. 1985. *The Mind's New Science: A History of the Cognitive Revolution*. Basic Books.

Gaser, C., and Schlaug, G. 2003. Brain structures differ between musicians and non-musicians. *Journal of Neuroscience* 23: 9240–9245.

Gell, A. 1998. *Art and Agency: An Anthropological Theory*. Oxford University Press.

Gelman, R., and Butterworth, B. 2005. Number and language: How are they related? *Trends in Cognitive Sciences* 9: 6–10.

Gelman, R., and Gallistel, C. R. 2004. Language and the origin of numerical concepts. *Science* 306: 441–443.

Gerber, B., Hiromu, T., and Heisenberg, M. 2004. An engram found? Evaluating the evidence from fruit flies. *Current Opinion in Neurobiology* 14: 737–744.

Gibbs, R. W. 2001. Intentions as emergent products of social interactions. In *Intentions and Intentionality: Foundations of Social Cognition*, ed. L. J. Moses and D. A. Baldwin. MIT Press.

Gibson, K. R. 1993. Tool use, language and social behavior in relationship to information processing capacities. In *Tools, Language and Cognition in Human Evolution*, ed. K. R. Gibson and T. Ingold. Cambridge University Press.

Gibson, K. R. 1996. The biocultural human brain, seasonal migrations, and the emergence of the Upper Palaeolithic. In *Modelling the Early Human Mind*, ed. P. Mellars and K. Gibson. McDonald Institute for Archaeological Research.

Gibson, J. J. 1977. The theory of affordances. In *Perceiving, Acting, and Knowing*, ed. R. E. Shaw and J. Bransford. Erlbaum.

Gibson, J. J. 1979. *The Ecological Approach to Visual Perception*. Houghton Mifflin.

Giddens, A., and Pierson, C. 1998. *Conversations with Anthony Giddens: Making Sense of Modernity*. Stanford University Press.

Goldin-Meadow, S. 2003. *Hearing Gesture: How Our Hands Help Us Think*. Belknap.

Goldin-Meadow, S., and Wagner, S. M. 2005. How our hands help us learn. *Trends in Cognitive Sciences* 9 (5): 234–241.

Goodall, J. 1964. Tool-use and aimed throwing in a community of free-ranging chimpanzees. *Nature* 201: 1264–1266.

Goodwin, C. 1994. Professional vision. *American Anthropologist* 96 (3): 606–633.

Goodwin, C. 2002. Time in action. *Current Anthropology* 43: S19–S35.

Goodwin, C. 2010. Things and their embodied environments. In *The Cognitive Life of Things*, ed. L. Malafouris and C. Renfrew. McDonald Institute for Archaeological Research.

Gordon, P. 2004. Numerical cognition without words: Evidence from Amazonia. *Science* 306: 496–499.

Gosden, C. 1994. *Social Being and Time*. Blackwell.

Gosden, C. 2001. Making sense: Archaeology and aesthetics. *World Archaeology* 33 (2): 163–167.

Gosden, C. 2004. Making and display: Our aesthetic appreciation of things and objects. In *Rethinking Materiality: The Engagement of Mind with the Material World*, ed. E. DeMarrais, C. Gosden, and C. Renfrew. McDonald Institute for Archaeological Research.

Gosden, C. 2005. What do objects want? *Journal of Archaeological Method and Theory* 12 (3): 193–211.

Gosden, C. 2008. Social ontologies. *Philosophical Transactions of the Royal Society of London Series B* 363: 2003–2010.

Gosden, C. 2010. The death of the mind. In *The Cognitive Life of Things: Recasting the Boundaries of the Mind*, ed. L. Malafouris and C. Renfrew. McDonald Institute for Archeological Research.

Gosden, C., and Marshall, Y. 1999. The cultural biography of objects. *World Archaeology* 31 (2): 169–178.

Gottdiener, M. 1995. *Postmodern Semiotics: Material Culture and the Forms of Postmodern Life*. Blackwell.

Gottlieb, G. 2002. Probabilistic epigenesis of development. In *Handbook of Developmental Psychology*, ed. J. Valsiner and K. J. Connolly. Sage.

Gottlieb, G. 2003. On making behavioral genetics truly developmental. *Human Development* 46: 337–355.

Gottlieb, G. 2007. Probabilistic epigenesis. *Developmental Science* 10 (1): 1–11.

Gottlieb, G., and Halpern, C. T. 2002. A relational view of causality in normal and abnormal development. *Development and Psychopathology* 14: 421–435.

Graham, G., and Stephens, G. L. 1994. Mind and mine. In *Philosophical Psychopathology*, ed. G. Graham and G. L. Stephens. MIT Press.

Griffiths, T., Chater, N., Kemp, C., Perfors, A., and Tenenbaum, J. B. 2010. Probabilistic models of cognition: Exploring representations and inductive biases. *Trends in Cognitive Sciences* 14 (8): 357–364.

Griffiths, P. E., and Gray, R. D. 1994. Developmental systems and evolutionary explanation. *Journal of Philosophy* 91: 277–304.

Griffiths, P. E., and Gray, R. D. 2001. Darwinism and developmental systems. In *Cycles of Contingency: Developmental Systems and Evolution*, ed. S. Oyama, P. E. Griffth, and R. D. Gray. MIT Press.

Griffiths, P. E., and Gray, R. D. 2004. The developmental systems perspective: organism—environment systems as units of evolution. In *The Evolutionary Biology of Complex Phenotypes*, ed. K. Preston and M. Pigliucci. Oxford University Press.

Griffiths, P. E., and Stotz, K. 2000. How the mind grows: A developmental perspective on the biology of cognition. *Synthese* 122: 29–51.

Guthrie, S. 1993. *Faces in the Clouds: A New Theory of Religion*. Oxford University Press.

Haggard, P., Aschersleben, G., Gehrke, J., and Prinz, W. 2002b. Action, binding and awareness. In *Common Mechanisms in Perception and Action: Attention and Performance*, volume XIX, ed. W. Prinz and B. Hommel. Oxford University Press.

Haggard, P., Clark, S., and Kalogeras, J. 2002a. Voluntary action and conscious awareness. *Nature Neuroscience* 5 (4): 382–385.

Halverson, J. 1992a. The first pictures: Perceptual foundations of Palaeolithic art. *Perception* 21: 389–404.

Halverson, J. 1992b. Paleolithic art and cognition. *Journal of Psychology* 126: 221–236.

Hansell, M., and Ruxton, G. 2008. Setting tool use within the context of animal construction behaviour. *Trends in Ecology and Evolution* 23: 73–78.

Haraway, D. 1991. A cyborg manifesto: Science, technology, and socialist-feminism in the late twentieth century. In Haraway, *Simians, Cyborgs and Women: The Reinvention of Nature*. Routledge.

Haslinger, B., Erhard, P., Altenmueller, E., Hennenlotter, A., Schwaiger, M., Graefin von Einsiedel, H., et al. 2004. Reduced recruitment of motor association areas during bimanual coordination in concert pianists. *Human Brain Mapping* 22: 206–215.

Hawkes, C. 1954. Archaeological theory and method: Some suggestions from the Old World. *American Anthropologist* 56: 155–168.

Head, H., and Holmes, G. 1911–12. Sensory disturbances from cerebral lesions. *Brain* 34: 102–254.

Heidegger, M. 1971. *Poetry, Language, Thought*. Harper and Row.

Heidegger, M. 1977. *The Question Concerning Technology and Other Essays*. Harper & Row.

Henare, A., Holbraad, M., and Wastell, S., eds. 2007. *Thinking through Things: Theorising Artefacts Ethnographically*. Routledge.

Henshilwood, C., and d'Errico, F., eds. 2011. Homo Symbolicus: *The Dawn of Language, Imagination and Spirituality*. Benjamins.

Henshilwood, C. S., d'Errico, F., and Watts, I. 2009. Engraved ochres from Middle Stone Age levels at Blombos Cave, South Africa. *Journal of Human Evolution* 57: 27–47.

Henshilwood, C. S., d'Errico, F., van Niekerk, K. L., Coquinot, Y., Jacobs, Z., Lauritzen, S., et al. 2011. A 100,000-year-old ochre-processing workshop at Blombos Cave, South Africa. *Science* 334: 219–222.

Henshilwood, C. S., d'Errico, F., Vanhaeren, M., van Niekerk, K., and Jacobs, Z. 2004. Middle Stone Age shell beads from South Africa. *Science* 384: 404.

Henshilwood, C. S., d'Errico, F., Yates, R., Jacobs, Z., Tribolo, C., Duller, G. A. T., et al. 2002. Emergence of modern human behaviour: Middle Stone Age engravings from South Africa. *Science* 295: 1278–1280.

Henshilwood, C. S., d'Errico, F. E., Marean, C. W., Milo, R. G., and Yates, R. 2001. An early bone tool industry from the Middle Stone Age at Blombos Cave, South Africa: Implications for the origins of modern human behaviour, symbolism and language. *Journal of Human Evolution* 41: 631–678.

Henshilwood, C. S., and Dubreuil, B. 2011. The Still Bay and Howiesons Poort, 77–59 ka: symbolic material cuture and the evolution of the mind during the African Middle Stone Age. *Current Anthropology* 52: 361–400.

Henshilwood, C. S., and Dubreuil, B. 2009. Reading the artefacts: Gleaning language skills from the Middle Stone Age in southern Africa. In *The Cradle of Language*, ed. R. Botha and C. Knight. Oxford University Press.

Henshilwood, C. S., and Marean, C. W. 2003. The origin of modern human behaviour: A review and critique of models and test implications. *Current Anthropology* 44 (5): 627–651.

Hicks, D., and Beaudry, M., eds. 2010. *The Oxford Handbook of Material Culture Studies*. Oxford University Press.

Hihara, S., Notoya, T., Tanaka, M., Ichinose, S., Ojima, H., Obayashi, S., Fujii. N., and Iriki, A. 2006. Extension of corticocortical afferents into the anterior bank of the intraparietal sulcus by tool-use training in adult monkeys. *Neuropsychologia* 44: 2636–2646.

Hodder, I. 1982. *Symbols in Action: Ethnoarchaeological Studies of Material Culture*. Cambridge University Press.

Hodder, I. 1986. *Reading the Past*. Cambridge University Press.

Hodder, I. 1987. The contextual analysis of symbolic meanings. In *The Archaeology of Contextual Meanings*, ed. I. Hodder. Cambridge University Press.

Hodder, I. 1991. Interpretative archaeology and its role. *American Antiquity* 56: 7–12.

Hodder, I. 1993. Social cognition. *Cambridge Archaeological Journal* 3: 247–270.

Hodder, I. 1999. *The Archaeological Process*. Blackwell.

Hodder, I. 2011a. Wheels of time: Some aspects of entanglement theory and the secondary products revolution. *Journal of World Prehistory* 24: 175–187.

Hodder, I. 2011b. Human-thing entanglement: Towards an integrated archaeological perspective. *Journal of the Royal Anthropological Institute* 17: 154–177.

Hodder, I., and Hutson, G. 2003. *Reading the Past*. Cambridge University Press.

Hodgson, D., and Helvenston, P. 2006. The emergence of the representation of animals in palaeoart: Insights from evolution and the cognitive, limbic and visual systems of the human brain. *Rock Art Research* 23 (1): 3–40.

Hoffecker, J. F. 2011. *Landscape of the Mind: Human Evolution and the Archaeology of Thought.* Columbia University Press.

Hollan, J., Hutchins, E., and Kirsh, D. 2000. Distributed cognition: Toward a new foundation for human-computer interaction research. *ACM Transactions on Computer-Human Interaction* 7 (2): 174–196.

Hollenback, K., and Schiffer, B. M. 2010. Technology and material life. In *The Oxford Handbook of Material Culture Studies,* ed. D. Hicks and M. Beaudry. Oxford University Press.

Holloway, R. 1999. Evolution of the human brain. In *Handbook of Human Symbolic Evolution,* ed. A. Lock and C. R. Peters. Blackwell.

Holmes, N. P., Calvert, G. A., and Spence, C. 2004. Extending or projecting peripersonal space with tools: Multisensory interactions highlight only the distal and proximal ends of tools. *Neuroscience Letters* 372 (1–2): 62–67.

Holmes, N. P., and Spence, C. 2006. Beyond the body schema: Visual, prosthetic, and technological contributions to bodily perception and awareness. In *Human Body Perception from the Inside Out,* ed. G. Knoblich, I. M. Thornton, M. Grosjen, and M. Shiffrar. Oxford University Press.

Hoopes, J., ed. 1991. *Peirce on Signs,.* University of North Carolina Press.

Hoskins, J. 1998. *Biographical Objects: How Things Tell the Stories of People's Lives.* Routledge.

Hoskins, J. 2006. Agency, biography and objects. In *Handbook of Material Culture,* ed. C. Tilley, W. Keane, S. Küchler, and M. Rowland. Sage.

Humphrey, N. 1998. Cave art, autism, and the evolution of the human mind. *Cambridge Archaeological Journal* 8 (2): 165–191.

Hurley, S. 1998. *Consciousness in Action.* Harvard University Press.

Hutchins, E. 1995. *Cognition in the Wild.* MIT Press.

Hutchins, E. 2005. Material anchors for conceptual blends. *Journal of Pragmatics* 37: 1555–1577.

Hutchins, E. 2008. The role of cultural practices in the emergence of modern human intelligence. *Philosophical Transactions of the Royal Society of London Series B* 363: 2011–2019.

Hutchins, E. 2010a. Imagining the cognitive life of things. In *The Cognitive Life of Things,* ed. L. Malafouris and C. Renfrew. McDonald Institute for Archaeological Research.

Hutchins, E. 2010b. Cognitive ecology. *Topics in Cognitive Science* 2: 705–715.

Hutchins, E. 2010c. Enaction, imagination, and insight. In *Enaction: Toward a New Paradigm for Cognitive Science*, ed. J. Stewart, O. Gapenne, and E. A. Di Paolo. MIT Press.

Ifrah, G. 1985. *From One to Zero: A Universal History of Numbers*. Viking.

Ingold, T. 1993. Tool-use, sociality and intelligence. In *Tools, Language and Cognition in Human Evolution*, ed. K. R. Gibson and T. Ingold. Cambridge University Press.

Ingold, T. 1998. Totemism, animism, and the depiction of animals. In *Animal, Anima, Animus*, ed. M. Seppala, J. P. Vanhala, and L. Weintraub. Pori Art Museum.

Ingold, T. 2000. *The Perception of the Environment: Essays in Livelihood, Dwelling and Skill*. Routledge.

Ingold, T. 2006. Rethinking the animate, re-animating thought. *Ethnos* 71 (1): 9–20.

Ingold, T. 2007. *Lines: A Brief History*. Routledge.

Ingold, T. 2008. Bindings against boundaries: Entanglements of life in an open world. *Environment & Planning A* 40: 1796–1810.

Ingold, T. 2010. The textility of making. *Cambridge Journal of Economics* 34: 91–102.

Iriki, A. 2005. A prototype of Homo faber: A silent precursor of human intelligence in the tool-using monkey brain. In *From Monkey Brain to Human Brain: A Fyssen Foundation Symposium*, ed. S. Dehaene, J.-R. Duhamel, M. D. Hauser, and G. Rizzolatti. MIT Press.

Iriki, A. 2006. The neural origins and implications of imitation, mirror neurons and tool use. *Current Opinion in Neurobiology* 16: 1–8.

Iriki, A., and Sakura, O. 2008. The neuroscience of primate intellectual evolution: Natural selection and passive and intentional niche construction. *Philosophical Transactions of the Royal Society of London Series B* 363: 2229–2241.

Iriki, A., Tanaka, M., and Iwamura, Y. 1996. Coding of modified body schema during tool use by macaque postcentral neurones. *Neuroreport* 7: 2325–2330.

Jancke, L., Shah, N. J., and Peters, M. 2000. Cortical activations in primary and secondary motor areas for complex bimanual movements in professional pianists. *Cognitive Brain Research* 10: 177–183.

Jeffares, B. 2010. The co-evolution of tools and minds: Cognition and material culture in the hominin lineage. *Phenomenology and the Cognitive Sciences* 9: 503–520.

Johnson, M. 1987. *The Body in the Mind: The Bodily Basis of Meaning, Imagination, and Reason.* University of Chicago Press.

Johnson-Frey, S. H. 2004. The neural bases of complex tool use in humans. *Trends in Cognitive Sciences* 8: 71–78.

Johnson-Frey, S. H., and Grafton, S. T. 2003. From "acting on" to "acting with": The functional anatomy of object-oriented action schemata. *Progress in Brain Research* 142: 127–139.

Jones, A. 2004. Archaeometry and materiality: Materials-based analysis in theory and practice. *Archaeometry* 46: 327–338.

Jones, A. 2007. *Memory and Material Culture.* Cambridge University Press.

Jordan, J. S. 2008. Wild agency: Nested intentionalities in cognitive neuroscience and archaeology. *Philosophical Transactions of the Royal Society of London Series B* 363: 1981–1991.

Karmiloff-Smith, A. 1992. *Beyond Modularity: A Developmental Perspective on Cognitive Science.* MIT Press.

Keane, W. 2003. Semiotics and the social analysis of material things. *Language & Communication* 23: 409–425.

Kelly, A. M. C., and Garavan, H. 2005. Human functional neuroimaging of brain changes associated with practice. *Cerebral Cortex* 15: 1089–1102.

Kingdom, J. 1993. *Self-Made Man and His Undoing.* Simon & Schuster.

Kingstone, A., Smilek, D., and Eastwood, J. D. 2008. Cognitive ethology: A new approach for studying human cognition. *British Journal of Psychology* 99: 317–345.

Kirsh, D. 1995. The intelligent use of space. *Artificial Intelligence* 73: 31–68.

Kirsh, D. 1996. Adapting the environment instead of oneself. *Adaptive Behavior* 4: 415–452.

Kirsh, D. 2009. Projection, problem space and anchoring. In *Proceedings of the 31st Annual Conference of the Cognitive Science Society*, ed. N. A. Taatgen and H. van Rijn. Cognitive Science Society.

Kirsh, D. 2010. Explaining artefact evolution. In *The Cognitive Life of Things*, ed. L. Malafouris and C. Renfrew. McDonald Institute for Archaeological Research.

Kirsh, D., and Maglio, P. 1994. On distinguishing epistemic from pragmatic action. *Cognitive Science* 18: 513–549.

Knappett, C. 2002. Photographs, skeuomorphs and marionettes: Some thoughts on mind, agency and object. *Journal of Material Culture* 7 (1): 97–117.

Knappett, C. 2004. The affordances of things. In *Rethinking Materiality: The Engagement of Mind with the Material World*, ed. E. DeMarrais, C. Gosden, and C. Renfrew. McDonald Institute for Archaeological Research.

Knappett, C. 2005. *Thinking Through Material Culture: An Interdisciplinary Perspective*. University of Pennsylvania Press.

Knappett, C. 2006. Beyond skin: Layering and networking in art and archaeology. *Cambridge Archaeological Journal* 16 (2): 239–251.

Knappett, C. 2011. *An Archaeology of Interaction: Network Perspectives on Material Culture and Society*. Oxford University Press.

Knappett, C., and Malafouris, L., eds. 2008. *Material Agency: Towards a Non-Anthropocentric Approach*. Springer.

Knoblich, G., and Sebanz, N. 2008. Evolving intentions for social interaction: From entrainment to joint action. *Philosophical Transactions of the Royal Society of London Series B* 363: 2021–2031.

Kohn, M., and Mithen, S. 1999. Handaxes: Products of sexual selection? *Antiquity* 73: 518–526.

Kopytoff, I. 1986. The cultural biography of things: Commoditization as process. In *The Social Life of Things*, ed. A. Appadurai. Cambridge University Press.

Kwint, M., Breward, C., and Aynsely, J., eds. 1999. *Material Memories: Design and Evocation*. Berg.

Lakatos, I. 1980. *The Methodology of Scientific Research Programmes*. Philosophical Papers, volume 1. Cambridge University Press.

Lakoff, G. 1987. *Women, Fire, and Dangerous Things: What Categories Reveal about the Mind*. University of Chicago Press.

Lakoff, G., and Johnson, M. 1980. *Metaphors We Live By*. University of Chicago Press.

Lakoff, G., and Johnson, M. 1999. *Philosophy in the Flesh: The Embodied Mind and Its Challenge to Western Thought*. Basic Books.

Lakoff, G., and Núñez, R. E. 2000. *Where Mathematics Comes From: How the Embodied Mind Brings Mathematics into Being*. Basic Books.

Laland, K. N., and Sterelny, K. 2006. Seven reasons (not) to neglect niche construction. *Evolution* 60: 1751–1762.

Laland, K. N., Odling-Smee, J., and Feldman, M. W. 2000. Niche construction, biological evolution and cultural change. *Behavioral and Brain Sciences* 23: 131–146.

Latour, B. 1991. Technology is society made durable. In *A Sociology of Monsters: Essays on Power, Technology and Domination*, ed. J. Law. Routledge.

Latour, B. 1992. Where are the missing masses? The sociology of a few mundane artefacts. In *Shaping Technology/Building Society: Studies in Sociotechnical Change*, ed. W. E. Bijker and J. Law. MIT Press.

Latour, B. 1993. *We Have Never Been Modern*. Harvard University Press.

Latour, B. 1994. Pragmatogonies. *American Behavioral Scientist* 37 (6): 791–808.

Latour, B. 1999. *Pandoras Hope: Essays on the Reality of Science Studies*. Harvard University Press.

Latour, B. 2005. *Reassembling the Social: An Introduction to Actor-Network-Theory*. Oxford University Press.

Lave, J. 1988. *Cognition in Practice*. Cambridge University Press.

Lave, J., and Wenger, E. 1991. *Situated Learning: Legitimate Peripheral Participation*. Cambridge University Press.

Law, J. 1999. After ANT: Complexity, naming and topology. In *Actor Network Theory and After*, ed. J. Law and J. Hassard. Blackwell.

Law, J., and Mol, A. 2008. The actor-enacted: Cumbrian sheep in 2001. In *Material Agency: Towards a Non-Anthropocentric Perspective*, ed. C. Knappett and L. Malafouris. Springer.

Leach, E. 1976. *Culture and Communication: The Logic by Which Symbols Are Connected*. Cambridge University Press.

Leder, D. 1990. *The Absent Body*. University of Chicago Press.

Legrand, D. 2006. The bodily self: The sensori-motor roots of pre-reflexive self-consciousness. *Phenomenology and the Cognitive Sciences* 5: 89–118.

Leroi-Gourhan, A. 1964/1993. *Gesture and Speech*. MIT Press.

Le Tensorer, J. M. 2006. Les cultures acheuleennes et la question de l'emergence de la pensée symbolique chez *Homo erectus* à partir des données relatives à la forme symetrique et harmonique des bifaces. *Comptes Rendus Palévol* 5: 127–135.

Lewis-Williams, D. 2002. *The Mind in the Cave: Consciousness and the Origins of Art*. Thames & Hudson.

Lewis-Williams, D. 2003. Review feature: A review of *The Mind in the Cave: Consciousness and the Origins of Art* by David Lewis-Williams. *Cambridge Archaeological Journal* 13 (2): 263–279.

Libet, B. 1985. Unconscious cerebral initiative and the role of conscious will in voluntary action. *Behavioral and Brain Sciences* 8: 529–566.

Libet, B. 1999. Do we have free will? *Journal of Consciousness Studies* 6: 47–58.

Lycett, S. J. 2008. Acheulean variation and selection: Does handaxe symmetry fit neutral expectations? *Journal of Archaeological Science* 35 (9): 2640–2648.

Lycett, S. J., and Gowlett, J. A. J. 2008. On questions surrounding the Acheulean "tradition." *World Archaeology* 40 (3): 295–315.

Lycett, S. J., and von Cramon-Taubadel, N. 2008. Acheulean variability and hominin dispersals: A model-bound approach. *Journal of Archaeological Science* 35 (3): 553–562.

Machin, A. J., Hosfield, R. T., and Mithen, S. J. 2007. Why are some handaxes symmetrical? Testing the influence of handaxe morphology on butchery effectiveness. *Journal of Archaeological Science* 34: 883–893.

Mack, J. 2003. *The Museum of the Mind*. British Museum Press.

Mackay, A., and Welz, A. 2008. Engraved ochre from a Middle Stone Age context at Klein Kliphuis in the Western Cape of South Africa. *Journal of Archaeological Science* 35: 1521–1532.

Maguire, E. A., Gadian, D. G., Johnsrude, I. S., Good, C. D., Ashburner, J., Frackowiak, R. S. J., and Frith, C. D. 2000. Navigation-related structural change in the hippocampi of taxi drivers. *Proceedings of the National Academy of Sciences* 97 (8): 4398–4403.

Maguire, E. A., Spiers, H. J., Good, C. D., Hartley, T., Frackowiak, R. S. J., and Burgess, N. 2003. Navigation expertise and the human hippocampus: A structural brain imaging analysis. *Hippocampus* 13: 208–217.

Maguire, E. A., Woollett, K., and Spiers, H. J. 2006. London taxi drivers and bus drivers: A structural MRI and neurophysiological analysis. *Hippocampus* 16: 1091–1101.

Malafouris, L. 2004. The cognitive basis of material engagement: Where brain, body and culture conflate. In *Rethinking Materiality: The Engagement of Mind with the Material World*, ed. E. DeMarrais, C. Gosden, and C. Renfrew. McDonald Institute for Archaeological Research.

Malafouris, L. 2007. Before and beyond representation: Towards an enactive conception of the Palaeolithic image. In *Image and Imagination: A Global History of Figurative Representation*, ed. C. Renfrew and I. Morley. McDonald Institute for Archaeological Research.

Malafouris, L. 2008a. Between brains, bodies and things: Tectonoetic awareness and the extended self. *Philosophical Transactions of the Royal Society of London Series B* 363: 1993–2002.

Malafouris, L. 2008b. Beads for a plastic mind: The "blind man's stick" (BMS) hypothesis and the active nature of material culture. *Cambridge Archaeological Journal* 18 (3): 401–414.

Malafouris, L. 2008c. At the potter's wheel: An argument for material agency. In *Material Agency: Towards a Non-Anthropocentric Perspective*, ed. C. Knappett and L. Malafouris. Springer.

Malafouris, L. 2009. "Neuroarchaeology": Exploring the links between neural and cultural plasticity. *Progress in Brain Research* 178: 253–261.

Malafouris, L. 2010a. The brain-artefact interface (BAI): A challenge for archaeology and cultural neuroscience. *Social Cognitive and Affective Neuroscience* 5: 264–273.

Malafouris, L. 2010b. Metaplasticity and the human becoming: Principles of neuro-archaeology. *Journal of Anthropological Sciences* 88: 49–72.

Malafouris, L. 2010c. Grasping the concept of number: How did the sapient mind move beyond approximation? In *The Archaeology of Measurement: Comprehending Heaven, Earth and Time in Ancient Societies*, ed. C. Renfrew and I. Morley. Cambridge University Press.

Malafouris, L. 2012. More than a brain: Human mindscapes. *Brain* 135: 3839–3844.

Malafouris, L. Forthcoming. How did the Mycenaean remember? In *Death Shall Have No Dominion*, ed. C. Renfrew and M. Boyd. Cambridge University Press.

Malafouris, L., and Renfrew, C. 2008. Steps to a "neuroarchaeology" of mind: An introduction. *Cambridge Archaeological Journal* 18 (3): 381–385.

Malafouris, L., and Renfrew, C. 2010a. An introduction to the cognitive life of things: Archaeology, material engagement and the extended mind. In *The Cognitive Life of Things: Recasting the Boundaries of the Mind*, ed. L. Malafouris and C. Renfrew. McDonald Institute for Archaeological Research.

Malafouris, L., and Renfrew, C., eds. 2010b. *The Cognitive Life of Things: Recasting the Boundaries of the Mind*. McDonald Institute for Archaeological Research.

Mania, D., and Mania, U. 1988. Deliberate engravings on bone artefacts of *Homo erectus*. *Rock Art Research* 5: 91–109.

Manzotti, R. 2006. Consciousness and existence as a process. *Mind and Matter* 4 (1): 7–43.

Maravita, A., Husain, M., Clarke, K., and Driver, J. 2001. Reaching with a tool extends visual-tactile interactions into far space: Evidence from cross-modal extinction. *Neuropsychologia* 39: 580–585.

Maravita, A., and Iriki, A. 2004. Tools for the body (schema). *Trends in Cognitive Sciences* 8: 79–86.

Mareschal, D., Johnson, M. H., Sirois, S., Spratling, M. W., Thomas, M. S. C., and Westermann, G. 2007. *Neuroconstructivism: How the Brain Constructs Cognition*. Oxford University Press.

Mareschal, D., Sirois, S., Westermann, G., and Johnson, M., eds. 2007. Neurocon-structivism, volume II: *Perspectives and Prospects*. Oxford University Press.

Marshack, A. 1972. Upper Paleolithic notation and symbol. *Science* 178: 817–828.

Marshack, A. 1996. The La Marche antler revisited. *Cambridge Archaeological Journal* 6 (1): 99–117.

Marzke, M. 1997. Precision grips, hand morphology, and tools. *American Journal of Physical Anthropology* 102 (1): 91–110.

Marzke, M. 2002. The psychobiology of the hand. *Journal of Human Evolution* 42 (3): 359–360.

Maturana, H. R., and Varela, F. J. 1980. *Autopoiesis and Cognition: The Realization of the Living*. Reidel.

Mauss, M. 1973. Techniques of the body. *Economy and Society* 2: 70–88.

Mauss, M. 1954. *The Gift*. Cohen & West.

McBrearty, S., and Brooks, A. 2000. The revolution that wasn't: A new interpretation of the origin of modern human behavior. *Journal of Human Evolution* 39 (5): 453–563.

McClelland, J. L., and Rumelhart, D. E. 1986. A distributed model of human learning and memory. In *Parallel Distributed Processing: Explorations in the Microstructure of Cognition*, volume 2, ed. J. L. McClelland, D. E. Rumelhart, and the PDP Research Group. MIT Press.

McIntosh, A. R. 1998. Understanding neural interactions in learning and memory using functional neuroimaging. *Annals of the New York Academy of Sciences* 855: 556–571.

McLuhan, M. 1964. *Understanding Media: The Extensions of Man*. MIT Press.

McPherron, S. P. 2000. Handaxes as a measure of the mental capabilities of early hominids. *Journal of Archaeological Science* 27: 655–663.

Mellars, P. 1989. Major issues in the emergence of modern humans. *Current Anthropology* 30: 349–385.

Mellars, P. 1991. Cognitive changes and the emergence of modern humans in Europe. *Cambridge Archaeological Journal* 1 (1): 63–76.

Mellars, P. 2006a. Why did modern human populations disperse form Africa ca. 60,000 years ago? A new model. *Proceedings of the National Academy of Sciences* 103: 9381–9386.

Mellars, P. 2006b. Going east: New genetic and archaeological perspectives on the modern human colonization of Eurasia. *Science* 313: 796–800.

Mellars, P., Boyle, K., Bar-Yosef, O., and Stringer, S., eds. 2007. *Rethinking the Human Revolution: New Behavioural and Biological Perspectives on the Origin and Dispersal of Modern Humans.* McDonald Institute for Archaeological Research.

Mellars, P., and Gibson, K., eds. 1996. *Modelling the Early Human Mind: Archaeological and Psychological Perspectives on the Evolution of Human Intelligence.* McDonald Institute for Archaeological Research.

Menary, R. 2006. Attacking the bounds of cognition. *Philosophical Psychology* 19: 329–344.

Menary, R., ed. 2010. *The Extended Mind.* MIT Press.

Merleau-Ponty, M. 1962. *Phenomenology of Perception.* Routledge.

Meskell, L. 2005. Introduction: Object orientations. In *Archaeologies of Materiality*, ed. L. Meskell. Blackwell.

Mesoudi, A. 2011. *Cultural Evolution: How Darwinian theory Can Explain Human Culture and Synthesize the Social Sciences.* University of Chicago Press.

Mesoudi, A., Whiten, A., and Laland, K. N. 2006. Towards a unified science of cultural evolution. *Behavioral and Brain Sciences* 29 (4): 329–383.

Miller, D. 1987. *Material Culture and Mass Consumption.* Blackwell.

Miller, D., ed. 1998. *Material Cultures. Why Some Things Matter.* University College London Press.

Miller, D., ed. 2005. *Materiality.* Duke University Press.

Miller, D. 2008. *The Comfort of Things.* Polity Press.

Miller, D. 2010. *Stuff.* Polity Press.

Miller, D., and Parrott, F. R. 2009. Loss and material culture in South London. *Journal of the Royal Anthropological Institute* 15: 502–519.

Miller, G. 2008. Neuroimaging: Growing pains for fMRI. *Science* 320: 1412–1414.

Mitchell, J. C. 1996. Studying biface utilisation at Boxgrove: Roe deer butchery with replica handaxes. *Lithics* 16: 64–69.

Mithen, S. 1996. *The Prehistory of Mind.* Thames & Hudson.

Mithen, S. 1998. Introduction. In *Creativity in Human Evolution and Prehistory*, ed. S. Mithen. Routledge.

Mithen, S., and Parsons, L. 2008. The Brain as a cultural artefact. *Cambridge Archaeological Journal* 18: 415–422.

Mockett, B. G., and Hulme, S. R. 2008. Metaplasticity: New insights through electrophysiological investigations. *Journal of Integrative Neuroscience* 7 (2): 315–336.

Munn, N. 1973. *Walpiri Iconography*. Cornell University Press.

Munn, N. 1983. Gawan kula: Spatiotemporal control and the symbolism of influence. In *The Kula: New Perspectives on Massim Exchange*, ed. J. Leach and E. Leach. Cambridge University Press.

Munte, T. F., Altenmuller, E., and Jancke, L. 2002. The musician's brain as a model of neuroplasticity. *Nature Reviews Neuroscience* 3: 473–478.

Nagel, T. 1979. What is it like to be a bat? In *Mortal Questions*, ed. T. Nagel. Cambridge University Press.

Neider, A. 2005. Counting on neurons: The neurobiology of numerical competence. *Nature Reviews Neuroscience* 6: 177–190.

Nicolelis, M. L. A. 2001. Actions from thoughts. *Nature* 409 (18): 403–407.

Nicolelis, M. L. A. 2003. Brain-machine interfaces to restore motor function and probe neural circuits. *Nature Reviews Neuroscience* 4: 417–422.

Nicolopoulou, A. 1997. The invention of writing and the development of numerical concepts in Sumeria: Some implications for developmental psychology. In *Mind Culture and Activity*, ed. M. Cole, Y. Engestrom, and O. Vasquez. Cambridge University Press.

Nithianantharajah, J., and Hannan, J. A. 2006. Enriched environments, experience dependent plasticity and disorders of the nervous system. *Nature Reviews Neuroscience* 7: 697–709.

Noble, W., and Davidson, I. 1996. *Human Evolution, Language and Mind: A Psychological and Archaeological Inquiry*. Cambridge University Press.

Noë, A. 2004. *Action in Perception*. MIT Press.

Noë, A. 2009. *Out of Our Heads: Why You Are Not Your Brain, and Other Lessons from the Biology of Consciousness*. Hill and Wang.

Norman, D. 1988. *The Psychology of Everyday Things*. Basic Books.

Norman, D. 1991. Cognitive artefacts. In *Designing Interaction: Psychology at the Human-Computer Interface*, ed. J. M. Carroll. Cambridge University Press.

Norman, D. 1993. Cognition in the head and in the world. *Cognitive Science* 17 (1): 1–6.

Nowell, A. 2010. Defining behavioural modernity in the context of Neandertal and anatomically modern human populations. *Annual Review of Anthropology* 39: 437–452.

Núñez, R. 1999. Could the future taste purple? In *Reclaiming Cognition: The Primacy of Action, Intention and Emotion*, ed. R. Núñez and W. J. Freeman. Imprint Academic.

O'Brien, M. J., and Lyman, R. L. 2002. Darwinian evolutionism in archaeology: Current status and prospects for synthesis. *Evolutionary Anthropology* 11: 26–36.

Odling Smee, F. J., Laland, K. N., and Feldman, M. 2003. *Niche Construction: The Neglected Process in Evolution.* Princeton University Press.

Ohel, M. Y. 1987. The Acheulean handaxe: A maintainable multi-functional tool. *Lithic Technology* 16: 54–55.

Olsen, B. 2003. Material culture after text: Remembering things. *Norwegian Archaeological Review* 36 (2): 87–104.

Olsen, B. 2010. *In Defense of Things: Archaeology and the Ontology of Objects.* Alta Mira.

Olsen, B., Shanks, M., Webmoor, T., and Witmore, C. 2012. *Archaeology: The Discipline of Things.* University of California Press.

Orban, G. A., Claeys, K., Nelissen, K., Smans, R., Sunaert, S., Todd, J. T., et al. 2006. Mapping the parietal cortex of human and non-human primates. *Neuropsychologia* 44: 2647–2667.

O'Regan, J. K. 1992. Solving the "real" mysteries of visual perception: The world as an outside memory. *Canadian Journal of Psychology* 46 (3): 461–488.

O'Regan, J. K., and Noë, A. 2001. A sensorimotor approach to vision and visual perception. *Behavioral and Brain Sciences* 24 (5): 939–973.

Ortman, S. 2000. Conceptual metaphor in the archaeological record: Methods and an example from the American Southwest. *American Antiquity* 65 (4): 613–645.

Oyama, S., Griffiths, P. E., and Gray, R. D., eds. 2001. *Cycles of Contingency: Developmental Systems and Evolution.* MIT Press.

Palaima, T. G. 1988. The development of the Mycenaean writing system. *MINOS* Suppl. 10: 269–342.

Peirce, C. S. 1955. *Philosophical Writings of Peirce,* ed. B. Justus. Dover.

Pelegrin, J. 1993. A framework for analysing prehistoric stone tool manufacture and a tentative application to some early stone industries. In *The Use of Tools by Human and Non-Human Primates,* ed. A. Berthelet and J. Chavaillon. Clarendon.

Pellegram, A. 1998. The message in paper. In *Material Cultures: Why Some Things Matter,* ed. D. Miller. UCL Press.

Penfield, W., and Rasmussen, T. 1950. *The Cerebral Cortex of Man.* Macmillan.

Penn, D. C., Holyoak, K., and Povinelli, D. J. 2008. Darwin's mistake: Explaining the discontinuity between human and nonhuman minds. *Behavioral and Brain Sciences* 31 (2): 109–178.

Penn, D. C., and Povinelli, D. J. 2007. Causal cognition in human and nonhuman animals: A comparative, critical review. *Annual Review of Psychology* 58: 97–118.

Petersen, S. E., van Mier, H., Fiez, J. A., and Raichle, M. E. 1998. The effects of practice on the functional anatomy of task performance. *Proceedings of the National Academy of Sciences* 95: 853–860.

Piazza, M., and Izard, V. 2009. How humans count: Numerosity and the parietal cortex. *Neuroscientist* 15 (3): 261–273.

Pica, P., Lemer, C., Izard, V., and Dehaene, S. 2004. Exact and approximate arithmetic in an Amazonian indigene group. *Science* 306: 499–503.

Pickering, A. 1995. *The Mangle of Practice*. Chicago University Press.

Pinker, S. 1997. *How the Mind Works*. Norton.

Polanyi, M. 1958. *Personal Knowledge*. Routledge & Kegan Paul.

Poldrack, R. A. 2000. Imaging brain plasticity: Conceptual and methodological issues—a theoretical review. *NeuroImage* 12: 1–13.

Popper, K. R. 1979. *Objective Knowledge: An Evolutionary Approach*, revised edition. Clarendon.

Powell, A., Shennan, S., and Thomas, M. G. 2009. Late Pleistocene demography and the appearance of modern human behavior. *Science* 324: 1298–1301.

Preucel, R. W. 2006. *Archaeological Semiotics*. Blackwell.

Putnam, H. 1975. The meaning of "meaning." In *Language, Mind, and Knowledge*, ed. K. Gunderson. University of Minnesota Press.

Putnam, H. 1982. *Reason, Truth, and History*. Cambridge University Press.

Quartz, S., and Sejnowski, T. 1997. The neural basis of cognitive development: A constructivist manifesto. *Behavioral and Brain Sciences* 20: 537–596.

Ragert, P., Schmidt, A., Altenmuller, E., and Dinse, H. R. 2004. Superior tactile performance and learning in professional pianists: Evidence for metaplasticity in musicians. *European Journal of Neuroscience* 19: 473–478.

Ramsey, A. 2000. Agency, personhood and the 'I' of discourse in the Pacific and beyond. *Journal of the Royal Anthropological Institute* 7: 101–115.

Ratner, C. 1991. *Vygotsky's Sociohistorical Psychology and Its Contemporary Applications*. Plenum.

Renfrew, C. 1994. Towards a cognitive archaeology. In *The Ancient Mind: Elements of Cognitive Archaeology*, ed. C. Renfrew and E. Zubrow. Cambridge University Press.

Renfrew, C. 2001a. Symbol before concept: Material engagement and the early development of society. In *Archaeological Theory Today*, ed. I. Hodder. Polity.

Renfrew, C. 2001b. Commodification and institution in group-oriented and individualizing societies. *Proceedings of the British Academy* 110: 93–117.

Renfrew, C. 2004. Towards a theory of material engagement. In *Rethinking Materiality: The Engagement of Mind with the Material World*, ed. E. DeMarrais, C. Gosden, and C. Renfrew. McDonald Institute for Archaeological Research.

Renfrew, C. 2006. Becoming human: The archaeological challenge. *Proceedings of the British Academy* 139: 217–238.

Renfrew, C. 2007. *Prehistory: the Making of the Human Mind*. Weidenfeld & Nicolson.

Renfrew, C., Frith, C., and Malafouris, L., eds. 2009. *The Sapient Mind: Archaeology Meets Neuroscience*. Oxford University Press.

Renfrew, C., Frith, C., and Malafouris, L. 2008. Introduction. The sapient mind: Archaeology meets neuroscience. *Philosophical Transactions of the Royal Society of London Series B* 363: 1935–1938.

Renfrew, C., and Scarre, C., eds. 1998. *Cognition and Material Culture: The Archaeology of Symbolic Storage*. McDonald Institute for Archaeological Research.

Renfrew, C., and Zubrow, E., eds. 1994. *The Ancient Mind: Elements of Cognitive Archaeology*. Cambridge University Press.

Riggins, S. H., ed. 1994. *The Socialness of Things: Essays in the Socio-Semiotics of Objects*. Mouton de Gruyter.

Rogoff, B. 1990. *Apprenticeship in Thinking: Cognitive Development in Social Context*. Oxford University Press.

Rogoff, B., and Lave, J. 1984. *Everyday Cognition: Its Development in Social Context*. Harvard University Press.

Rosenkranz, K., Williamon, A., and Rothwell, J. C. 2007. Motorcortical excitability and synaptic plasticity is enhanced in professional musicians. *Journal of Neuroscience* 27 (19): 5200–5206.

Roux, V., and Bril, B., eds. 2005. *Stone Knapping: The Necessary Conditions for a Uniquely Hominin Behaviour*. McDonald Institute for Archaeological Research.

Rowlands, M. 1999. *The Body in Mind*. Cambridge University Press.

Rowlands, M. 2009. Extended cognition and the mark of the cognitive. *Philosophical Psychology* 22: 1–19.

Rowlands, M. 2010. *The New Science of the Mind*. MIT Press.

Rupert, R. 2004. Challenges to the hypothesis of extended cognition. *Journal of Philosophy* 101: 389–428.

Rupert, R. 2009. *Cognitive Systems and the Extended Mind*. Oxford University Press.

Rupert, R. 2010a. Extended cognition and the priority of cognitive systems. *Cognitive Systems Research* 11: 343–356.

Rupert, R. 2010b. Systems, functions, and intrinsic natures: On Adams and Aizawa's *The Bounds of Cognition*. *Philosophical Psychology* 23: 113–123.

Ryle, G. 1949. *The Concept of Mind*. Barnes & Noble.

Saussure, F. D. 1966. *Course in General Linguistics*. McGraw-Hill.

Schaefer, M. C. A., Rothemund, Y., Heinze, H. J., and Rotte, M. 2004. Short-term plasticity of the primary somatosensory cortex during tool use. *Neuroreport* 15 (8): 1293–1297.

Schick, K. D., and Toth, N. 1993. *Making Silent Stones Speak: Human Evolution and the Dawn of Technology*. Weidenfeld and Nicolson.

Schick, K. D., Toth, N., and Garufi, G. 1999. Continuing investigations into the stone tool-making and tool-using capabilities of a Bonobo (*Pan paniscus*). *Journal of Archaeological Science* 26: 821–832.

Schiffer, M. B., and Miller, A. 1999. *The Material Life of Human Beings: Artifacts, Behavior, and Communication*. Routledge.

Schlanger, N. 1994. Mindful technology: Unleashing the chaine opératoire from an archaeology of mind. In *The Ancient Mind: Elements of Cognitive Archaeology*, ed. C. Renfrew and E. Zubrow. Cambridge University Press.

Schmandt-Besserat, D. 1992. *Before Writing*, volume I: From Counting to Cuneiform. University of Texas Press.

Schmandt-Besserat, D. 1996. *How Writing Came About*. University of Texas Press.

Schmandt-Besserat, D. 2010. The token system of the ancient Near East. In *The Archaeology of Measurement: Comprehending Heaven, Earth and Time in Ancient Societies*, ed. C. Renfrew and I. Morley. Cambridge University Press.

Searle, J. R. 1983. *Intentionality: An Essay in the Philosophy of Mind*. Cambridge University Press.

Seed, A., and Byrne, R. 2010. Animal tool-use. *Current Biology* 20: 1032–1039.

Semaw, S. 2000. The world's oldest stone artifacts from Gona, Ethiopia: Their implications for understanding stone technology and patterns of human evolution between 2.6 and 1.5 million years ago. *Journal of Archaeological Science* 27: 1197–1214.

Semaw, S., Renne, P., Harris, J. W. K., et al. 1997. 2.5-million-year-old stone tools from Gona, Ethiopia. *Nature* 385: 333–336.

Semaw, S., Roger, M. J., Quade, J., et al. 2003. 2.6-million-year-old stone tools and associated bones from OGS-6 and OGS-7, Gona, Afar, Ethiopia. *Journal of Human Evolution* 45: 169–177.

Shanks, M. 2007. Symmetrical archaeology. *World Archaeology* 39 (4): 589–596.

Shanks, M., and McGuire, R. H. 1996. The craft of archaeology. *American Antiquity* 61 (1): 75–88.

Shapiro, L. 2004. *The Mind Incarnate*. MIT Press.

Shapiro, L. 2008. Functionalism and mental boundaries. *Cognitive Systems Research* 9: 5–14.

Shapiro, L. 2011. *Embodied Cognition*. Routledge.

Shea, J. 2011. *Homo sapiens* is as *Homo sapiens* was. *Current Anthropology* 52 (1): 1–35.

Shea, J. 2012. Lithic Modes A–I: A new framework for describing global-scale variation in stone tool technology illustrated with evidence from the East Mediterranean Levant. *Journal of Archaeological Method and Theory* (online).

Shelmerdine, C. W. 1997. Review of Aegean prehistory VI: The palatial Bronze Age of the southern and central Greek mainland. *American Journal of Archaeology* 101: 537–585.

Sheng-zhi, W., and Huizhong, W. T. 2009. History matters: Illuminating metaplasticity in the developing brain. *Neuron* 64 (2): 155–157.

Shennan, S. 2002. *Genes, Memes and Human History*. Thames and Hudson.

Shore, B. 1996. *Culture in Mind*. Oxford University Press.

Simao, J. 2002. Tools evolve: The artificial selection and evolution of Paleolithic stone tools. *Behavioral and Brain Sciences* 25: 419.

Smith, A. T. 2001. The limitations of doxa. *Journal of Social Archaeology* 1 (2): 155–170.

Solso, R. L. 1991. *Cognitive Psychology*. Allyn & Bacon.

Sowell, E. R., Peterson, B. S., Thompson, P. M., Welcome, S. E., Henkenius, A. L., and Toga, A. W. 2003. Mapping cortical change across the life span. *Nature Neuroscience* 6: 309–315.

Stamatopoulou, D. 2011. Symbol formation and the embodied self: A microgenetic case-study examination of the transition to symbolic communication in scribbling activities from 14 to 31 months of age. *New Ideas in Psychology* 29: 162–188.

Steels, L. 2007. Fifty years of AI: From symbols to embodiment—and back. In *50 Years of Artificial Intelligence: Essays Dedicated to the 50th Anniversary of Artificial Intelligence*, ed. M. Lungarella, F. Iida, J. Bongard, and R. Pfeifer. Springer.

Stewart, J. O. Gappene, and di Paolo, E., eds. 2010. *Enaction: Towards a New Paradigm in Cognitive Science*. MIT Press.

Steiner, P. 2010. The bounds of representation. *Pragmatics & Cognition* 18 (2): 235–272.

Sterelny, K. 2004. Externalism, epistemic artefacts and the extended mind. In *The Externalist Challenge: New Studies on Cognition and Intentionality*, ed. R. Schantz. De Gruyter.

Stiegler, B. 1998. *Technics and Time, 1: The Fault of Epimetheus*. Stanford University Press.

Stout, D. 2002. Skill and cognition in stone tool production: An ethnographic case study from Irian Jaya. *Current Anthropology* 45 (3): 693–722.

Stout, D. 2005. The social and cultural context of stone-knapping skill acquisition. In *Stone Knapping: The Necessary Conditions for a Uniquely Hominin Behaviour*, ed. V. Roux and B. Bril. McDonald Institute for Archaeology.

Stout, D. 2011. Stone toolmaking and the evolution of human culture and cognition. *Philosophical Transactions of the Royal Society of London Series B* 366: 1050–1059.

Stout, D., and Chaminade, T. 2007. The evolutionary neuroscience of tool making. *Neuropsychologia* 45: 1091–1100.

Stout, D., and Chaminade, T. 2009. Making tools and making sense: Complex, intentional behaviour in human evolution. *Cambridge Archaeological Journal* 19: 85–96.

Stout, D., Toth, N., Schick, K., and Chaminade, T. 2008. Neural correlates of Early Stone Age toolmaking: Technology, language and cognition in human evolution. *Philosophical Transactions of the Royal Society of London Series B* 363: 1939–1949.

Strathern, M. 1988. *The Gender of the Gift*. University of California Press.

Streeck, J. 2009. *Gesturecraft. The Manu-Facture of Meaning*. Benjamins.

Suchman, L. A. 1987. *Plans and Situated Action*. Cambridge University Press.

Sutton, J. 2008. Material agency, skills and history: Distributed cognition and the archaeology of memory. In *Material Agency: Towards a Non-Anthropocentric Perspective*, ed. C. Knappett and L. Malafouris. Springer.

Sutton, J. 2010. Exograms and interdisciplinarity: History, the extended mind, and the civilizing process. In *The Extended Mind*, ed. R. Menary. MIT Press.

Sutton, J., Harris, C. B., Keil, P. G., and Barnier, A. J. 2010. The psychology of memory, extended cognition, and socially distributed remembering. *Phenomenology and the Cognitive Sciences* 9 (4): 521–560.

Synofzik, M., Vosgerau, G., and Newen, A. 2008a. I move, therefore I am: A new theoretical framework to investigate agency and ownership. *Consciousness and Cognition* 17 (2): 411–424.

Synofzik, M., Vosgerau, G., and Newen, A. 2008b. Beyond the comparator model: A multifactorial two-step account of agency. *Consciousness and Cognition* 17 (1): 219–239.

Tallis, R. 2011. *Aping Mankind: Neuromania, Darwinitis and the Misrepresentation of Humanity*. Acumen.

Tang, Y., Zhang, W., Chen, K., et al. 2006. Arithmetic processing in the brain shaped by cultures. *Proceedings of the National Academy of Sciences* 103 (10): 775–780.

Taylor, C. 1985. Theories of meaning. In *Human Agency and Language*, ed. C. Taylor. Cambridge University Press.

Texier, J. P., Porraz, G., Parkington, J., Rigaud, J. P., Poggenpoel, C., Miller, C., et al. 2010. A Howiesons Poort tradition of engraving ostrich eggshell containers dated to 60,000 years ago at Diepkloof Rock Shelter, South Africa. *Proceedings of the National Academy of Sciences* 107 (14): 6180–6185.

Thagard, P. 1996. *Mind: Introduction to Cognitive Science*. MIT Press.

Thelen, E., and Smith, L. 1994. *A Dynamic Systems Approach to the Development of Cognition and Action*. MIT Press.

Thomas, J. 1996. *Time, Culture and Identity*. Routledge.

Thomas, J. 2004. *Archaeology and Modernity*. Routledge.

Thomas, J. 2007. The trouble with material culture. *Journal of Iberian Archaeology* 9/10: 11–23.

Thomas, N., and Pinney, C., eds. 2001. *Beyond Aesthetics: Art and the Technologies of Enchantment*. Berg.

Thompson, E. 2007. *Mind in Life: Biology, Phenomenology, and the Sciences of Mind*. Harvard University Press.

Thompson, E., and Stapelton, M. 2009. Making sense of sense-making: Reflections on enactive and extended mind theories. *Topoi* 28: 23–30.

Tilley, C. 1991. *Material Culture and Text: The Art of Ambiguity*. Routledge.

Tilley, C. 1994. *A Phenomenology of Landscape*. Berg.

Tilley, C. 1996. *An Ethnography of the Neolithic*. Cambridge University Press.

Tilley, C. 1999. *Metaphor and Material Culture*. Blackwell.

Tilley, C. W., Keane, S., Küchler, M., Rowlands and Spyer, P., eds. 2006. *Handbook of Material Culture*. Sage.

Tomasello, M. and Call, J. 1997. *Primate Cognition*. Oxford University Press.

Tomasello, M., Carpenter, M., Call, J., Behne, T., and Moll, H. 2005. Understanding and sharing intentions: The origins of cultural cognition. *Behavioral and Brain Sciences* 28: 675–735.

Tomasello, M., and Herrmann, E. 2010. Ape and human cognition: What's the difference? *Current Directions in Psychological Science* 19: 3–8.

Toth, N., Schick, K. D., Savage-Rumbaugh, E. S., Sevcik, R. A., and Rumbaugh, D. 1993. Pan the tool-maker: Investigations into the stone tool-making and tool-using capabilities of a Bonobo *(Pan paniscus)*. *Journal of Archaeological Science* 20: 81–91.

Tsakiris, M., Haggard, P., Franck, N., Mainy, N., and Sirigu, A. 2005. A specific role for efferent information in self-recognition. *Cognition* 96 (3): 215–231.

Tsakiris, M., and Haggard, P. 2005a. Experimenting with the acting self. *Cognitive Neuropsychology* 22 (3/4): 387–407.

Tsakiris, M., and Haggard, P. 2005b. The rubber hand illusion revisited: Visuotactile integration and self-attribution. *Journal of Experimental Psychology Human Perception and Performance* 31 (1): 80–91.

Tsakiris, M., Hesse, M., Boy, C., Haggard, P., and Fink, G. R. 2007b. Neural correlates of body-ownership: A sensory network for bodily self-consciousness. *Cerebral Cortex* 17: 2235–2244.

Tsakiris, M., Prabhu, G., and Haggard, P. 2006. Having a body versus moving your body: How agency structures body-ownership. *Consciousness and Cognition* 15 (2): 423–432.

Tsakiris, M., Schütz-Bosbach, S., and Gallagher, S. 2007a. On agency and body-ownership: Phenomenological and neurocognitive reflections. *Consciousness and Cognition* 16 (3): 645–660.

Turing, A. M. 1950. Computing machinery and intelligence. *Mind* 59: 433–460.

Turner, M. 1996. *The Literary Mind*. Oxford University Press.

Tulving, E. 2002. Chronesthesia: Conscious awareness of subjective time. In *Principles of Frontal Lobe Function*, ed. D. T. Stuss and R. C. Knight. Oxford University Press.

Turkle, S., ed. 2007. *Evocative Objects: Things We Think With*. MIT Press.

Van der Leeuw, S. 2008. Agency, networks, past and future. In *Material Agency: Towards a Non-Anthropocentric Perspective*, ed. C. Knappett and L. Malafouris. Springer.

Van Gelder, T. 1995. What might cognition be if not computation? *Journal of Philosophy* 92: 345–381.

Van Gelder, T. 1999. Defending the dynamical hypothesis. In *Dynamics, Synergetics, Autonomous Agents*, ed. W. Tschacher and J. Dauwalder. World Scientific.

Van Gelder, T., and Port, R. 1995a. It's about time: A perspective to dynamical system approach to cognition. In *Mind as Motion*, ed. R. Port and T. Van Gelder. MIT Press.

Van Gelder, T., and Port, R. 1995b. Preface. In *Mind as Motion*, ed. R. Port and T. Van Gelder. MIT Press.

Varela, F. J., Thompson, E., and Rosch, E. 1991. *The Embodied Mind: Cognitive Science and Human Experience*. MIT Press.

Ventris, M., and Chadwick, J. 1973. *Documents in Mycenean Greek*. Cambridge University Press.

Verbeek, P. P. 2005. *What Things Do: Philosophical Reflections on Technology, Agency, and Design*. Pennsylvania State University Press.

Verbeek, P. P. 2011. *Moralizing Technology: Understanding and Designing the Morality of Things*. University of Chicago Press.

Visalberghi, E., and Tomasello, M. 1998. Primate causal understanding in the physical and psychological domains. *Behavioural Processes* 42: 189–203.

Vygotsky, L. S. 1978. *Mind in Society*. Harvard University Press.

Vygotsky, L. S. 1986. *Thought and Language*. MIT Press.

Wadley, L. 2001. What is cultural modernity? A general view and a South African perspective from Rose Cottage Cave. *Cambridge Archaeological Journal* 11: 201–221.

Wadley, L. 2010. Compound-adhesive manufacture as a behavioral proxy for complex cognition in the Middle Stone Age. *Current Anthropology* 51 (S1): 111–119.

Wadley, L., Hodgskiss, T., and Grant, M. 2009. Implications for complex cognition from the hafting of tools with compound adhesives in the Middle Stone Age, South Africa. *Proceedings of the National Academy of Sciences* 106 (24): 9590–9594.

Walter, S., and Kastner, L. 2012. The where and what of cognition: The untenability of cognitive agnosticism and the limits of the Motley Crew Argument. *Cognitive Systems Research* 13: 12–23.

Walter, W. G. 1953. *The Living Brain*. Duckworth.

Warnier, J. P. 2001. A praxeological approach to subjectivation in a material world. *Journal of Material Culture* 6 (1): 5–24.

Watanabe, D., Savion-Lemieux, T., and Penhune, V. B. 2007. The effect of early musical training on adult motor performance: Evidence for a sensitive period in motor learning. *Experimental Brain Research* 176: 332–340.

Webmoor, T. 2007. What about "one more turn after the social" in archaeological reasoning? Taking things seriously. *World Archaeology* 39 (4): 547–562.

Webmoor, T., and Witmore, C. L. 2008. Things are us! A commentary on human/things relations under the banner of a "social" archaeology. *Norwegian Archaeological Review* 41 (1): 53–70.

Wegner, D. M. 2002. *The Illusion of Conscious Will*. MIT Press.

Wegner, D. M. 2003. The mind's best trick: How we experience conscious will. *Trends in Cognitive Sciences* 7 (2): 65–69.

Wegner, D. M. 2004. Précis of the illusion of conscious will. *Behavioral and Brain Sciences* 27: 649–692.

Wertsch, J. V. 1991. *Voices of the Mind: A Sociocultural Approach to Mediated Action.* Harvard University Press.

Wertsch, J. V. 1998. *Mind as Action.* Oxford University Press.

Westermann, G., Mareschal, D., Johnson, M. H., Sirois, S., Spratling, M. W., and Thomas, M. S. C. 2007. Neuroconstructivism. *Developmental Science* 10 (1): 75–83.

Wexler, B. E. 2006. *Brain and Culture: Neurobiology, Ideology, and Social Change.* MIT Press.

Wheeler, M. 2005. *Reconstructing the Cognitive World: The Next Step.* MIT Press.

Wheeler, M. 2010a. In defense of extended functionalism. In *The Extended Mind*, ed. R. Menary. MIT Press.

Wheeler, M. 2010b. Minds, things, and materiality. In *The Cognitive Life of Things*, ed. L. Malafouris and C. Renfrew. McDonald Institute for Archaeological Research.

Wheeler, M., and Clark, A. 2008. Culture, embodiment and genes: Unraveling the triple helix. *Philosophical Transactions of the Royal Society of London Series B* 363: 3563–3575.

Whiten, A., Goodall, J., McGrew, W. C., Nishida, T., Reynolds, V., Sugiyama, Y., et al. 1999. Cultures in chimpanzees. *Nature* 399: 682–685.

Whiten, A., Schick, K., and Toth, T. 2009. The evolution and cultural transmission of percussive technology: Integrating evidence from palaeoanthropology and primatology. *Journal of Human Evolution* 57: 420–435.

Wiener, N. 1948. *Cybernetics, or, Control and Communication in Animal and the Machine.* Wiley.

Wilson, F. R. 1998. *The Hand: How Its Use Shapes the Brain, Language, and Human Culture.* Pantheon Books.

Wilson, R. 1994. Wide computationalism. *Mind* 103: 351–372.

Wilson, R. 2004. *Boundaries of the Mind.* Cambridge University Press.

Wilson, R., and Clark, A. 2009. How to situate cognition: Letting nature take its course. In *The Cambridge Handbook of Situated Cognition*, ed. P. Robbins and M. Aydede. Cambridge University Press.

Witmore, C. 2007. Symmetrical archaeology: Excerpts of a manifesto. *World Archaeology* 39 (4): 546–562.

Wylie, A. 2002. *Thinking from Things: Essays in the Philosophy of Archaeology.* University of California Press.

Wynn, T. 1995. Handaxe enigmas. *World Archaeology* 27: 10–24.

Wynn, T. 2000. Comment on F. d'Errico and A. Nowell, "A new look at the Berekhat Ram figurine: Implications for the origins of symbolism." *Cambridge Archaeological Journal* 10: 151–152.

Wynn, T. 2002. Archaeology and cognitive evolution. *Behavioral and Brain Sciences* 25: 389–403.

Wynn, T., and Coolidge, F. 2004. The expert Neandertal mind. *Journal of Human Evolution* 46: 467–487.

Wynn, T., and Coolidge, F. 2010. Beyond symbolism and language: An introduction to supplement 1, *Working Memory. Current Anthropology* 51 (1): 5–16.

Zhang, W., and Linden, D. 2003. The other side of the engram: Experience driven changes in neuronal intrinsic excitability. *Nature Reviews Neuroscience* 4: 885–900.

Zilhão, J. 2007. The emergence of ornaments and art: An archaeological perspective on the origins of "behavioural modernity." *Journal of Archaeological Research* 15 (1): 1–54.

Index

Abduction, 114, 134
Acheulean handaxe, 157, 160, 167,
    169, 177, 235, 243
Actant, 130
Actor-Network Theory, 122–129
Actualistic studies, 160, 163, 190
Adams, Frederick, 37, 73, 80, 81
Affordance(s), 18, 66, 72, 81, 82, 91,
    111, 126, 141–144, 176, 193, 209,
    213, 220
Agency
  and archaeology, 120–122
  attribution of, 219, 220
  and causality, 175, 207
  of clay, 116
  and creativity, 20, 207–209, 212,
    213
  decentralized, 123
  feeling of, 215, 218, 224, 225
  illusion of, 214, 219
  judgment of, 215–219, 225
  locus of, 219
  loss of, 224
  of markings, 191
  material, 17, 18, 51, 79, 110, 119,
    130–135, 147–149, 207, 214, 236
  meaning of, 208, 211
  moral, 230
  non-anthropocentric conception of,
    122, 123
  object, 12

  and ownership, 223
  question of, 18, 119, 207, 218–221
  relational, 145
  sense of, 159, 172, 176, 213, 214, 217,
    224
  of things, 18, 119, 144–149
Aizawa, Kenneth, 37, 73, 80, 81
Ambrose, Stanley, 153, 157, 158
Anchoring
  emotional, 86
  intellectual, 86
  material, 102–104
  temporal, 246
Anderson, Michael, 10, 57, 65
Anthropomorphism, 130–132
Anti-localization, 37
Appadurai, Arjun, 12, 122, 133, 248
Arithmetic, approximate and exact,
    105, 109–111
Artificial intelligence, 28, 29, 227
Artificiality, 184, 185
Authorship, sense of, 218
Automaticity, 224

Bateson, Gregory, 4, 6, 34, 89, 91, 207,
    217, 243, 244, 248
Bell, James, 23, 25
Bergson, Henri-Louis, 154
Binding
  intentional, 223
  temporal, 247

Blind man's stick, 4–7, 243, 244
Blombos cave engravings, 181,
  186–192, 243
Boden, Margaret, 212
Body (or bodies)
  and brains and things, 6, 208, 219
  enculturated, 221
  inhabiting mind, 60
  knapper's, 174
  ownership of, 218, 224
  potter's, 209, 213, 221
  and proprioceptive awareness, 223
  prosthetic, 223
  situated, 221
Body schema, 5, 166, 167, 233
Boivin, Nicole, 11, 24, 30, 95, 231
Boundaries
  between disciplines, 13
  between "inner" and "outer," 84, 177,
    230
  between mental and physical
    domains, 73, 84, 177
  between minds and things, 13, 84,
    162, 179, 192, 230, 244
  between persons and things, 122,
    130
  biological, 4, 85
  dissolution of, 65
  of mind, 2–4, 13, 17, 24, 37, 38, 66,
    162, 228, 230, 246
  organismic, 81, 84
  permeable, 2, 179
  temporal, 249
  of units of analysis, 36, 38, 66, 67, 80,
    162, 179, 236
Brain
  as biological constant, 45
  clay tablets and, 76
  and culture, 11, 39, 45, 46, 49, 84,
    115, 168, 169
  and development, 40, 46
  embodied, 82
  evolution of, 46

  and hand, 60
  hominin, 169, 174
  imaging, 109, 229, 249
  interactivity and, 48
  monkey's, 164, 165
  naked, 30, 116
  plastic, 42, 45–49
  potter's, 212, 213, 217–220
  primate, 60
  super-, 231
  and things, 67, 77, 82–85
  in vat, 29
  visual, 197, 203
Brain-artifact interface, 244, 245
Brain-culture spiral, 30
Brooks, Rodney, 28, 219, 237
Byers, Martin, 96, 98

Cartesian dichotomy, 25
Cartesian doctrine, 59
Cartesian genealogy, 118
Cartesian metaphysics, 57, 163
Cartesian predicament, 17, 25, 148.
  See also Modernity
Cartesian prison, 16
Cartesian self, 220
Cartesian universe, 25
Cartesian way of thinking, 15, 234
Category mistake, 25, 34, 208
Causal cognition, 214
Causal efficacy of things, 8, 44
Chadwick, John, 68–72, 78
Chaîne opératoire, 160, 161. See also
  Operational sequence
Chauvet cave, 183, 185, 195–200, 205
Chemero, Anthony, 10, 57, 59, 222,
  236
Chronesthesis, 1
Chrono-architecture, 213, 222
Chronostratigraphy, 190
Clancey, William, 37, 58
Clark, Andy, 2, 7, 10, 13, 16, 26–29,
  37, 48, 57, 58, 73–77, 81, 85, 104,

153, 155, 161, 177, 192, 208, 214,
  228, 232, 233, 237, 238, 244, 246,
  249
Clark, Grahame, 156
Clay tokens, 106–108, 111–116
Coalitions
 dynamic, 191, 245
 emergent, 5
 hybrid, 177
 ontological, 5, 245
 of tools, 233
Cognitive
 mark of, 8, 57, 162
 yardstick for, 76, 83
Cognitive agnosticism, 8
Cognitive archaeology, 1–3, 6, 8, 13,
  17, 20, 23–25, 29, 32, 33, 38, 43, 46,
  49, 53, 69, 83, 153, 227–230, 241,
  243, 246, 248
Cognitive artifact, 50, 67, 69, 72, 76,
  111, 155
Cognitive assemblies, 82, 84, 245
Cognitive becoming, 2, 11, 39–41, 53,
  242
Cognitive components, 84
Cognitive continuity, 155, 231
Cognitive discontinuity, 232
Cognitive ecologies, 5, 36, 78, 81, 205,
  207, 223, 234, 245
Cognitive economy, 196
Cognitive ethnography, 208
Cognitive extensions, 4, 5, 59, 81, 82,
  228, 233
Cognitive impartiality, 37
Cognitive landscape, 2
Cognitive life of things, 30, 33, 44, 45,
  76, 80, 84, 133, 134, 181, 203, 230,
  238, 248
Cognitive mappings, 62, 100
Cognitive network, 10
Cognitive projections, 99–102
Cognitive realm, 24, 162
Cognitive residue, 162

Cognitive science, 2, 3, 6, 7, 10, 11,
  26–31, 35, 43, 50, 52, 57, 61, 67, 70,
  73, 208, 228, 230, 236, 240
 embodied, 10, 16, 35, 50, 67, 236
 non-Cartesian, 58
Cognitive system, 27, 35, 46, 48, 71,
  72, 76, 79–85, 114, 180, 228, 237,
  238, 246–249
Cognitive topology, 213
Comparative anthropology of lines,
  180
Comparative cognition, 232, 233
Comparative primatology, 164
Composite person, 123
Composite tools, 163, 175
Compound adhesives, 163
Conceptual integration, 90, 99,
  103–106
Connectivity, 36, 48, 81
Contextual archaeology, 127, 128
Counting, 111–114
Coupling-constitution fallacy, 80, 81
Creative conflation of appearance with
  reality, 198
Creative ecology of recursiveness,
  193
Creative engagement, 204, 207, 211
Creative performance, 211
Creative process, 209–215
Creativity, 20, 207–209, 224, 235,
  240
 combinational, 212
 exploratory, 212
 externalist approach to, 211, 212
 internalist approach to, 211, 212
 transformational, 212
Cyborgs, 15, 155, 177, 232

Damerow, Peter, 111
Darwin, Charles, 155, 233
Davidson, Iain, 154, 157, 160, 161,
  170, 171, 176, 179, 184
Dehaene, Stanislas, 105–109

Deleuze, Gilles, 235
Deliberate engravings, 185, 187, 189.
    See also Blombos cave engravings
Deliberate imposed form, 192
Deliberate marking, 186
Deliberateness, 184, 185
Deliberate planning, 236
DeLoache, Judy, 199
Dennett, Daniel, 241
d'Errico, Francesco, 181–189, 234, 240
Descartes, René, 233
Developmental systems theory, 40
Di Paolo, Ezequiel, 50, 58, 84
Dobres, Marcia-Anne, 120, 121
Donald, Merlin, 73, 82, 83, 243
Dreyfus, Hubert, 142

Ecological validity, 29, 179, 208
Ellen, Roy, 131–134
Embodied action-taking, 59, 115, 153,
    193, 207, 211, 219, 234
Embodied being, 221, 222
Embodied cognition, 59, 60, 64, 66
Embodied cognitivism, 64
Embodied cultural practices, 248
Embodied dynamics, 2
Embodied engagement, 50, 105, 208
Embodied imagination, 105
Embodied mind, 2, 6, 57–66
Embodied praxis, 233
Embodied routines, 87
Embodied semiotic field, 116
Embodied thinking process, 222
Embodiment, profound, 48, 208
Emergence
  of agency, 148, 159, 212
  of depiction, 183
  of human signification, 189
  of material sign, 99
  of numerical thinking, 18, 113, 110,
    111, 202
  of Palaeolithic image, 203
  of symbolism, 105, 191, 202

Enactive approach, 50, 85
Enactive cognition, 58, 219, 220
Enactive cognitive prostheses, 154,
    163, 164, 175, 245
Enactive discovery, 110
Enactive perception, 102
Enactive projections, 180, 191, 193
Enactive sensorimotor account, 203
Enactive thinking, 205, 235
Enactivism, 50, 236
Enframing, 122
Engrams, 76, 83, 84
Engravings
  as cognitive scaffolds, 190, 239
  earliest examples of, 185, 186
  as enactive projections, 193
  epistemic and ontological status of,
    190
Entanglement Theory, 33
Environmental enrichment, 45
Epistemic actions, 117, 194
Epistemic artifacts, 116
Epistemic asymmetry, 7
Epistemic debate, 52
Epistemic engineering, 246
Epistemic landscape, 205
Epistemic neglect of object, 10, 240
Epistemic obligation, 13
Epistemic power of neuroimage,
    168
Epistemic significance of incised lines,
    187
Epistemic status, 185, 187
Epistemological barrier of modernity,
    242
Epistemological obligation, 248
Epistemological position of Material
    Engagement Theory, 52
Epistemological status of archaeological
    record, 232
Epistemological use or abuse of
    boundaries, 162
Evans, Arthur, 70

Everett, Daniel, 110
Evocative nature of things, 86
Evolution
  biological, 39, 229, 231
  cognitive, 4, 5, 11, 13, 15, 23, 39, 167,
    168, 171, 183, 185, 227–231, 241,
    243, 245
  cultural, 39
  Darwinian, 230
  hominid, 166
  hominin, 30
  human, 10, 14, 161, 230–232
  ongoing, 45, 243
  technological, 167
  things and, 245
Evolutionary archaeology, 38, 39
Evolutionary dynamics, 245, 246
Evolutionary epistemology, 39
Evolutionary narrative, 15
Evolutionary psychology, 39, 42
Evolutionary studies, 11
Exograms, 76
Experiential realism, 61
Externalism, 73, 74, 134, 142, 248
Externalization, 180, 189, 193, 231,
  236

Fauconnier, Gilles, 61, 100, 103
Finished artefact fallacy, 171
Foley, Robert, 156–159
Fritz, Carole, 201

Gallagher, Shaun, 60, 214, 222, 223
Gamble, Clive, 231, 242
Garavan, Hugh, 45, 48, 115
Gell, Alfred, 12, 95, 123, 130, 134–137,
  143–146, 218
Genetic mutation, 239–241
Gesture, 3, 14, 60, 65, 148, 190, 191,
  245
  crafting, 193
  and markings, 191
  technical, 194

temporality of, 201
  and tools, 155
  prosthetic, 154
Ghost in machine, 65
Gibson, James, 144, 176, 193, 204
G-intentionality, 142
Goodwin, Charles, 66, 105
Gosden, Chris, 10, 16, 24, 32, 57, 85,
  87, 122, 135, 136, 246
Gottlieb, Gilbert, 40, 41
Griffiths, Paul, 40, 42
Guattari, Félix, 235
Guthrie, Stewart, 131

Habitus, 116, 120, 141
Haggard, Patrick, 223, 224
Hands, freeing of, 155
Haraway, Donna, 236
Hawkes, Christopher, 25, 31, 32
Heidegger, Martin, 122, 163, 237
Henshilwood, Christopher, 181,
  184–189, 201, 234, 240
Hodder, Ian, 16, 32, 33, 44, 52, 89, 91,
  96, 121, 127, 247
Hoffecker, John, 231, 235
Homo erectus, 157, 170
Homo faber, 153, 154, 232, 233
Homo sapiens, 11, 24, 45, 106, 154,
  159, 230, 231
Homo symbolicus, 232, 234
Human becoming, 1, 5, 11, 39–41, 53,
  215, 231, 242
Human cognition, topology of, 37
Human condition, 51
Human embodiment, 165, 166, 225
Human intelligence
  emergence of, 5, 11
  modern, 239, 240
  reorganization of, 243
Human mindscape, 49, 248
Human-nonhuman interaction, 48
Human perception, 191, 193, 196,
  204

Humans
  as cyborg species, 155, 232
  distinctive mental architecture of, 163
  entangled with things, 33
  entangled with tools, 155
  mark making by, 155, 180, 184
  modern, 230, 240
  uniqueness of, 46, 108, 232
Humility of things, 7
Hurley, Susan, 26, 74
Hutchins, Edwin, 5, 29, 36, 38, 66–68,
  79, 102–105, 110, 207, 208, 236, 238
Hylonoetic field, 227
Hylozoism, 7

Iconicity, 114, 198
Imposition of form, 236
Ingold, Tim, 29, 36, 171, 179, 180,
  191, 192, 200, 207, 235
Inhabitation, 192, 201
Integrative projections, 101–104, 202
Intentionality
  and affordance, 149
  and agency, 119, 121, 125, 129,
    136–144, 172, 207
  and background, 140–144
  and mark making, 191, 185
  in philosophy, 136, 137
  in pottery making, 207, 214, 219
  and stone tools, 162, 163, 170–174,
    177, 234, 235
Intention-in-action, 137–140, 191
Internalism, 73
Internalist fallacy, 12
Iriki, Atsushi, 154, 165–167, 233, 245

Jeffares, Ben, 229
Johnson, Mark, 58, 61, 62, 65
Jordan, Scott, 42, 242

Kelly, Clare, 45, 48, 115
Kirsh, David, 57, 66, 72, 100, 102, 117,
  194

Knappett, Carl, 24, 25, 30, 33, 34, 77,
  79, 86, 95, 121, 127, 176, 228, 229,
  242
Knapping
  as act of thought, 164, 236
  as form of embodying, 163, 236
  intentions, 153, 172–174, 236
  and neural activation, 174, 175
  process of, 161, 172, 176, 177
  techniques of, 160
Know-how, 209

Lahr, Marta, 156–159
Lakoff, George, 58–62, 65, 102
La Marche antler, 181, 182, 185
Language, 11, 18, 38, 60–65, 184, 204,
  240, 245
  and arithmetic, 105–111, 238
  and material culture, 91, 94, 95
  and semiotics, 90–96, 99
Latour, Bruno, 11, 15, 16, 43, 44, 77,
  120–131, 145, 147, 220, 221,
  244
Law, John, 43, 123, 221
Leach, Edmund, 91
Leroi-Gourhan, André, 14, 154,
  177
Levallois, 158, 160
Lewis-Williams, David, 198
Linear B, 17, 68–86, 238
Linguistic sign, fallacy of, 91
Lithic technologies, 158, 160, 164
Locational fallacy, 80, 82
Logic
  arbitrary, 91
  of boundaries, 36, 236
  computational, 28
  enactive, 18, 90, 96, 190, 194,
    203
  of inhabitation, 192
  of inversion, 192
  non-representational, 191
  of substantive participation, 65

Maguire, Eleanor, 49
Mapping
 conceptual, 61
 cross-domain, 62
 external, 100
 integrative, 61
 internal, 100
 metaphoric, 61, 65, 102, 103
Mark making
 comparative study of, 19, 180, 190, 192, 239
 as epistemic action, 193, 194
 as form of enactive signification, 192
 and human signification, 180, 193, 239
 and intent, 180, 190, 194
 ontology of, 179
 phenomenology of, 180
 and scribbling, 193
 symbolic properties of, 179, 180, 184, 187
Marshack, Alexander, 181, 182
Material culture
 active nature of, 32, 121, 135, 148, 248
 and agency, 134
 as analytic object for the sciences of mind, 230
 and brain, 43, 48, 115, 247
 causal efficacy of, 132, 166, 237–240
 and cognition, 3, 5, 7, 10, 13, 17–20, 24, 29–35, 43, 50, 52, 59, 64, 73, 77, 81, 83, 90, 180, 201, 237, 242, 248
 cognitive efficacy of, 2, 44, 198, 238
 and extended mind, 228, 229
 representational dimension of, 30
 and semiotics, 11, 30, 90–98, 103, 104
 studies of, 11–16, 48, 83, 120, 135
 symbolic, 191
 taking seriously, 8, 43, 44, 120, 230
 thinking through, 24
Materiality
 absence of, 6
 inscribed, 66
 missing masses of, 11
 nature of, 7
 question of, 11
 semiotic of, 90, 123
 vital, 43, 44, 248
Materiality turn, 12
Material metaphors, 32, 65
Maturana, Humberto, 50
Mauss, Marcel, 122
McIntosh, Randal, 48
McPherron, Shannon, 157, 162, 170
Mediated action, 38, 147, 148, 153, 175, 208, 212, 215, 221, 224, 226, 245
Mediation, 65, 66, 126, 133, 221, 227, 234, 244
Mediational effects, 245, 246
Melanesian person, 123, 218
Memory, 1, 19, 46, 47, 68–70, 74–84, 155, 177, 218, 223
 amplifying, 81
 biological, 75, 83
 ecology of, 82
 economy of, 86
 external, 82, 83
 exteriorization of, 154
 and forgetting, 86
 internal, 82
 Mycenaean, 73, 76, 78, 81, 82, 84
  (see also Linear B)
 social construction of, 83
 technology of, 76
 working, 82, 83, 163, 193, 240
Mental causation, apparent, 219
Merleau-Ponty, Maurice, 4, 51, 143, 207, 243
Metacognition, 77, 193, 239
Metaphor, 5, 62, 65
Metaplasticity, 43–47, 80, 168, 241, 245
Methodological fetishism, 119, 133–135, 145–149
Methodological individualism, 25, 228
Microlithic technologies, 159, 180

Middle Stone Age markings, 181,
185–186, 189–194
Miller, Daniel, 7, 13, 32, 44, 83, 86, 87,
120
Mind
active, 85, 172
archaeology of, 1, 5–8, 12, 17, 18,
23–25, 30, 33, 57, 159, 162, 169,
172, 228, 238, 242
as artifact of our own making, 231
behind artefact, 23, 25, 34
as brain-bound, 6, 37
computational, 17, 26, 28, 67, 227
concept of, 8, 9, 57
constitutive intertwining with the
material world, 227
decentralized view of, 37
distributed, 2, 6, 12, 19
dualist view of, 3
embodied, 2, 6, 59, 60, 66
enacted, 2, 6
enactive perspective on, 219
extended, 2, 6, 11, 12, 17, 19, 59, 66,
73–81, 85–87, 144, 227, 228, 233,
248
in context, 36
internalist view of, 3, 6, 30, 141
immanent, 217
as leaky organ, 7
limited by skin, 6
location of, 81
making of, 8, 19, 34, 155, 242
material basis of, 4
modular, 46
neurocentric view of, 3
not limited by skin, 248
philosophy of, 10, 25, 73, 97, 136,
146, 161, 171
plasticity of, 5, 46
potter's, 220
profoundly embodied, 244
projective, 177
relational, 9

representational view of, 25–27, 141,
189
stuff of, 2–4, 23, 37
symmetric view of, 77
as unfinished project, 244
whereabouts of, 4, 14, 248
Mind-body problem, 3, 13, 25, 28, 59,
162
Mithen, Steven, 45
Microscopic analysis, 186, 190, 201
Modern cognition, 239
Modernity
cognitive, 4, 11, 30, 180, 184, 239,
242
concept of, 239, 242
behavioral, 4, 30, 180, 239, 242
divisions, 53
ontological tidiness of, 16
origin of, 242, 243
tyranny of, 183
unlearning of, 239, 242
Modern mind, 205, 239, 243
Modern predicament, 15
Mol, Annemarie, 221
Morphometric analysis, 181
Mundurukú, 109
Munn, Nancy, 122

Nagel, Thomas, 53
Neo-evolutionary comparative
cognition, 232
Neo-evolutionary theories, 45, 231, 233
Neural activation, 31, 41, 48, 174, 175,
213
Neural architecture, 247
Neural circuits, 46
Neural constructivism, 31, 40, 46
Neural context, 48
Neural correlates of action, 219
Neural networks, 4, 82, 116, 217
Neural plasticity, 46, 49, 245
Neural presentations, 213
Neural structures, 4, 27

Neural substrates, 43, 167
Neural system, 40
Neural tissue, 29, 197
Neural vehicles, 27
Neuroarchaeology, 168, 229
Neurocentrism, 169, 229
Neuroimaging, 3, 48, 164, 167–169,
    222
Neurophenomenology, 208
Neuroscience, 3, 4, 13, 45–48, 164,
    168, 196, 212, 214, 217
Niche construction, 40, 246
Noë, Alva, 50, 58, 102, 203, 228
Number sense, 105–109, 114, 115, 202
Numerical concepts, 109, 238
Numerocity, 108, 109, 115
Núñez, Rafael, 62–64, 102

Objectification, 32, 97, 126, 133, 143,
    163, 193
Occupation, 192, 201
Ochre, incised, 181, 184
Oldowan industrial complex, 156, 167
Oldowan technologies, 157, 160, 243
Olsen, Bjørnar, 14, 43, 247
Ontological asymmetry, 18, 233
Ontological boundaries of cognition,
    37, 65, 230
Ontological commitment, 53, 77, 163,
    172
Ontological compound, 14, 77, 248
Ontological configurations, 17, 80
Ontological deprivation, 7
Ontological description about minds
    and things, 9
Ontological gulf of representation, 32
Ontological ingredients of human
    thought, 248
Ontological inseparability, 19
Ontological moments, 145
Ontological locus of cognition, 25
Ontological priority of signified over
    signifier, 90, 97

Ontology
    hylomorphic, 235, 236
    hylonoetic, 236
    of lines, 191
    of markings, 179, 184
    of material culture, 11, 148
    of material signs, 2
    of mind, 43
    of relatedness, 53
    relational, 50, 146, 228
    representational, 229
    semiotic, 11, 91
    social, 57
    of tools, 172
Operational sequence
    and knapping, 162
    and Linear B tablets, 78
    in pottery making, 216–219, 223
O'Regan, Kevin, 102, 203
Originary technicity, 154
Ostrich egg shells, 181, 185
Ownership, sense of, 213, 214, 224

Parietal art, 195
Parity principle, 74–77, 83, 84
Parrott, Fiona, 86, 87
Partible person, 123
Peirce, Charles Sanders, 93–96, 134
Pellegram, Andrea, 92, 93
Peripersonal space, 244, 245
Phenomenological description,
    220
Phenomenological osmosis, 7
Phenomenological requirements, 20,
    207
Phenomenology, 9, 13, 32, 120, 190,
    208, 219, 222
Pickering, Andrew, 129, 130, 148, 149,
    220
Pictorial competence, 199
Pictures, 195
Pirahã, 109, 110
Plastic effects, 247

Plasticity
activity-dependent, 45
cross-modal neural, 5, 48
cultural, 245, 249
hippocampal, 49
in musicians, 47
neural, 245, 249
practice-related developmental, 40
synaptic, 46, 47
in taxi drivers, 49
Polanyi, Michael, 4, 207, 243
Pottery making, 207, 213, 223
Practice effects, 224
Probabilistic epigenesis, 40, 41
Prostheses, 154
Prosthetic beings, 154
Prosthetic body, 223
Prosthetic gesture, 154, 155, 193
Prosthetic image, 203
Putnam, Hilary, 29, 74

Ratner, Carl, 234
Readiness potential, 220
Relational causality, 41
Relational comparisons, 155
Relational domain, 50, 77
Relational entities, 16
Relational instantiations, 97
Relational networks of persons and
  things, 123
Relational transactions between
  persons and things, 9
Relational ways of thinking, 127, 230
Renfrew, Colin, 1, 3, 12, 23, 25, 30, 33,
  44, 46, 61, 97–99, 229, 242
Reorganization, extended, 81, 115, 247
Representational capacities, 30, 194
Representational device, 31
Representational economy, 194
Representational fallacy, 237
Representational idiom, 117, 149
Representational illusion, 195
Representational image, 183

Representational inputs, 28
Representational intent, 185–190
Representational logic, 18, 90, 163
Representational mobility, 195
Representational objects, 180, 200
Representational ontology, 229
Representational predicament, 200
Representational realm, 219
Representational stability, 110
Representational stance, 64, 243
Representational structures, 26–29, 67,
  90
Representational substitute or
  replicator, 27
Representations
cultural, 134
engraved, 189
external, 26, 27, 30, 31, 67, 89, 90,
  162, 191, 238, 239
intentional, 138, 139
internal, 26, 27, 31, 64, 67, 71, 89,
  162, 197
material, 31, 90
mental, 27, 73, 162, 163, 237
meta-, 39, 194, 239
non-derived, 37, 81
and pictures, 199
in pottery making, 211, 213
somatosensory, 47
spell of, 130
symbolic, 19, 180
R-intentionality, 142
Robb, John, 120, 121
Ryle, Gilbert, 25, 34

Sakura, Osamu, 165–167, 245
Saussure, Ferdinand de, 91–96
Scaffolding, 102, 190, 202, 204, 224,
  239, 249
Schmandt-Besserat, Denise, 111, 112
Scribbling, 193
Searle, John, 136–145
Self, loss of, 224

Self-engineering, 231
Self-made species, 232
Self-referential narratives, 218
Self-transforming human
  predisposition, 155
Semiology, 91–94
Semiotics, 90–95, 187, 198
Sense making, 100, 180, 191, 236
Sensorimotor engagement, 202, 203
Sensual properties of things, 87
Shapiro, Larry, 37, 57, 59
Shore, Bradd, 93
Sight, liberation of, 204
Signification
  arbitrariness of, 93
  early human, 180, 189, 234
  enactive, 30, 51, 99, 110, 115,
    191–194, 235
  material, 113, 116, 191, 237
  metaphoric, 191
  pragmatic, 98
  prehistory of, 236
  warranting model of, 98
Signs
  denotative meaning of, 96
  designative meaning of, 96
  enactive, 18, 96, 113, 116, 124, 134,
    201
  expressive meaning of, 96, 97
Skills
  acquisition of, 169, 209, 213, 224
  bodily, 203, 207, 217
  cognitive, 74, 111, 155, 159, 229
  embodied, 7, 141, 174, 209
  motor and sensory, 47
  pictorial, 194
  practical, 141, 209
  tactile, 47
Smith, Adam, 132
Social archaeology, 14
Socio-technical network, 221
Socio-technical trajectory, 125,
  128–129

Stamatopoulou, Despina, 193
Steiner, Pierre, 31
Sterelny, Kim, 42, 246
Stiegler, Bernard, 154
Stone tools
  as enactive cognitive prostheses, 164
  and human thinking, 229, 233, 245
  imaging studies of, 164, 167
  making of, 153–158, 161, 162
Stotz, Karola, 40, 42
Stout, Dietrich, 157, 160, 161, 164,
  167, 168, 174, 175
Strathern, Marilyn, 123, 218
Surrogate material structures, 104, 192
Sutton, John, 57, 82
Symbol, constitutive, 97, 98
Symbolic, and cognitive, 25
Symbolic abilities of children, 193
Symbolic archaeology, 91, 92, 95, 98
Symbolic equivalency, 97
Symbolic externalization, 189
Symbolic function, 28
Symbolic intent, 183, 187, 190, 198
Symbolic material culture, 91, 191
Symbolic thinking, 11, 38, 39, 113
Symbolic representation, 25
Symbolic storage, 30, 73, 74, 237, 238
Symbolic species, 234
Symbolism, 30, 33, 38, 89, 105, 180,
  183, 184, 189, 191, 202, 234, 237,
  238
Synofzik, Matthis, 215, 225

Tacit knowledge, 209
Tallis, Raymond, 229–232, 242
Taylor, Charles, 96
Technical choices, 216
Tectonoetic awareness, 194, 236
Temporal anatomy of action, 222
Temporal dynamics, 212
Temporal effects of things, 246, 247
Temporal stratigraphy of creative
  action, 213

Temporal scales and stages of action, 224
Temporal web of interactions, 176
Thagard, Paul, 28
Thinking
  as action, 235
  about thinking, 175, 239
  tools for, 190
Thompson, Evan, 50, 58, 86, 236
Tilley, Christopher, 11, 16, 32, 33, 65, 91, 94, 95
Time, 35, 36, 38, 45, 49, 52, 223–225, 246
Tool making, 11, 153, 161, 235, 236
  cognitive requirements of, 11
  imaging studies of, 164, 167, 168
  non-human primates and, 164
Tool use, 153
  by animals, 154, 155
  as hallmark of human cognition, 232
  and functional anatomy of monkey's brain, 165
Tosello, Gilles, 201
Tsakiris, Manos, 213, 223
Turkle, Sherry, 86
Turner, Mark, 62, 100, 103

van der Leeuw, Sander, 216
Varela, Francisco, 50, 58, 219
Ventris, Michael, 69
Verbeek, Peter-Paul, 230
Vygotsky, Lev, 35, 58, 221, 227

Wadley, Lyn, 163
Walter, Grey, 28
Warnier, Jean-Pierre, 66, 120
Webmoor, Timothy, 14, 44
Wegner, Daniel, 214, 219, 220
"We have never been modern," 243, 244
Wheeler, Mike, 10, 44, 57, 59, 73, 76, 80–85, 228, 246
Wilson, Frank, 60

Wilson, Robert, 58, 73, 85
Witmore, Christopher, 14, 44, 77
Wynn, Thomas, 23, 156, 157, 170–173, 177, 234